One for the Road

One for the Road

DRUNK DRIVING SINCE 1900

Barron H. Lerner

The Johns Hopkins University Press

Baltimore

The Johns Hopkins University Press
2715 North Charles Street
Baltimore, Maryland 21218-4363
www.press.jhu.edu

Lyrics for "Wasn't That a Party?" reprinted by permission of Alfred Publishing Co., Inc. All rights reserved. Words and music by Tom Paxton, copyright © 1973 (renewed) EMI U Catalog, Inc. All rights controlled by EMI U Catalog, Inc. (publishing) and Alfred Publishing Co., Inc. (print).

Lyrics from "Ddamm" and "Hooray for Beer" reprinted by permission of Hal Leonard Corporation. International copyright secured. All rights reserved.

"Ddamm," words and music by Jeff Hanneman, copyright © 1996 Pennemunde Music (ASCAP). All rights administered by Universal Music—MGB Songs.

"Hooray for Beer," words and music by Jaret Reddick and James Dotson, copyright © 2009 Universal Music—Z Tunes LLC, Drop Your Pants Publishing, Figs D. Music, Inc., and I Can't Believe It's Not Music. All rights for Drop Your Pants Publishing administered by Universal Music—Z Tunes LLC. All rights for Figs D. Music, Inc., and I Can't Believe It's Not Music administered by The Bicycle Music Company.

Library of Congress Cataloging-in-Publication Data
Lerner, Barron H.
     One for the road : drunk driving since 1900 / Barron H. Lerner.
        p. cm.
     Includes bibliographical references and index.
     ISBN-13: 978-1-4214-0190-4 (hardcover : alk. paper)
     ISBN-10: 1-4214-0190-8 (hardcover : alk. paper)
     1. Drunk driving—United States. 2. Drunk driving—United States—Prevention. I. Title.
     HE5620.D72L47 2011
     363.12'5140973—dc22   2010051484

A catalog record for this book is available from the British Library.

Special discounts are available for bulk purchases of this book. For more information, please contact Special Sales at 410-516-6936 or specialsales@press.jhu.edu.

The Johns Hopkins University Press uses environmentally friendly book materials, including recycled text paper that is composed of at least 30 percent post-consumer waste, whenever possible.

To those individuals who, having experienced a drunk driving tragedy, subsequently spent parts of their lives trying to make sure this did not happen to other people

Those who would give up essential liberty to purchase a little temporary safety deserve neither liberty nor safety.

—BENJAMIN FRANKLIN (1759)

Freedom is a hard thing to preserve. In order to have enough you must have too much.

—CLARENCE DARROW (1928)

Contents

Preface

Have you ever wondered, after having had a few drinks at a party, how drunk you would have to be to be considered a drunk driver? You might be surprised by the answer.

If you have the time and money and are age 21 or over, you might try the following experiment. Go to Amazon.com and purchase a Breathalyzer. One that is not too expensive and has good reviews is the AlcoHAWK Slim model. Before using it, read the instructions carefully in order to get accurate readings. For example, one should not use a Breathalyzer within twenty minutes of one's last drink because lingering alcohol in the mouth can lead to artificially high readings.

Then, select your drink of choice: hard liquor, wine, or beer. If you are drinking liquor, your portion size will be one shot, which is equivalent to 1.5 ounces. In the case of wine, you will be imbibing five ounces at a time. Beer drinkers should drink by the bottle.

Then get a friend to help you. Ask this person not to drink. His or her role is to stop the experiment if you are getting too intoxicated to document what happens to you as you drink. Also, be sure not to have eaten for two hours prior to beginning this experiment, which is best done on an empty stomach.

If you are a man, consume three drinks—liquor, wine, or beer—over the next hour. If you are a woman, drink two. At the end of the hour, describe to your friend how you feel, both while sitting down and taking a walk. Have your friend engage you in a discussion about current events and see how well you do. Try the old trick of highway patrolmen: say "Methodist Episcopal." Finally, if you like, get into your car and contemplate driving in your current state. Please do not actually drive.

Based on body weight, metabolism, and personal tolerance to alcohol, people will react very differently to this experiment. However, most will be mildly euphoric, feeling "buzzed" or "tipsy." They will have poor concentration, poor judgment, and slow reaction times. They will be less able to perform complex tasks. Behind the wheel, they may drive acceptably if there are no obstacles, but they will respond slowly or clumsily when encountering an unexpected event, such as a pedestrian running across the street or a car that unexpectedly brakes or cuts them off.

In the United States, in contrast to many other countries, it is absolutely legal for individuals who have drunk this much alcohol to drive. The vast majority of them will have blood alcohol levels of less than 0.08%, the current upper legal limit for driving. Of course, if police officers stop such drivers and request roadside sobriety tests, and the drivers do poorly, a driving while intoxicated (DWI) arrest is still possible. But even then, if the blood alcohol level turns out to be under 0.08%, such a person may not ultimately be convicted or punished.

Now it is time for part two of the experiment. Imagine having two more drinks, which would raise your blood alcohol level to roughly 0.12%. At this point, most people who are not heavy drinkers will be, well, plastered, or getting there. They will feel giddy, have few inhibitions, and be mentally unfocused. They will be physically clumsy and may stagger and slur their speech.

Anyone who gets into a car in this condition and simulates driving will perceive, one hopes, that this idea is utterly absurd. Nevertheless, for decades following the repeal of Prohibition in 1933, being stopped for erratic driving and having a blood alcohol level of 0.12% was unlikely to lead to a DWI conviction, unless a driver was unlucky enough to kill or injure someone. To ensure an arrest and possible conviction, his or her level would have had to be even higher: 0.15%, the equivalent of six or more drinks on an empty stomach. It was not until the 1960s that some states lowered their legal blood alcohol levels to 0.10%. And, regardless of what the cutoff was, even bodily harm caused to an innocent victim by a drunk driver was no assurance of a substantial punishment.

Not inclined to try this experiment? That's perfectly fine. But as a driver or a pedestrian, you should care. It is estimated that, despite decades of anti–drunk driving messages, millions of arrests, and countless horror stories, there are still more than 80 million car trips taken annually by impaired drivers—this in a country with a legal and public health system that seeks to protect its citizens from harm. Very few people leave their homes expecting their lives to be catastrophically changed by a drunk driver, but it can happen at any second.

A number of people who read drafts of this book commented on my moral outrage about drunk driving, immediately assuming that I had lost a loved one to a drunk driver. Thankfully, I have not. Maybe my passion stems from being the parent of teenagers who are either already driving or who will drive in the near future. But to me, the history I tell offers no other conclusion. Let's see if you agree.

Acknowledgments

I am dedicating this book to those individuals who, having experienced a drunk driving tragedy, subsequently spent parts of their lives trying to make sure this did not happen to other people. My three previous books all featured activists: forcibly detained Skid Row tuberculosis patients who stood up for their rights; women with breast cancer who took on and triumphed over a patronizing male medical profession; and celebrities whose own illnesses led them to become spokespersons and fundraisers for various diseases.

In the case of drunk driving, no one would have criticized the family members of victims if they had simply grieved for the loss of their loved ones. But these individuals—mostly, but not all, women—channeled that grief and its accompanying anger into a phenomenally successful social movement that has saved many lives. Most of their efforts, moreover, were not glamorous but entailed real grunt work: holding vigils, pestering legislators, issuing press releases. I have only met a tiny fraction of these people, but I remain impressed with all of them. Fortunately, I was able to speak with three of the main early activists, Candace Lightner, Cindi Lamb, and Doris Aiken. Doris deserves special praise and thanks. When she became involved in anti–drunk driving activism in 1978, there was no anti–drunk driving activism. The tragedy that inspired her involved two teenagers whom she knew only peripherally. As of the writing of this book, at the age of 84, she still devotes most of her waking hours to her organization, Remove Intoxicated Drivers. She has been a source of endless knowledge and dusty old papers, gold to a historian.

Another group of individuals crucial to this project are those who have researched and fought drunk driving professionally. I have learned an enormous amount from—and sent far too many e-mails to—Robert Voas and James Fell, of the Pacific Institute for Research and Evaluation; David Sleet, of the Centers for Disease Control and Prevention (CDC); Kurt Dubowski, who was present at a famous 1958 conference on drunk driving and remembers it as if it were yesterday; and Ben Kelley, a coauthor of the 1968 government report that first put drunk driving on the map. Others whom I spoke with include C. Everett Koop, Amy Barkin, Bill Bronrott, Robert Denniston, George Hacker, Jere Joiner, J. Marse Grant, Marion Grant, Joseph Gusfield, John Moulden, Grant Baldwin, Ann Dellinger, Justin McNaull, and Ralph Hudson. William Dikant put me on his e-mail list for articles about drunk driving. Frank Kelly Rich gave me permission to use images from *Modern Drunkard Magazine*. I greatly benefited from participating in a public health grand rounds at the CDC at the invitation of Tom Frieden. Other helpful feedback came from talks I gave at the State University of New York Stony Brook, Montefiore Medical Center, and a conference on health activism at Yale University organized by Naomi Rogers. Sarah Tracy read parts of the manuscript and gave great suggestions. So did anonymous readers from the Johns Hopkins and Yale University Presses. Allan Brandt was especially helpful while I was writing grants.

Speaking of which, the generosity of granting agencies is why this book exists, pure and simple. I obtained funding from both the National Library of Medicine's G13 program and the Greenwall Foundation. William Stubing, Greenwall's president, has always been a great supporter of my work. Others who have generously helped me over the years include Angelica Berrie, the Arnold P. Gold Foundation, Jay Meltzer, the Rudin Foundation, and the Ewig Foundation.

Finding primary research materials is essential for a book like this, and I greatly benefited when Gene Haddon, the widow of William Haddon, gave me access to her late husband's papers. Gene and Jim Metzger showed me great hospitality during two visits to Bethesda, Maryland. Others who helped me to tell the Bill Haddon story were Susan Baker, Robert Haddon, Michael Guarnieri, and Stephen Merrill. Especially helpful archivists included Shelly Williams, of the Ronald Reagan Presidential Library; Penny Page, of the Rutgers Center of Alcohol Studies; Bradley Cook, of the Indiana University Archives; Andrea Bainbridge, of the American Medical Association Archives; and Amy Bray and Melissa Bush, of the University of Georgia's Hargrett Library. The entire staff of the State Historical Society of Iowa was of great help in navigating the William Plymat Papers. Paul Anderson Jr. helped me get permission to use the Margaret Mitchell papers. The staff of the National Library of Medicine alerted me to the C. Everett Koop papers.

Closer to home at Columbia University, David Rosner, Ronald Bayer, Amy Fairchild, James Colgrove, Janlori Goldman, Gerald Oppenheimer, and NiTanya Nedd, of the Center for the History and Ethics of Public Health, gave me helpful feedback and provided an important intellectual home. In the Division of General Medicine, Steven Shea, Rafael Lantigua, Rita Charon, and all my colleagues help me to balance my research and clinical work. Grant funding being as it is these days, my chief research assistant for this book was Barron H. Lerner. But he was ably assisted by several terrific medical and graduate students: John LeGall, Alison Bateman-House, Resham Patel, Erica Satin-Hernandez, and Alex Kertzner.

My family, as always, is very supportive. My teenagers, Ben and Nina, had so little interest in interacting with me that it freed up time to work on the book. My parents, Ronnie and Phillip Lerner, and my mother-in-law, Ellen Seibel, always encouraged me but knew when to stop asking if I had finished the manuscript. As usual, my wife, Cathy Seibel, read the entire book and provided perceptive comments. Our beloved dog, Akeela, also read the whole manuscript and picked up on several spelling errors that Cathy missed.

My agent, Robert Shepard, did not work directly with me on this project, explaining that the only way one could truly sell a book about drunk driving to a trade publisher was to be in favor of it. I was not (quite) willing to do that. Nevertheless, Robert helped me to conceptualize the project and write my proposal. Which brings me to Jacqueline Wehmueller, who has now edited three of my books for the Johns Hopkins University Press. It is simply a joy to work with Jackie. She and her colleagues at the press are all top-notch professionals.

Lastly, I would also like to thank all our family and friends who have heard about this project for years. Inviting someone working on a history of drunk driving to dinner or a party does not exactly increase the "fun index." But if even one person had one drink less before driving home from the party as a result of my presence, I did my job.

One for the Road

What's the Harm?

Readers of the Long Island, New York, section of the June 3, 1984, *New York Times* had the opportunity to read an opinion piece by Philip B. Linker, an associate professor of English at the local Suffolk County Community College. Linker's piece, entitled "Drinking and Driving Can Mix," began with a description of how he had driven home legally drunk the previous Saturday night. He then continued: "I drove home drunk the Saturday before that, and the one before that, in what probably amounts to a fairly consistent pattern over the last 25 years, ever since I have been licensed to drive." But, Linker wrote, he had never been pulled over or arrested. The same was true for many of his friends. Hence, he concluded, it was possible to drive drunk successfully.[1]

The timing of Linker's article was no coincidence. For several years, the United States had been experiencing a surge of interest in drunk driving and the damage it caused. Mothers Against Drunk Drivers (MADD), which dated from 1980, was the best-known activist group, but Remove Intoxicated Drivers (RID), founded two years earlier, was based in New York. The professor admired the efforts of these groups to publicize the issue of drunk driving and get stronger laws passed, but he was concerned about possible excesses.

Linker's piece touched on a series of issues that would ultimately hinder the anti–drunk driving crusade. For example, that he and his friends seemed able to drive while inebriated suggested that drunk driving might not be such a grave societal problem. Linker also emphasized the concept of moderate liquor intake, comparing his own childhood drinking experiences to what happened in Europe, where children learned to enjoy alcohol "sensibly and responsibly."

The related notion of "responsible drinking," which implied moderate intake without harmful repercussions, would consistently be invoked as something that had no relationship to drunk driving and thus was acceptable.[2]

Linker's article also had a libertarian flavor, underscoring another type of objection that would emerge. Some of what MADD, RID, and state legislatures proposed, he wrote, were "draconian measures which severely encroach upon the rights and liberty of the vast majority of New Yorkers." True liberty, in contrast, "entails the responsibility, in effect, to police ourselves." Not surprisingly, Linker compared the current efforts to an earlier anti-alcohol movement. "Let us eliminate once and for all," he declared, "the mystique and the myths about alcohol along with the attitudes that led to such follies as Prohibition and the WCTU (Woman's Christian Temperance Union)."[3]

It is not known how many letters the *Times* received in response to Linker. It is possible that some were supportive. But the three writers whose letters were printed were highly negative. Twenty-five thousand Americans had died in alcohol-related crashes in 1983, one writer pointed out, with ninety-seven in Suffolk County alone. For a professor to advocate publicly any degree of drinking and driving was especially unfortunate, he added—"a tremendous disservice to our young." "What scares me to death," one of the other correspondents wrote, "is Mr. Linker's utter sincerity."[4]

This book, the first history of drunk driving and efforts to control it in the United States, chronicles the century-long saga of one of the most controversial offenses committed by members of the public.[5] At first glance, drunk driving is among the clearest of crimes, one in which impaired individuals knowingly place themselves behind the wheel of vehicles that can wreak destruction when out of control. But, as Linker's piece reveals, such a viewpoint collides with other factors, notably, Americans' love of alcohol, love of driving, and more abstractly, love of freedom and individual liberties.

This book tells the stories of a diverse group of individuals:

- doctors and advocates for alcoholics who promoted the sympathetic concept of "alcoholism" in the years after the repeal of Prohibition;
- scientists and policymakers who first conceptualized drunk driving as a major public health problem that was inexplicably being ignored;
- representatives from the alcoholic beverage industry who promoted the idea of responsible drinking while carefully ensuring the continued sales of their product;

- mothers and other victims of drunk driving whose anger at lax punishment finally led to pure moral outrage;
- academicians who, while opposed to drunk driving, nevertheless challenged some of the statistics that justified the new activism;
- libertarian critics who derided organizations like MADD as paternalistic and neoprohibitionist; and
- the drunk drivers themselves, who ranged from star athletes to factory workers to housewives, all of whom had knowingly chosen to commit an act that was both illegal and morally dubious.

The old joke goes that the definition of a conservative is a liberal who has been mugged. It might similarly be said that a libertarian is someone who has never lost a loved one in a drunk driving crash. The point, of course, is that passionately held beliefs are more likely to be based on emotion than reason. Thus, this history of drunk driving may not alter anyone's beliefs about the subject. Those already vehemently opposed to impaired driving will see a story of unnecessary death and missed opportunities. To them, the notion of condoning any type of drinking and driving will remain inexplicable. At the same time, other readers will find resonance in the words of Philip Linker. Although they may not applaud his specific behavior, they are apt to sympathize with two very "American" themes that he raised: individual responsibility and rejection of governmental intrusion into citizens' lives. As the old basketball expression goes, "No harm, no foul." Yet even if this book ultimately changes few minds, it provides an excellent opportunity to demonstrate how we have become a society that concurrently condemns and tolerates drunk driving.

Opposition to drunk driving is as old as the automobile. In the early years of the twentieth century, state and local legislators in certain areas passed laws making impaired driving illegal. But prohibitions varied greatly. Although publicly on the record as opposed to drinking and driving, the automobile and beverage industries carefully avoided any black-and-white characterization of the problem. The suburbanization of America after World War II, followed by the development of the interstate highway system, helped to transform the automobile—and the act of driving—into a vital cultural and economic activity. The car, the "freedom machine," became the primary mode of transportation for those in suburban or rural areas going to work, visiting friends, and most importantly for this book, going to restaurants and bars. It was one thing to leave a bar in a city and stagger home or onto a bus or subway; it was quite another to literally have "one for the road" and get into one's car, either in an impaired or a fully inebriated state.[6]

If anything, alcohol was even more all-American than driving. Prohibition, which lasted from the passage of the Volstead Act in 1919 until its repeal in 1933, represented only a temporary triumph of the "dry" forces, which conceived of liquor as the root of all evil—not only drunk driving but public drunkenness, indolence, disease, and crime. Historians have argued that Prohibition actually succeeded in lowering the rates of alcohol-related social and medical problems. But after 1933, the pendulum would swing far in the other direction, strongly discouraging governmental intervention in the world of liquor. Concurrent with this development was the rise of the alcoholism movement, which situated drinking problems not with alcohol but with the person drinking it. Those who abused alcohol were no longer regarded as sinners but were seen to be sick, the victims of a disease. The notion of alcoholism as a disease, while surely well meaning, could not help but throw a monkey wrench into anti–drunk driving efforts.[7]

It was not only those with an obvious alcohol problem who drank and drove. There was also the middle-class "social drinker" who, at first glance, seemed nothing like the skid row bum or other stereotypical drunks. Some were likely alcoholics and others were not. Regardless, few caused alarm among police departments, judges, and juries, who generally freed the reckless drivers with a fine and, in later years, an appointment at "drunk driving school." "There but for the grace of God go I" seemed to be the motto of those who, when confronted by incontrovertible evidence that someone had endangered hundreds of people and perhaps maimed or killed some, preferred to look the other way. As longtime *Washington Post* columnist Jonathan Yardley wrote in 1981, "Most of the people who slide boozily behind their steering wheels are not criminal types . . . but nice middle-class folks, just like you and me."[8]

Of course, a term like *social drinker* was itself what we might call "socially constructed." When a social drinker was caught driving drunk, it was seen as a single instance of bad judgment in an otherwise exemplary life, but this was rarely the case. Experts liked to point out that persons caught driving drunk for the first time had, like Linker, probably done so dozens of times before without incident. The language chosen to characterize these particular individuals, however, reflected the forgiving way that society viewed them. The same could be said for the word *accident*, which was the common term used to describe automobile crashes well into the 1980s. An accident connoted an unfortunate act of God, not something that could—or should—be prevented.

This relative indifference to drunk driving persisted even when the development of the first breath-testing systems meant that police could now quantify just how inebriated a suspect was. Before this, an officer could rely only on a series of dexterity tests, all of which were subjective. But with Rolla Harger's 1937 Drunkometer and Robert F. Borkenstein's 1954 Breathalyzer, it was increasingly possible to know just how much impairment was related to alcohol. The values chosen for most Driving While Intoxicated (DWI) laws, however, reflected the conservative tenor of the times. Someone caught driving recklessly with a blood alcohol level greater than 0.15%—equivalent to 0.15 grams of alcohol per 1,000 milliliters of blood, or six to eight drinks on an empty stomach—was assumed to be drunk, but lower values, which still often caused marked inebriation, were considered only one piece of evidence and not definitive. As a result, probably millions of Americans who could not walk a straight line for a policeman walked free from the police station or the courtroom—and got into their cars. "Safety interests obviously were superseded by an unusual concern for the offender," one critic would later write. "This national embarrassment and disgrace has not been just the accumulation of death and injury, but, rather, the strange acceptance of such death and injury as the way of life."[9] In contrast, Scandinavian countries set their level of presumed intoxication much lower, between 0.05% and 0.08%.

The history of drunk driving is also a story of perception versus reality. Prior to the advent of blood alcohol content (BAC) testing, defense lawyers and their clients were often able successfully to challenge the testimony of arresting officers. Even after BACs became available, challenges persisted. Defendants and their lawyers argued that the new machines were not accurate, that experienced drinkers could drive safely with high BACs, and that testing violated the constitutional rights of Americans. As the twentieth century progressed, state and federal courts, including the Supreme Court, would become involved in adjudicating these competing claims.

All along, there were activists charging that the problem of drunk driving was being minimized or ignored. The largest group of such individuals, who belonged to Baptist churches and other remnants of the old dry movement, took an unabashedly moral view. Drinking and driving, like other inappropriate alcohol-related activities, was simply wrong. "Alcohol at the Wheel," a 1953 pamphlet written by a psychiatrist and a chemist, made essentially the same argument about the ills of drunk driving that MADD would advance a quarter of a century later.[10] A different approach, which might best be called epidemiological, emerged in the mid-1960s, initially under the auspices of the newly formed National Highway Safety Bureau. If Dwight D. Eisenhower's name would be indelibly associated with the highway system, it was Lyndon B. Johnson's administration that finally acknowledged the massive problems, including speeding, crashes, and trauma, brought on by the expansion of the interstates.

This book explores these efforts, particularly those of the first traffic "czar," William Haddon Jr., who studied drunk driving through the larger prism of automobile-injury prevention. Befitting his public health training, Haddon's approach focused on the epidemiology of drunk driving, studying its incidence and exploring its causes. Haddon had first tackled the problem of intoxicated drivers while working for the New York State Health Department in the late 1950s with a young Daniel Patrick Moynihan, who would later become an adviser to presidents and a senator from New York. With all the publicity given to MADD and other victims' rights organizations after 1980, the largely forgotten efforts of earlier federal and state policymakers, positive and negative, bear special scrutiny. Pointing fingers at the inadequate safety features of American cars and roads, these individuals anticipated modern innovations, such as air bags and ignition interlock devices, that lower the death rate from drunk driving.

Yet this painstaking devotion to science and careful study increasingly failed to appease the many victims of drunk driving. Whether or not one believed the figure of 25,000 and 800,000 annual alcohol-related deaths and crashes, respectively, there seemed to be remarkably little justice occurring. It was utterly routine for police, prosecutors, and judges to either let drunk drivers off or reduce their charges to lesser misdemeanors. License suspensions, let alone jail time, were infrequent. Moreover, this tradition of lax punishment extended to cases in which victims were severely injured or killed. Although certain judges, lawyers, and social critics had for decades argued that drunk drivers who killed should be prosecuted for manslaughter or even murder, this rarely occurred. Much more common was vehicular homicide, generally punishable by fines, license revocation, and trivial jail sentences. "I just feel that some of these people have suffered more than I could impose on them," admitted one sympathetic judge.[11]

More remarkably, by the 1990s, bookstores and libraries were filled with books, generally written by defense attorneys, instructing readers how to avoid drunk driving convictions. To be sure, the American legal system protected accused persons whose guilt could not be established beyond a reasonable doubt, but the number and content of these volumes were striking. Representative titles, such as *How to Avoid a Drunk Driving Conviction* and *Drunk Driving Defense: How to Beat the Rap*, instructed readers to deceive police officers, trick juries, and at times, even leave the site of an accident. Similar material appeared on the Internet. Imagine, for a moment, the overwhelmingly negative response that would greet information on how to escape conviction for arson, fraud, or child abuse. Those who beat a drunk driving rap, in contrast, wore it like a badge of honor.

In popular culture, drunkenness, and at times drunk driving, was a constant source of humor. In his 1973 song, *Wasn't That a Party?*, folk singer and songwriter Tom Paxton penned the following:

> Could-a been the whisky,
> Might a-been the gin,
> Could-a been the three or four six packs,
> I don't know,
> But won't you look at the mess I'm in?
> My head's like a football,
> I think I'm going to die.
> But tell me, a-me oh me oh my,
> Wasn't that a party?

In the 1978 comedy *Animal House*, four fraternity boys go out for a night of drinking and end up wrecking the car lent to them by one of the boy's brothers. Although the dean admonishes one of them, warning that "Fat, drunk, and stupid is no way to go through life, son," the film's irreverent message was, of course, exactly the opposite.

Television personalities like Dean Martin and Jackie Gleason developed on-air personas in which they drank liquor and appeared intoxicated, usually for laughs. Perhaps the best-known television drunk was a gifted comedian and real-life teetotaler named Foster Brooks. Brooks's popularity surged in the 1970s, when he regularly appeared as a befuddled drunk on the *Dean Martin Show* and the *Dean Martin Roasts*. Gags about drinking and driving were not off limits. In one skit, Brooks, playing an obviously inebriated airline pilot, meets Dean Martin in a bar for a drink prior to a flight. Here was a typical interchange:

> Martin: How did you get to be an airline pilot?
> Brooks: I used to be a b-b-b-bus driver but I quit. T-t-too many drunks on the road.[12]

The alcohol industry, and its sister industries that made money from selling alcohol, never condoned or made light of drunk driving in this manner. But throughout the twentieth century, they fiercely guarded the right to advertise and sell alcohol, even though the language and imagery they used—which connected the consumption of beer, wine, and liquor to the good life—almost surely promoted irresponsible acts such as drunk driving. At the same time, however, Seagrams and a few other manufacturers became involved early on in "being part of the solution"[13]—that is, promoting moderate and responsible drinking and admitting that their products could be misused. This strategy was in contrast to that of the tobacco industry, which continued to insist that cigarettes were harmless long after it knew the truth and which only became involved in control efforts after being pressured to do so. Were the beverage industry's efforts altruistic or merely an effort to co-opt anti–drunk driving activists and other critics?

It is hard to know just what drunk driving victims and their relatives thought of the laissez-faire attitude toward drunk driving in the United States. Aside from periodic lawsuits or newspaper articles, there was little public discussion of the apparent laxity of drunk driving enforcement. And because victims were commonly said to have been "in the wrong place at the wrong time," they could, paradoxically, be blamed for having created the circumstances that had led to their own injury or death. Lacking any type of organized movement, the individual stories of those harmed by drunk driving, at once poignant and exasperating, stayed largely private.

But a "stiff upper lip" was becoming a thing of the past. Thanks to the civil rights movement, the unpopular Vietnam War, and the rise of feminism and consumerism in the 1960s and 1970s, Americans had begun to criticize authoritarian behaviors they found unacceptable. Exemplified by the feminist health book *Our Bodies, Ourselves*, which questioned male domination of the birthing process, women with breast cancer who refused radical mastectomies, and the nascent environmental movement, the ability of powerful people in society to dictate cultural norms was under attack. This largely liberal activism drew the attention of both newspapers and television news programs, which eagerly reported stories of individuals who had fought the system.

Enter another angry group: mothers whose children had been killed or injured at the hands of drunk drivers. Of course, not all the activists were mothers and not all the victims were children. Nor were all located on the left of the political spectrum. During the 1980s, concurrent with Ronald Reagan's presidency, a more conservative brand of activism, concerned with issues such as drug addiction, domestic violence, the protection of fetuses, and rising crime rates, emerged. The driving force for many of these initiatives was victims' rights, the notion that the legal system had paid too much attention to the rights of criminals as opposed to those who suffered. Drunk driving control, with its emphasis on arrests and prosecution, was a natural fit.

In such an environment, the use of actual stories of individual people—often children—victimized by those who drove drunk proved especially powerful. "I did not believe that such pain was possible nor that I could reach such depths of despair," wrote a San Diego woman who had lost her son. "I feel so cheated."[14] MADD and other anti–drunk driving groups used such accounts liberally. Indeed, the stories were so profoundly sad and moving it was hard to understand why they had so rarely come to the public's attention before. In general, these stories followed a predictable plot line in which a wanton and uncaring drinking driver, often a recidivist with prior drunk driving convictions, killed an innocent (and sober) victim. Central to these narratives was the idea that what had occurred was no accident, but rather the conscious act of someone who had deliberately disregarded both the law and any semblance of decent behavior. These were morality tales, pure and simple, and represented a throwback to the Prohibition era's disapprobation of excessive alcohol use.

Exemplary of these stories was that of MADD founder Candy Lightner, a California woman whose 13-year-old daughter Cari was killed by a drunk driver in 1980. The man had been convicted for drunk driving several times before, in each case being given a lenient punishment. Remarkably, his most recent arrest had been only two days earlier. The judge had not only let him go home awaiting trial but had not even taken away his license. The fury generated by stories such as these—reaching the American public for the first time—was both breathtaking and understandable.

MADD was not the first grassroots organization to take on drunk driving. In 1978, a journalist named Doris Aiken had founded Remove Intoxicated Drivers in upstate New York. But Mothers Against Drunk Drivers, which later changed its name to the somewhat softer-sounding Mothers Against Drunk Driving, rapidly gained moral authority, becoming the nation's best-known foe of drunk driving. Part of this success stemmed from Lightner's personal appeal. Attractive, media-savvy, and unwilling to take no for an answer, Lightner generated an enormous amount of sympathy. By 2000, MADD, working with RID, other organizations, legislators, and the press, had spearheaded a series of new deterrence laws designed at curbing drunk driving. One was getting state governments to lower the acceptable legal blood alcohol level—first to 0.10% and then 0.08%—thus finally beginning to convert the scientific findings generated by the Breathalyzer into appropriate public policy. More importantly, however, the new activism created an entirely new cultural image of the drunk driver, not as some type of all-American rebel or comic figure, but as an outlaw, pure and simple.

Was it the efforts of MADD and its sister organizations that led to a reduction in drunk driving deaths in the United States from more than 25,000 in 1980 to roughly 17,000 in 1992? It was nice to think so, because it honored the efforts of the activists. When Charles Gibson interviewed Candy Lightner on *Good Morning America* in 2000, he movingly stated that 110,000 people were alive because Cari Lightner had died.[15] But, demonstrating the continuing competing tensions between the moralistic and epidemiological approaches to drunk driving, such claims did not go unchallenged. A series of academicians following in the footsteps of William Haddon, including sociologists, statisticians, and policy experts, revived his approach, which closely scrutinized—and often criticized—standard data being generated about drunk driving–related crashes and casualties. For example, some of these researchers believed that activists routinely inflated the incidence of the problem because they falsely assumed that alcohol was necessarily the cause of any crash in which one or more parties had been drinking. Others made the point that anecdotes about drunk driving victims, while moving and important, had the potential to distract the public from embracing the most effective public health strategies to deal with a complicated and evolving problem. These conflicts, which had important ramifications for research funding and media attention, at times caused strained relations within the anti–drunk driving crusade.

Still, the successes of the movement were undeniable. By the start of the twenty-first century, drunk driving was no longer a laughing matter. The activists had made it one of the nation's foremost health concerns (alongside AIDS) for much of the 1980s. And even if there was disagreement about actual numbers and causation, rates of drunk driving and related injuries and deaths were clearly down. A series of interventions, ranging from tougher laws to more reliable punishments to sobriety checkpoints to ignition interlocks, represented successful strategies for combating intoxicated driving.

But, as is so often the case, the successes of MADD and other activist groups generated a backlash. A broad range of critics accused MADD of using its money to build a self-sustaining bureaucracy, of taking compromising funding from the alcohol industry, and most interestingly, of secretly being "neoprohibitionist," opposed not just to drunk driving but to the ingestion of alcohol more broadly. MADD became the punching bag for Internet pundits and publications such as *Modern Drunkard Magazine*, which used libertarianism to argue for the inalienable right of Americans to get sloshed and then, perhaps, to try to drive home.

Assessing these rebukes is difficult, and they may have had more symbolic than substantive effects on anti–drunk driving efforts. But one thing was clear: the movement's moment in the sun was to be brief. With dozens of competing public health issues, including ones pertaining to traffic safety, such as road rage and the use of cell phones when driving, the goal of eliminating most drunk driving deaths—which had seemed so pressing and even possible in the 1980s— once again became one of just many important social issues.

As described in Chapter 1, the history of drunk driving in the United States begins at the turn of the twentieth century, with the growing use of the automobile. It was not until the 1930s, however, that there was substantial scientific research into the problem. These first studies consistently showed that even small amounts of alcohol caused impairment behind the wheel. This work was enhanced by the introduction of the Drunkometer, the first machine that could measure blood alcohol levels using exhaled air. The chapter concludes with a forgotten episode in the history of drunk driving: the death of the beloved Margaret Mitchell, author of *Gone with the Wind*, at the hands of a likely drunk driver in 1949. At one point it looked as if Mitchell's death would spur a nationwide movement to crack down on intoxicated drivers, but such a crusade never materialized.

Chapter 2 covers the 1950s and 1960s, when the growth of the suburbs and interstate highways practically ensured an explosion of drunk driving. Reflecting back on his own "vehicular carousing" from this era, Jonathan Yardley later remarked that it was "a miracle" that he was alive to write about it.[16] But others were not so lucky, as injuries and fatalities mounted. Help was on the way, however, first in the form of the Breathalyzer and then the Grand Rapids Study, the first research project to definitively quantify the increased risk of driving at various BACs. This study induced the federal government to begin to characterize drunk driving as a public health emergency.

But, as Chapter 3 shows, there was no real anti–drunk driving movement until there were "public" victims and survivors who insisted on telling their moving and tragic stories. RID and MADD were the two main activist groups, but there was also Students Against Drunk Driving (SADD) and the Alliance Against Intoxicated Motorists. Harnessing the notion of victims' rights to images of grieving parents and their dead children, these activists proved remarkably adept at capturing the attention of the media and, by extension, the public. The alcohol industry also increased its anti–drunk driving efforts at this time, mostly by promoting responsible drinking, and, when possible, influencing the policies of the grassroots activist organizations. The chapter ends with Ronald Reagan's creation of the Presidential Commission on Drunk Driving in 1982. Drunk driving was front and center.

But was there more than one way to fight drunk driving? Chapter 4 answers yes to this question, chronicling the early efforts of academicians to both deconstruct the problem and shift the emphasis of control efforts. Also emerging in the mid-1980s was a renewed effort to conceptualize the anti–drunk driving crusade as a public health as opposed to a law-and-order issue. Politically progressive groups like the Center for Science in the Public Interest increasingly stressed preventive measures, such as restricting alcohol sales and advertising, as a way to lower the availability of alcohol and, in turn, drunk driving. But the alcohol industry and its allies fought back, pushing their familiar themes of personal choice and individual responsibility when it came to the use of alcohol. Was drunk driving a moral and legal transgression that demanded remorse and punishment? Or was it a public health problem that needed to be carefully studied and prevented? And, if it was both, did this dichotomy fatally impede the campaign? These tensions erupted in 1988, when Surgeon General C. Everett Koop held a controversial workshop on drunk driving, which some industry groups boycotted in protest.

By the 1990s, the backlash against anti–drunk driving activists, particularly the mothers of MADD, was in full flower. Critics ranged from industry to scholarly researchers questioning how much actual harm drunk driving caused to libertarians asserting their right to be left alone. It is no exaggeration to suggest that the fury directed at the women trying to control drunk driving at times dwarfed the original anger these women had shown to the killers of their children. Rather than serve as an impetus for constructive change, events like the 1997 death of Princess Diana of Wales in a drunk driving crash became moratoria on how MADD used propaganda to further its cause. Still, as detailed in Chapter 5, progress continued to be made as scientists generated substantial data about the value of various interventions. Most notably, by 2004, all fifty states had lowered their legal BACs to 0.08%—close to, but not at, the 0.05% level at which impairment generally begins.

Chapter 6 looks at drunk driving today, more than a hundred years after it was identified and thirty years after the crusade to stop it began. The chapter tells a series of stories, such as that of Donte Stallworth, an athlete who killed a man when driving drunk but who served less than thirty days in prison, and Diane Schuler, a mother who inexplicably got drunk and high with seven children in her minivan and killed herself and all but one of them. These stories demonstrate not only the pervasiveness of drunk driving but also the continued difficulty in explaining, preventing, and punishing such behavior. For every Internet discussant declaring alcohol-related deaths on the road to be "murder," there is another commentator citing extenuating circumstances and even, at times, characterizing the drunk drivers as the real victims.

Perhaps nothing better demonstrates the ambiguities and contradictions of drunk driving than the stories of two women involved in the founding of MADD: Candy Lightner and Cindi Lamb. Both women lost daughters to drunk drivers, although Lamb's daughter, Laura, was paralyzed for six years before dying. In the early 1990s, both women went to work for the alcohol industry, the very people who manufactured and vigorously advertised the exact product that had, indirectly, led to their children's deaths. As we will see, Lightner and Lamb were not naïve at all and had good reasons for doing what they did. But former colleagues were truly aghast.

One of the best articles written on drunk driving appeared in the journal *Philosophy and Public Affairs* in the summer of 1985. In it, the philosopher and bioethicist Bonnie Steinbock carefully laid out the case that American society inadequately prevented people from driving drunk and inadequately punished them when they did, even when injury or death resulted. She summarized her conclusions in an understated phrase: "It is not unreasonable to require people to undergo great inconvenience to avoid killing other people."[17] This book tells the story of how, in the case of drunk driving, this eminently rational proposition has too often been ignored.

CHAPTER ONE

The Discovery of Drunk Driving

There has probably been drunk driving for as long as there has been driving. Even before the invention of the automobile in the 1890s, the problem of impaired vehicle operators had been publicly discussed. But the rapid multiplication of "horseless carriages" on the roads of America quickly made the question of drunk driving a pressing subject.

The identification of a "new" social problem can provide a brief opportunity to explore what we might call the knee-jerk response of society. Within a few decades of learning that certain people drank intoxicating liquors and then chose to drive, what did Americans think? Were they appalled? Did they think it was inevitable? Acceptable? Acceptable under certain conditions?

Recognizable interest groups began to register opinions on this issue fairly quickly. Of course, alcohol was very much in the news at this time. The first two decades of the twentieth century witnessed the triumph of the temperance movement, which culminated in the passage of the Eighteenth Amendment (also known as the Volstead Act) in 1919. To Prohibitionists, drunk driving was another of the unambiguous evils produced by "demon rum" and other alcoholic beverages. But when the Twenty-First Amendment, which overturned Prohibition in 1933, ushered in the acceptance of drinking, it also signified Americans' willingness to tolerate and even celebrate drunk driving, though this position was never quite stated as such. This societal acceptance of drunk driving persisted for nearly five decades, until the rise of citizen activism in the late 1970s.

One of the most ironic aspects of this story is that as the twentieth century progressed, the ability to gauge which drivers were and which were not impaired dramatically increased. Yet blood alcohol levels and other scientific innovations were used as often to exonerate obviously drunk drivers as to convict them of serious crimes—even when innocent victims died as the result of these reckless escapades.

Americans welcomed the new automobiles with great excitement. Annual car sales, which had totaled eight thousand in 1900, leapt to more than eight million by 1920. The new vehicles transported people long distances in a short period of time, and they also quickly became status symbols. But there was trepidation as well. Within cities and on rural roads, automobiles upset the daily rhythms of life. After all, horse-driven carriages, the primary mode of transportation at this time, moved slowly. Accidents involving horses and buggies occurred, but there was usually time for pedestrians or other drivers to get out of the way of a wayward horse.

Of course, other motorized conveyances had existed for decades, most notably electric trolley cars within cities and trains that traveled between cities. The problem of periodic drunkenness among operators of these vehicles was well known. "The Conductor Was Drunk," read the headline of a January 10, 1887, *New York Times* story about a two-car train crash in Delaware on the Wilmington and Northern Railroad. Less than a week earlier, a drunken engineer had been the possible cause of a horrific accident on the Baltimore & Ohio Railroad near Tiffin, Ohio, which killed sixteen people. "Tyler, the engineer, is said to have been intoxicated," reported the *Washington Post*, "and a brakeman on his train said that he had four drinks with him the evening previous."[1]

Accidents such as these had begun to attract the attention of critics, such as editorial writers. In "Some Morals about Drink and Drunkards," "Howard," a Boston Globe columnist, commented on the Tiffin crash, in which the victims were "roasted alive in that horrible furnace, some of them with their heads and arms out of the windows." Underscoring the primary dilemma addressed by this book, Howard went on to state: "There is so much to be said as to a man's right on the one hand to do as he pleases [but also] as to a community's duty on the other hand to restrain individuals from doing as they please, if their pleasure brings discomfort, distress, expense upon the Commonwealth."[2]

Articles appeared in newspapers, magazines, and professional journals both at the time of such crashes and when they led to civil or criminal trials. Depending on the damage that had occurred, local laws, and the preferences of prosecutors, charges brought in such cases varied widely. The same proved true as the numbers of cars increased and drivers increasingly drove drunk. Should driving while intoxicated be considered a traffic violation or a more serious misdemeanor? Should this assessment change if damage occurred to people or property as the result of the driver's transgression? Finally, what charges were appropriate if people died at the hands of a drunk driver? Was such a crime manslaughter? Or, as some argued, was it murder to knowingly drive in an impaired state, which, by definition, put people's lives at risk?

There were no easy answers to these questions, and, indeed, they persist today. But crashes involving drunk drivers, especially those that involved prominent individuals, surely grabbed the public's attention. An oft-quoted 1904 article from the *Quarterly Journal of Inebriety* reported on twenty-five recent "alcohol-related accidents occurring to automobile wagons," which had led to twenty-three deaths. "Inebriates and moderate drinkers," the author concluded, "are the most incapable of all persons to drive motor wagons."[3]

A case that achieved particular notoriety in this era occurred in Los Angeles in 1905. On March 26, a "heavy touring automobile" driven by Barbee Hook, son of the late W. S. Hook, a wealthy streetcar manufacturer, hit a 22-year-old "obscure and humble" pedestrian named Margaret Birtwistle. Thrown a hundred feet, Birtwistle died of a fractured skull several days later. Hook had been speeding, perhaps as fast as 50 miles per hour in a residential area.

The *Los Angeles Times* covered the story very closely, because of the 21-year-old Hook's notoriety as a society playboy and because the case was California's first prosecution of a drunk driver on felony charges. It turned out that Hook and his two traveling companions had been drinking whiskey from pint flasks prior to the crash. The local prosecutor charged Hook with the felony of manslaughter, which was defined as the unlawful killing of a human being without malice. Meanwhile, as the hearing approached, Hook's mother offered to pay Birtwistle's mother $400 annually as a way to make amends. The reparations were accepted.

The case went to trial in July 1905. Those who testified included the physician who attended to the injured Birtwistle and various eyewitnesses, including the conductor and the motorman of the streetcar from which Birtwistle had just emerged before the crash. Although the motorman estimated that Hook's car was going 40 miles per hour, Esther Babler, one of Hook's passengers, testified that Hook had paid close attention to the road and had not been speeding. Hook himself took the stand on July 12, telling the jury that he had done everything possible to avoid hitting Birtwistle, whom he had seen only at the last moment.

"I could not have changed my action a bit if I had a week to think it over," he stated.[4]

After a four-day trial, it took the jury just fifty-two minutes to acquit Hook of manslaughter. The *Times* speculated that Hook's lawyers had successfully challenged the credibility of the prosecution's witnesses, thereby creating reasonable doubt. Whatever the exact details, the encounter between Barbee Hook and Margaret Birtwistle can be seen as emblematic of hundreds of thousands of similar events that occurred in America in the twentieth century: an innocent victim was injured or killed by an automobile driven in a reckless manner by someone who had chosen to both drink and get behind the wheel. Although many drivers would be found guilty of a serious crime in such cases, acquittals were commonplace, as were instances in which prosecutors would offer plea-bargains down to misdemeanors. At times, the only punishment might be a fine.

What also made the Hook case representative of other drunk driving cases was that it was less a fact-finding mission than a game. The reporter for the *Times* remarked that, during the trial, Hook had looked self-possessed, almost expecting acquittal. As he left the courtroom after the verdict, Hook blew rings of smoke from a cigarette. Over succeeding decades, defense lawyers would successfully work the legal system to free drunk drivers—many of whom were recidivists—whom they surely knew to be guilty.

And Barbee Hook proved to be one such recidivist. On December 29, 1907, according to the *Los Angeles Times*, he drove into a crowd of people at a Los Angeles intersection, nearly crushing a woman. Then, when police attempted to apprehend him, he sped away. Although the use of alcohol was not mentioned in the article, Hook had clearly not learned any lessons from the Birtwistle tragedy two years earlier.[5]

In its assessment of the Hook case prior to the trial, the *Times* was not nearly as forgiving as the jury ultimately was. The automobile, read an editorial, was "manifestly a great danger to the public when it is directed by hands made unsteady, or by brains made indecisive and reckless, through the use of liquor." The writer went on to question the use of the word *accident* to describe acts that were due "to the carelessness, incompetency, recklessness or inebriety of the man at the controls."[6] Nevertheless, the notion of automobile crashes caused by drunk drivers as accidental or an act of fate would persist for decades.

As acquittals like that of Barbee Hook became commonplace, local government officials sought to pass laws with more teeth. In Massachusetts in 1909, for example, the state's highway commission implemented a fine of not more than $200 and imprisonment of not more than six months for "operation of an automobile recklessly or while under the influence of liquor."[7] In New York, a state legislator named Albert S. Callan sponsored a law that both licensed automobiles and made it a felony to drive while intoxicated.

Even though the Callan law was strict on paper, within a few years it was being criticized as far too lenient. A cartoon in a New York City newspaper showed a tipsy driver mowing down women and children while a police officer stood idly by. A sign on the car announced "The Callan Joke Law." "It is ridiculous," said one New York City judge in 1912, "that a man should be able to drive a car in the streets of Manhattan Borough, at least, while intoxicated, and escape with a fine of $25."[8] Another judge favored a minimum of five years in prison for first-time offenders.

As the 1910s progressed, though, it appeared that a solution other than tougher punishments might solve the problem of drunk driving: getting rid of alcohol altogether. The push for Prohibition was in full flower, with twenty states having prohibited the sale of liquor by 1915. With the passage of the Volstead Act in 1919, the entire United States was technically "dry." Despite what the temperance movement had hoped, the new amendment did not make alcohol disappear; rather, it went underground, at speakeasies and private homes. Still, with alcohol now much harder to obtain and public consumption a potential crime, rates of drinking went down.[9] Although there were few statistics from the era specifically about drunk driving, it seems to have declined as well. So did attention to the issue.

By 1928, however, even though the "dry" candidate Herbert C. Hoover had defeated "wet" candidate Alfred E. Smith for the presidency, Prohibition's days were numbered. When Franklin D. Roosevelt became the thirty-second president in 1933, one of his first acts was to push for repeal of the Volstead Act, which occurred on December 5 of that year. The reasons for this turn of events were several. For one thing, as alcoholism historians Mark E. Lender and James K. Martin have written, the increasingly pluralistic nature of American society was causing "a rapid collapse of the moral authority of the sober republic." In addition, with the United States mired in an economic depression, tax receipts from legal liquor sales were highly appealing. Finally, most of the country, spurred on by a group of brewers, distillers, and other business leaders who called themselves the Association Against the Prohibition Amendment, judged Prohibition to have been a total failure. The Volstead Act had seemingly increased—not decreased—the vice associated with alcohol, by promoting bootlegging, bathtub gin, and the operation of mobster-run speakeasies. The drys, of course, disagreed, and anticipated that widespread legal use of alcohol would once again foster the exact problems that had led the country to try the "noble experiment."[10]

As the pendulum swung away from a dry mindset, literature and the cinema increasingly celebrated alcohol and inebriation. Alcohol played a central role in F. Scott Fitzgerald's 1925 novel of the Jazz Age, *The Great Gatsby*, and eased the ennui and alienation of characters in Ernest Hemingway's *The Sun Also Rises* (1926) and *A Farewell to Arms* (1929). Thorne Smith's 1926 novel *Topper*, which became a 1937 movie starring Cary Grant, romanticized the heavy-drinking couple George and Marion Kerby, who were killed when an inebriated George drives into a tree. Friends and acquaintances are none too distraught over the demise of the Kerbys, who wind up coming back as good-natured—and still drunk—ghosts. "A gay life and a quick death," remarked one character. "They liked it that way and they got what they wanted," mused another.[11] Nick and Nora Charles, hero and heroine of *The Thin Man* films of the 1930s, liked to compete with one another to see how many martinis they could down at one sitting.

Beyond this renewed love affair with alcohol, another factor was changing public opinion. Perhaps as a backlash against the obsession with alcohol that had characterized the Prohibition era, Americans shifted their focus increasingly to the alcoholic and the new "disease" of alcoholism. From the newly founded Research Council on Problems of Alcohol (1937) to the Yale School of Alcohol Studies (1943) to the voluntary agency known as the National Council for Education on Alcoholism (1944) to Alcoholics Anonymous (1935), the long vilified drunk was getting a makeover. No longer a sinner responsible for his own misguided ways, he was the victim of a disease—and thus in need of medical treatment instead of scorn. "Our concern," wrote NCEA President and recovered alcoholic Marty Mann, "is a disease called alcoholism and its victims, those hapless, suffering human beings who are known as alcoholics." The time had come to prevent the "thousands of unnecessary deaths" from alcoholism.[12]

If treating the disease of alcoholism was one strategy for preventing the abuse of liquor post-repeal, an emphasis on moderate drinking was another. In 1934, a New Jersey lawyer and politician named Everett Colby formed the Council for Moderation, a voluntary agency that sought to urge the public to enjoy alcohol in modest amounts. By devilifying liquor, Colby hoped to strike a compromise between the drys and the wets. What better way, after all, to reassure

Americans that the repeal of Prohibition did not simply presage a return to the "bad old days" of public drunkenness and seedy saloons?[13]

The dual concepts of alcoholism and moderation found favor within the beverage industry. Cautiously reintroducing their product to an America that still, in some sense, distrusted alcohol, distillers and other manufacturers of alcoholic beverages were drawn to the notion that only a small diseased subset of the population abused the product. Indeed, segments of the alcohol industry quietly began to provide funds to both the Research Council and the Yale School, which eventually raised questions as to the objectivity of research into the concept of alcoholism. This effort to shift attention away from the notion of liquor itself as the root of all evil made the remaining drys, such as the members of the Woman's Christian Temperance Union and other religious Protestants, highly skeptical of the new "science." As a result, these individuals, once largely seen as embodying social respectability, increasingly came to be perceived in some circles as fanatics. Meanwhile, the perception that most drinkers used liquor properly promoted growing sales among the bulk of the population. Over the succeeding decades, middle-class Americans, who had previously avoided alcohol or drunk it in private, openly embraced it. Moderation, historian Patricia A. Morgan has written, "became a key marketing, public relations and advertising . . . strategy" for decades.[14]

Liquor advertisements from the 1930s played up the virtues of moderation. For example, the Distilled Spirits Institute, a lobbying group established by the liquor industry in 1933, developed a Code of Good Practice urging the use of slogans such as "We who make whiskey say: drink moderately." The company in the forefront of these efforts was Joseph E. Seagram & Sons, which ran newspaper advertisements portraying Seagram's customers as cultured individuals who drank sophisticated blended whiskies and did not get drunk. "One man who is guilty of excess in drinking," announced Seagram's spokesperson H. I. Peffer in 1934, "can make a spectacle of himself while a thousand men who drink moderately go unnoticed."[15] Peffer readily admitted these ads were a strategic move to help the distilling industry "perpetuate itself," but Samuel Bronfman, the head of Seagram's parent company and the creative force behind this campaign, also appears to have had a genuine interest in marketing a safer, socially acceptable product. Seagram's even publicly praised the actor Ray Milland for his performance as an end-stage alcoholic in *The Lost Weekend*, the 1945 Hollywood film that did not hide its anti-alcohol bent.[16]

It was one thing to talk about the disease of alcoholism and the importance of moderation when discussing individual drinkers who potentially harmed themselves. But how did these concepts apply when others were being harmed? This was not an academic question. Data compiled soon after repeal suggested that the increased availability of liquor had quickly accelerated the problem of drunk driving. In Chicago, for example, injuries and deaths due to drunk driving were four times higher during the first six months of 1934 than the first six months of 1933. Also in 1934, Los Angeles officials reported a "vast increase in drunk driving since repeal" and a 40 percent increase in deaths attributed to drunk drivers. "During the past year," a *Los Angeles Times* editorial read, "the country has been shocked, if not sobered, by the alarming rate of increase of traffic casualties directly traceable to the effects of hard liquor on bibulous automobile drivers."[17]

What, then, was society to do with those who drove while intoxicated? To some degree, it depended on who was doing the drunk driving. Broadly, two different ways had emerged for classifying those who drank and drove. One was to distinguish between the alcoholic and the so-called social drinker. Another was to distinguish between drivers who were extremely intoxicated and those who were merely impaired. There was some degree of correlation between the categories. Alcoholics, experts believed, were more likely to be very drunk and social drinkers "buzzed," although this was not always the case.

If one looks at the anti–drunk driving rhetoric that emerged in the 1930s, no amount of drinking and driving was deemed acceptable. "A drunken man at the wheel of an automobile," wrote the *Los Angeles Times*, "is about as safe as a stick of dynamite with the fuse lighted." "No man who has been drinking is a safe driver," stated the head of the California Highway Patrol.[18] Whereas Seagram's and other liquor manufacturers emphasized moderation for the average drinker, this option did not apply to those who chose to drive after imbibing. A series of advertisements begun by Seagram's in 1935 to promote "safer, saner driving" definitively declared that "alcohol and gasoline do not mix." "This conviction must be shared," a later advertisement reiterated, "by everyone who reads the newspapers and by every thinking person who drives a car."[19]

Drinking and driving was also strongly discouraged by the National Safety Council, a nonprofit, nongovernmental organization comprising corporate and individual members that was America's foremost authority on drunk driving from the 1930s into the 1970s. When the NSC was founded in 1913, its primary aim was the prevention of workplace injuries. Founding organizations included steel and railroad companies. As the NSC gradually expanded its aegis to non-workplace issues, such as highway safety, drunk driving became a logical focus,

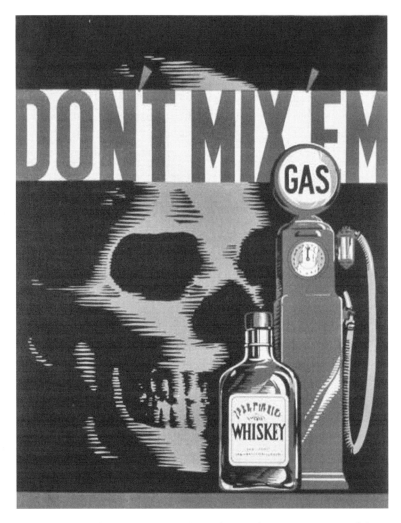

Works Project Administration print by Robert Lachenmann warning of the dangers of drinking and driving. Courtesy of the Library of Congress

especially following repeal. The NSC established a Committee on Alcohol and Other Drugs in 1936 and quickly initiated an educational campaign with the slogan "If you drink, don't drive." In later years, the NSC would be best known for its warning announcements that estimated how many Americans would die in automobile crashes over various holiday weekends.

The NSC blamed workplace accidents on a complex combination of human error and mechanical hazards, but ultimately, drawing on the work of industrial safety pioneer Herbert W. Heinrich, it cited unsafe acts by workers as the more common cause. These included "improper attitude" and "lack of knowledge or skill." The NSC's relative downplaying of corporate responsibility has led some historians to see the organization as industry-dominated and devoted to protecting the interests of business. What seems clear is that its focus on the individual responsibility of workers jibed well with its efforts to control drunk driving, which emphasized the problem of recalcitrant alcoholics on the roads—as opposed to scrutinizing the safety initiatives of automobile manufacturers or the promotion of drinking by the alcohol industry.[20]

It is difficult to know the degree to which the new paradigm, which viewed alcoholism as a disease, interfered with efforts to prosecute alcoholic drivers. For one thing, even though academia and Alcoholics Anonymous were pushing the disease paradigm, it hardly achieved immediate acceptance by the public. Nevertheless, the new emphasis probably generated a degree of sympathy for alcoholics that permeated certain courtrooms. More specifically, to the degree that treatment of the underlying illness was becoming increasingly important for alcoholics, punishing them for drunk driving seemed counterproductive—a point that would be made most explicitly in the early 1970s by the first head of the National Institute on Alcohol Abuse and Alcoholism.

A similar tolerance characterized the attitude of law enforcement toward social drinkers who chose to drive. One explanation for this situation stemmed from the common use of the term *drunk driving* itself. If it was *drunk* drivers who were menaces on the road, the implication was that it was the heaviest drinkers—that is, the alcoholics—who were mostly at fault.

But the term *social drinker* deserves equal scrutiny. Its origins are not clear, but as early as the late nineteenth century it was being used to describe individuals who partook of liquor as part of other activities, such as eating out, going to the theater, or attending sporting events. Unlike the alcoholic, who drank to get inebriated, the ostensible goal of drinking for such people was not to get drunk but to better enjoy the activity in question. As such, *social drinker* retained a positive connotation, suggesting that such an individual was both sociable and harmless. It followed that if he or she caused some type of disturbance, it was surely a one-time mistake. These assumptions were especially commonplace when intoxicated "social drinkers" were of the same social class as the local prosecutor and judge, thus tempting these officials to look the other way and do a favor for a friend. This situation likely characterized the Barbee Hook case.

If the categories of alcoholic and social drinker proved equally unhelpful in bringing drunk drivers to justice, perhaps the actual degree of intoxication could provide a better guidepost. That is, there surely had to be a level of impairment that represented such a clear danger that society would find it unacceptable. The trouble, though, was that such assessments in this era were by definition subjective. Since the first drunk driving laws went on the books in the early twentieth century, police performing roadside examinations had basically gauged drunkenness by how well drivers could perform a series of tests, such as identifying themselves, answering questions, walking a straight line, maintaining their balance during a series of tasks, and acting sober. Another favorite was asking drivers to say "Methodist Episcopal" to reveal a drunken lisp. Because the findings relied on the testimony of the police officer only, drivers could later dispute what had happened, a loophole large enough for defense lawyers to, figuratively, drive through. And witnesses always seemed available with alibis, swearing that the driver in question had imbibed no more than two drinks.

But science was about to change things dramatically. Concerned about the subjectivity of police examinations, researchers had been working since the 1920s on various tests to ascertain degrees of inebriation. Among the earliest scientists was Erik Widmark, a Swedish physician and physiologist who, in the late 1910s, developed a mechanism for quantifying the amount of alcohol in the blood obtained by a fingertip sample. He also provided kits to the police enabling them to collect the blood of suspected drunk drivers. Widmark's method, like those of subsequent scientists in the field, would be criticized by some as inaccurate, but most experts believed that it could reliably estimate how much alcohol had been ingested.[21]

The next major advance was the Drunkometer, invented in 1931 by Rolla N. Harger, a cigar-smoking biochemist at Indiana University, which became available for use in 1937. Harger's great accomplishment was the ability to estimate blood alcohol levels by having drivers blow air into his device, a latex balloon connected to a series of chemicals that turned various colors depending on the degree of intoxication. Such testing obviated the need to draw blood. There were high hopes for what the new device might achieve, making prosecution of accused drunk drivers less ambiguous and less adversarial. "The use of the Drunkometer assures an honest prosecution and eliminates the chance of error under the Drunk Motor Law," a Detroit police official stated. Commentators often remarked that science had now entered the field. As a *New York Times* reporter wrote, "Science is replacing guesswork in obtaining evidence in drunken-driving cases."[22] Harger quickly began a course at Indiana University to teach law enforcement officials and others how to use the machine. In January 1939, owing to its experience with the Drunkometer, Indiana passed the country's first law equating various blood alcohol levels with degrees of intoxication. Harger donated all royalties from the Drunkometer to the Indiana University Foundation.

Even before there were ways to check blood alcohol levels, there was a consensus in the scientific community that alcohol's effects occurred at low levels. "Many investigators have shown," wrote Ohio physician Herman M. Gunn in 1938, "that even small amounts of alcohol ingested by most people will produce a sufficient depressant action to interfere with their various mental functions." Such impairment, Gunn added, made drinkers more "accident prone."[23] Yet did this mean that drinkers should never drive? Could such individuals still operate cars safely? Was it possible that they actually paid closer attention to the road if they had "had a few"?

The only way to answer such questions definitively was through scientific research, which could now employ the new technology of blood alcohol testing. Among the first investigators to do so was a Wisconsin physician named Herman A. Heise. Prior to the widespread emergence of the field of epidemiology, it was not uncommon for physicians—and the American Medical Association—to champion this type of public health research, although topics like alcoholism and certainly drunk driving were largely absent from medical school curricula. Heise had an interesting personal connection to drunk driving. In 1917, while a young physician serving in the Medical Corps at Fort Oglethorpe, Georgia, he found himself performing autopsies on soldiers who got into car crashes while racing home before the midnight curfew. Although this was the era before blood alcohol testing, Heise concluded that those killed were "all loaded with alcohol."[24]

One of Heise's earliest studies, presented at the 1934 annual meeting of the American Medical Association and then published in *JAMA*, the *Journal of the American Medical Association*, involved a group of volunteer subjects who were not driving. First, he gave them 30 cc (1 oz.) of whisky and had them perform various tasks at a typewriter. "All subjects in this group," Heise reported, "suffered a measured loss of efficiency, generally gaining increased speed at the expense of accuracy." When Heise measured blood alcohol content (BAC) and urine alcohol levels in this group, they did not exceed 0.02%, which meant 20 mg of alcohol in 1,000 mL of blood, or just slightly above negative.

Then Heise moved specifically to the question of drunk driving, giving his subjects five times as much whiskey and putting them behind the wheel. He had managed to get the mayor of Uniontown, Pennsylvania, where he was then working as a police physician, to cordon off several streets and provide police escorts for the drivers. Interestingly, Heise's subjects proved able to do routine driving and even to pass typical roadside sobriety tests. But, he reported, when various obstacles and complicated tasks were added, "reaction times were somewhat increased and all subjects displayed a lack of appreciation of changes in judgment and motor control." All subjects in the study, Heise added, admitted to being disoriented and either exhilarated or depressed. Their blood alcohol levels were all below 0.10%.[25]

Testing outside of the United States also revealed impairment after ingestion of small amounts of alcohol. For example, researchers in Dresden, Germany, found that 20 percent of drivers drove recklessly with a blood alcohol level of 0.02%, 49 percent with a level of 0.05% (two and one-half small bottles of beer), and 87.5 percent with a level of 0.10%. A 1937 article in the *Edinburgh Medical Journal* reported on data from London's Westminster Hospital that found that blood alcohol levels between 0.01% and 0.08% produced the following behaviors: "fewer inhibitions, delayed reaction times and diminished judgment, attention and control." Later work would confirm that a 0.05% BAC generally led to an inability to process information and make rational decisions.[26]

Meanwhile, researchers sought to quantify and analyze the blood alcohol levels of actual apprehended drunk drivers, particularly those involved in crashes. In another study conducted in Uniontown, Heise reviewed 119 crashes that had occurred in the area over two years. He found that 74 of the crashes (62%) had involved alcohol. In addition, 155 of the 199 injured people (78%) and 10 of the 17 killed (59%) had been involved in the alcohol-related crashes. Through newspaper articles and public lectures, Heise attempted to alert the public that "little nips" of liquor should not be ignored.[27]

Later in the 1930s, Richard L. Holcomb, of the Traffic Institute of Evanston, Illinois, performed a more sophisticated case-control study comparing the BACs of drivers involved in crashes in Evanston with other drivers using the same roads during the same hours. He found that 25 percent of those who crashed had consumed enough alcohol to impair their driving ability (a 0.10% BAC) compared to only 2 percent of his controls. The conclusion: drunk drivers were much more likely to be involved in crashes, as high as 33 times more likely, if their blood alcohol levels were 0.15% or more.[28]

So how were these data to be used to create more just and effective drunk driving laws? Europe, particularly Widmark's native Scandinavia, had already begun to weigh in. In 1936, Norway adopted a national law making it a criminal offense to drive with a blood alcohol level higher than 0.05%, roughly equivalent to two or three shots of whiskey or two or three 12-ounce beers in one hour on an empty stomach. Sweden followed suit in 1941, opting for a level of 0.08%, which it then lowered to 0.05% in 1957. Denmark and Finland also relied heavily on BAC testing and strict punishments. The laws were known as *per se*, meaning that exceeding the stated limit itself constituted a crime, regardless of the apprehended person's physical or mental state. These low legal BACs, plus the relatively strict penalties that ensued for violators—often imprisonment— became celebrated as the Scandinavian approach to drunk driving. Although some criticized it as state paternalism, it seemed to have a substantial deterrent effect. For example, between 1935 and 1959 in Sweden, convictions for drunk driving increased from 1,255 to 8,190. Concurrently, the percentage of motor vehicle crashes involving alcohol declined by 40 percent. "When a man goes to a party where alcoholic drinks are likely to be served, and if he is not fortunate enough to have a wife who drives but does not drink," Norwegian lawyer and drunk driving researcher Johannes Andenaes wrote, "he will leave his car at home or he will limit his consumption to a minimum." Others took taxis. In one Scandinavian country, it was apparently acceptable for a drunken person to request that the police take him and his car home.[29]

Lund University legal scholar Hans Klette traced this model to the legal philosophy of Sweden's renowned Uppsala University, which was that "criminal law can be used to educate or create morality." Central to such a strategy was the concept of deterrence. In the case of drunk driving, those previously arrested for driving while intoxicated and others at risk for doing so would "think twice," owing to the possibility of severe punishment. A *New York Times* reporter met a civil engineer, an insurance agent, and a bookbinder chopping wood at a prison work camp north of Stockholm. The men were serving one- to three-month sentences for driving with a BAC of roughly 0.15%.[30]

Some of the momentum for these strict laws came from a culture that embraced temperance, especially when it improved safety. As the United States lurched from Prohibition to repeal, a Union of Temperance Drivers formed in Sweden to discourage drinking and driving, mostly through public education. In 1934, it linked forces with groups in Norway, Finland, and Denmark to form the Scandinavian Union for Non-Alcoholic Traffic. This notion of voluntarily avoiding drinking before driving greatly impressed Rolla Harger, who regretted that no similar organization (or philosophy) existed in America.[31]

What was occurring in the United States by 1938 was that committees from the National Safety Council and the American Medical Association had joined forces to study the problems of motor vehicle accidents and testing for intoxication. The committees, comprising physicians, scientists, and administrators interested in drunk driving, overlapped in membership. Herman Heise, for example, sat on the NSC committee and chaired the AMA committee. Ultimately, the AMA committee issued a series of reports, with which the NSC committee concurred.

The first AMA report, dated May 1939, detailed a series of "physical and mental defects" apt to lead to accidents, including various diseases, visual deficits, sleep deprivation, and even "feeblemindedness." But the major cause of the "slaughter" on America's highways, Heise and colleagues believed, was "alcoholic intoxication." Citing Holcomb's data, other research correlating blood alcohol concentrations with "detrimental effects" and Indiana's new law, the committee established a framework to guide police and other officials seeking to control drunk driving. Despite periodic objections from critics who found these standards to be extremely lax and even counterproductive, the committee's criteria had an enormous influence on America's drunk driving policy for decades.

In brief, the committee defined three separate situations:

1. Less than 0.05%: no prosecution for driving under the influence of alcohol
2. Greater than 0.15%: should be prosecuted as under the influence
3. Between 0.05% and 0.15%: prosecution only if the circumstances and results of physical examination "give definite confirmation of such influence."

In other words, the committee deliberately created a "liberal, wide zone" between unimpaired and impaired, which gave local officials great leeway in deciding whether to arrest and prosecute those apprehended.[32]

The quintessence of historical research is understanding why particular decisions were made at a given historical time. As the historian David Hackett Fischer has written, history is the study of "a series of real choices that living people actually made."[33] The AMA-NSC guidelines, later codified by the National Committee on Uniform Traffic Laws and Ordinances and eventually adopted in large part by all forty-eight states, are a wonderful case study for this type of analysis. Even though it was the committee's chairman, Heise, who had performed much of the groundbreaking research demonstrating impairment for blood levels *less* than 0.05%, and even though the committee cited Holcomb's research suggesting a much higher risk of crashes for blood alcohol levels approaching 0.15%, the committee nevertheless promulgated guidelines that can only be called highly forgiving of impaired drivers.

Relatively little information about the AMA-NSC committee's decision-making process was released at the time of its original deliberations. Committee members had liked the idea of an intermediate zone owing to the well-known variability with which people tolerated alcohol. And even though it was known that some individuals were impaired at 0.02% or 0.03%, a floor value of 0.05% was chosen. Choosing not to prosecute below 0.05%, the committee wrote, "vindicates the nondrinking or temperate driver."[34] This decision to exonerate *temperate drivers*—a term synonymous with *social drinkers*—would carve out an exception that persists today for nonalcoholics who wished to drive and drink (ostensibly in moderation) as part of their social lives.

As far as the upper limit of 0.15% goes, more information came to light twenty years later, when the AMA was developing a manual on chemical testing for intoxication. Heise, who was involved with this effort, took the opportunity to provide some back history to the 1938 deliberations, which had been quite controversial. The manual, coauthored by Heise, Ralph F. Turner, and Clarence W. Muehlberger, explained that the first upper limit chosen had been 0.11%, but because there were "a few tolerant persons" among heavy drinkers at this level, 0.13% was proposed instead. Eventually, the AMA-NSC committee had decided to go even higher, to 0.15%, because BAC testing had a margin of error and because "somewhere some person might be found who was still more tolerant than any seen by American experimenters."[35]

Committee members had realized full well that 0.15% was "inordinately high and extremely conservative," Heise and his colleagues wrote, but they rationalized their decision not only on the issue of tolerance but of individual liberties as well. "One of the cornerstones of our American way of life," the chemical testing manual explained, "is the element of personal freedom, the maximum liberty of the individual to do as he pleases within the restrictions of majority-approved laws." Put another way, they opted to respect the American tradition of justice, "wherein it is believed to be better for a guilty man to go free rather than have an innocent one convicted."[36]

It is hard to know what Heise and the other members of the original joint 1938 AMA-NSC committee, among the country's experts on the deaths and injuries caused by drunk driving, really thought of their decision. After all, they knew that even if Holcomb's early data were not definitive, a 33-times-greater chance of crash for a 0.15% blood alcohol level meant that those between 0.10% and 0.15% were dozens of times more likely to cause a crash and thus had absolutely no business being behind the wheel. One clue as to the joint committee's state of mind comes from one of its own follow-up reports, issued in 1942, which stated that "driving a car is such a hazardous occupation, even in the best of circumstances, that no driver should have the legal or moral right to lower his driving ability deliberately to any extent."[37] This statement obviously completely contradicts the earlier decision to essentially condone driving with mild impairment and to create a major exception for people whose blood alcohol tests indicated significant intoxication. Committee members surely realized that, due to the 0.15% upper limit, utterly intoxicated drivers, many of whom had already done terrible damage behind the wheel, would be let off scot-free and continue to drive drunk. That is, the committee simultaneously condemned such individuals as morally bankrupt and then gave them back their keys. In later years, Heise somewhat ruefully referred to the 0.05%–0.15% zone as his "illegitimate child."[38]

Ultimately, the AMA-NSC committee's decisions were the product of a distinct set of historical circumstances. Well aware of the recently concluded and highly criticized Prohibition experiment, committee members erred far on the side of leniency when it came to the apprehension and prosecution of impaired and drunk drivers. As Stanford University neurologist and alcoholism expert Henry W. Newman later explained, "We would not like to see a parallel to prohibition occur here, with the subsequent revulsion of feeling and the license that followed after prohibition and which still prevails to a certain extent at the present time."[39] At one point Newman even suggested that it was inappropriate to convict someone for drunk driving if he could still drive better than the least-skilled sober driver—a standard that would let just about any drinking driver off the hook.[40] Also, it is important to remember that the two sponsoring organizations, the AMA and the NSC, were basically conservative. In addition, by the 1930s, NSC member organizations included representatives of the alcohol industry. Although no correspondence exists documenting that they influenced the AMA-NSC committee's deliberations, it is reasonable to assume they would have objected to harsher drunk driving standards, which would have potentially reduced liquor sales in the United States just as the product had once again been made legal. Indeed, in later years, the beverage industry would explicitly challenge attempts to lower legal BACs and to allow police officers to randomly stop drivers and check their BACs.

Of course, it can be argued that Herman Heise, his fellow committee members, Indiana legislators, and others promulgating the new laws based on blood alcohol levels thought that sobriety testing would confirm inebriation among those with intermediate BACs and thus lead to both punishments and deterrence. In practice, however, the opposite occurred. Drunk drivers and, not infrequently, their lawyers, seized on the ambiguity of the committee's language to argue that those with blood levels between 0.05% and 0.15% should be given the benefit of the doubt. "In practice," Rolla Harger told attendees of the First International Conference on Alcohol and Road Traffic, held in Stockholm in 1950, "very few people are convicted in our country below 0.15%."[41] In turn, police and prosecutors became less enthusiastic about pressing charges against such drivers given the probability of plea-bargaining or outright acquittal. One California highway patrol superintendent even stopped getting BACs for fear they would exonerate obviously drunk individuals.[42] Ironically, therefore, the objective science designed to distinguish between safe and unsafe drivers actually further blurred this distinction. It was not until the late 1950s and early 1960s that state—and finally federal—agencies genuinely began to revisit what had become the status quo: a remarkable tolerance for a problem that killed tens of thousands of Americans every year.

This is not to say that the issue disappeared. All along, critics—mostly former drys, certain members of the media, and health officials—continued to rail against drunk driving. Most of these individuals, however, were "preaching to the choir," communicating their concerns to others already appalled by the situation. Public interest in drunk driving did increase after someone was killed or maimed by an impaired driver. Local newspapers covered the event and, if there was a trial, the legal proceedings. The problem was sustaining interest in the topic, something that proved nearly impossible.

At times, drunk driving cases achieved national attention. One such example was the sad story of Margaret Mitchell, the charming Atlantan whose 1936 novel *Gone with the Wind* had sold eight million copies and been made into an Oscar-winning motion picture by the time she was hit by a car on August 11, 1949. The 43-year-old Mitchell was crossing her beloved Peachtree Street, which she had made famous in her book, heading to the theater with her husband, advertising executive John R. Marsh. Suddenly, a car going 50 miles per hour in a 25-mph zone, driven by 29-year-old Hugh D. Gravitt, an off-duty taxi driver driving his private car, hit Mitchell, dragging her some fifteen feet.

It was readily apparent that the injuries were grave. Mitchell was not responsive. A disturbing and graphic Associated Press photograph distributed to newspapers across the country showed an unconscious Mitchell lying face down in the street in front of onlookers prior to the arrival of an ambulance. Mitchell was taken to Atlanta's famed Grady Memorial Hospital, where doctors initially diagnosed her with a brain concussion, leg injuries, and possible internal injuries. Two of the South's most prominent brain surgeons consulted on her case and concluded that she was too sick for an operation. Although newspapers reported some improvement in her condition on August 12, the famed author deteriorated four days later. She was rushed to the operating room but died on the table, presumably of a brain hemorrhage.

The Mitchell story was big news, covered on the front pages of newspapers across the country. Not only was Mitchell beloved, especially in the South, but it turned out that Gravitt had twenty-two prior traffic infractions since 1944, including seven for speeding and five for "reckless driving." Moreover, he admitted to having drunk beer at some point before the accident, although he later insisted it had been only one beer four hours earlier. The arresting officers later stated that they had smelled alcohol on Gravitt's breath, but apparently his blood alcohol level was not checked. Local officials initially charged Gravitt with speeding, drunken driving, and driving on the wrong side of the road.

Editorials and letters appearing in the *Atlanta Journal,* the *Atlanta Constitution,* and other newspapers across the country expressed astonishment and dismay that Gravitt had previously received only slaps on the wrist and had thus simply continued driving. The *Constitution* printed a list of Gravitt's past traffic offenses on August 13, 1949. The paper's editorial page concurrently posed two questions, asking why his license had never been revoked and how he had simply been allowed to pay the same small fines over and over. "This man," the writer concluded, "has habitually endangered lives for four years." Ten days later, the *Journal* published the same list along with the names of the judges who had continually freed Gravitt rather than taking away his license. "An astonishing angle to this story of death in the American streets," wrote an editorialist in Texas, "was that the accused driver had a police record of 22 arrests for traffic law violations."[43] Although it was never specified whether Gravitt's numerous offenses had occurred when he was driving his cab, some writers nevertheless called for a crackdown on "reckless taxi driving"—ironic, perhaps, as future anti–drunk driving campaigns would strongly urge inebriated bar and restaurant patrons to call for cabs.

Certain members of the public were considerably angrier. Interestingly, while some of these writers took Gravitt to task, most leveled their criticism at the police and judges for excessive leniency and at the general public for its apathy. "Atlanta has just committed another murder," read a typical letter to the *Journal*. "Margaret Mitchell was killed," *New York Sun* columnist Dave Boone wrote, "as much by Police-Court prosecutors, Judges and automobile–law enforcement bureaus as by the actual driver of the auto that ran her down."[44] Letters sent directly to John Marsh made similar points. "Atlanta must be seething with indignation," wrote a South Carolina lawyer, "at this useless extinction of a life so valuable." Anger piqued when a photograph of a jailed Gravitt and two grinning policemen was published in the September 19, 1949, issue of *Life* magazine. "I'd like to know," asked a New York woman, "what's so funny about having a record of 22 traffic violations and then being responsible for the death of one of the greatest writers?" Another correspondent to *Life* termed the image the "most contemptible picture I've ever seen."[45]

The possibility that Gravitt was drunk generated special enmity. "Let's take effective action," urged an *Atlanta Journal* editorial, "against the innumerable drunken drivers who menace us all in their alcoholic daze." *Journal* columnist Pierce Harris mocked the common excuse "I just had a couple of beers," writing that "more and more space is required every day to tell about the people getting killed by drunken drivers." Harris also presaged anti–drunk driving activists in criticizing liquor advertising that proclaimed the "virtues of beer," especially to young people. The result, according to Harris: "more slaughtered citizens under spinning wheels." A reader of the *Journal* perceptively took its editors to task for printing both an anti–drunk driving editorial and liquor advertisements in the same issue. "Is the revenue received from these advertisements," the writer asked, "sufficient to compensate for the lives of our people who are maimed and killed by the stuff you advertise?"[46]

Mitchell's was perhaps the first drunk driving death that had the potential to mobilize the entire country to take action on the problem. The Margaret Mitchell papers at the University of Georgia contain editorials from newspapers, such as the *Spokane* (WA) *Review*, the *St. Charles* (MO) *Cosmo-Monitor*, and the *Pine Bluff* (AR) *Commercial*, with headlines such as "Murder by Auto Must Be Stopped," "Margaret Mitchell Was Murdered," and "Drunk at the Wheel."

Ned H. Dearborn, president of the National Safety Council, saw an opportunity as well, urging the public to care as much about drunk driving as it did contagious diseases such as typhoid fever. "It's time we quarantined traffic killers just as we quarantine disease carriers," he told the Associated Press.[47]

Locally, several Georgians approached John Marsh with the idea of using his wife's name to spur measures to control drunken and otherwise reckless drivers. A Boy Scout leader from Forsyth, Georgia, upset not only at Mitchell's death but at the death of two local boys at the hands of a drunk driver, proposed a "Margaret Mitchell Minute," in which Americans would pause for one minute at noon on August 16, 1950, the one-year anniversary of Mitchell's death. Marsh agreed, and also approved the founding of the Margaret Mitchell Safety Foundation, a Georgia organization that sought to save lives and reduce injuries from traffic accidents through educational programs for secondary school and college students.[48]

Mitchell's death also spurred one newspaper to produce what may have been the first investigative report into the problems of drunk driving. In December 1949, the *Los Angeles Times* ran a five-part series by a reporter, Bill Dredge. That the investigation took place in Los Angeles and California was no surprise. Beginning with Depression era workers in search of jobs and continuing into the war years, the population of California had dramatically increased. There were roughly 3.5 million people living in the state as of 1920; by 1950, this figure would triple, to over 10.5 million. The number of cars had increased commensurately. Los Angeles County, itself home to more than 4 million people by 1950, lacked an extensive public transportation system, meaning that city and suburban streets—and later a series of highways—were crammed with drivers and pedestrians.

"Drunk Driving Toll Highest in History" blared the front-page headline in the December 5, 1949, edition of the *Times*. Dredge went on to explain how police in Los Angeles expected to arrest 4,500 people for drunk driving in 1949, nearly double the total for 1939. But this figure still represented only a fraction of the city's drunken drivers, "usually those so drunk they lose control of their cars, cause accidents, block traffic or otherwise call public attention to their sodden plight." Moreover, Dredge reported, those arrested were generally "patted" through the courts with fines, probationary sentences, and generally only brief license suspensions.[49]

This enormous leniency occurred even though there was a felony drunk driving law on the books. The problem, according to Dredge, was that the law was rarely used to its full extent. A survey conducted by the *Times* found that the local district attorney had pursued only 34 of 176 cases of drunk drivers originally charged with a felony and had obtained only 9 convictions. In the remaining 25 instances, as with the 142 cases not considered as felonies, the charges had either been dropped or lowered to lesser misdemeanors, even if they did not reflect what had actually happened. These included reckless driving, parking violations, bald tires, or violation of the city drunk ordinance, and carried fines of only $10 to $20. As a result, less than 6 percent of people charged with DWI ever went to jail. Moreover, even when prosecutors obtained DWI convictions, the guilty parties were likely to remain free. For example, there was only a 50 percent chance that people convicted of DWI three times would spend any time in jail.

One problem, Dredge reported, was the strict nature of the felony law, which required prosecutors to show that the defendant was drunk, was driving, was simultaneously guilty of a second driving offense, and had inflicted serious injury on another person. Meanwhile, earlier in 1949, the California state legislature had actually weakened the existing misdemeanor laws, overturning an earlier mandatory license suspension for people convicted of drunk driving. The result of this weak law enforcement, according to the newspaper, was that "two, three, four and up to 10-time drunk driving offenders are able to flout the law and drive on Southland highways, killing, maiming, wrecking and laughing at the law."[50]

Hyperbolic? Perhaps, but Dredge supplemented his reporting with a vivid and horrifying case study of a man the paper unsubtly called "John Death." Over a ten-year period, this person, described as "a woodworker and a family man," regularly drove drunk despite having killed two people in 1938. After being released from prison in 1940, having served two years for manslaughter, he was arrested for drunk driving at least seven other times, including hit-and-runs and instances of resisting arrest and driving without a license. In several of these cases, John Death was released after only paying fines. At the time of the five-part series, he was evidently out of jail and free to drive. The explanation was "careless judges, thoughtless prosecutors, inaccurate filing systems and . . . pressures exerted by friends."[51]

Dredge concluded his reporting by providing a series of recommendations made by experts in the field: mandatory license suspensions, including permanent suspensions for repeat offenders; increased use of blood alcohol devices, such as Harger's Drunkometer, and legal support for such testing; and jail terms for felony drunk driving convictions. In addition, the experts interviewed by Dredge called for increased "public pressure" as a way to help achieve these tighter restrictions.

The public did respond—at least to Dredge's series. As had been true with the cases of Barbee Hook, Hugh Gravitt, and other drunk drivers whose stories had received coverage in local and national newspapers, ordinary citizens were appalled by what they read. "Your tackling the drunken and drinking driver situation is about the most worth-while undertaking for many a day," wrote a man from Palos Verdes Estates. A writer from Lancaster, California, agreed, writing that "death marches on" because of inadequate laws that force judges to hand down "soft-pedal sentences." "It is to be hoped," wrote a man from Los Angeles, "that our apathetic citizens may be so shocked that they may take the necessary action to eliminate, or at least lessen, this outstanding evil." Hearkening back to the days of the temperance movement, he concluded that "John Barleycorn is our public enemy No. 1."[52]

Four years after Dredge's series appeared, Baltimore psychiatrist Robert V. Seliger and Ohio criminologist Lloyd M. Shupe published a pamphlet for "young people and their parents" called *Alcohol at the Wheel*. Using graphic pictures from police files, the authors told stories of "killers at the wheel," drinking drivers whose automobiles were as "deadly as the loaded gun." In a typical case, a drunk driver had fallen asleep at the wheel and crossed into oncoming traffic. The resulting crash killed him and severely injured the two people in the second car. The driver's blood alcohol level was 0.155%. "We are horrified at the Korean War casualties," Seliger and Shupe wrote, "but we seemingly shrug our shoulders at the much heavier casualties on our highways and streets."[53]

The first drunk driving public service announcements aired on radio and television also dated from this era. Typical was "A Few Too Many," which told the story of Tom, who drove himself and a friend home from a bar after drinking more than he had planned. A crash ensues in which Tom loses his leg. Jim, meanwhile, is in the operating room, where his life hangs by a thread. When Tom is told this, he soberly intones, "If Jim dies, it's my fault. If Jim dies, I murdered him." Happily, Jim survives and Tom is extremely remorseful, regretting his trip on "Highball Highway" and vowing never to make the same mistake again. The announcement concludes with an appearance by the actor Robert Young of television's *Father Knows Best*, who, later in his career, admitted to being an alcoholic. Young explained that the first things to be affected by alcohol were judgment and the ability to distinguish right from wrong. "Those same few drinks that bring out the best in your personality," he warned, "can only accentuate your worst driving habits."

But like everything else, outrage is historically contingent. Young's words, like those of Seliger and Shupe and those of Dredge, largely fell on deaf ears. By the late 1950s, however, the first voices would emerge characterizing the problem of intoxicated drivers as a public health emergency.

CHAPTER TWO

Science and Government Enter the Fray

It might sound crude, but it is reasonable to call the 1950s and early 1960s the "golden age of drunk driving." One person who might have agreed was the New York Yankees' all-star center fielder Mickey Mantle, who was not only a heavy drinker but thought nothing of driving home after a binge. Like most drunk drivers, he got lucky for a while, but in 1963, a drunken Mantle, speeding at over 60 miles per hour, crashed into a telephone pole, ejecting his wife, Merlyn. Happily, she only required stitches. Mantle, thanks to sympathetic police officers, paid $400 to replace the pole but was never charged with DWI. The crash never made it into the papers.[1]

Even though many Americans during these decades personally witnessed the carnage produced by intoxicated drivers, and others heard stories through the media, the cultural, political, and economic factors that directly or indirectly promoted drinking and driving simply overwhelmed efforts to identify, arrest, convict, and punish offenders. These factors included postwar prosperity, the growth of suburbs, a new interstate highway system, declining restrictions on alcohol sales, and clever marketing by the beverage industry, particularly of beer. In Mantle's case, fame also helped.

It was not until the 1960s, when a workaholic government bureaucrat named William Haddon Jr. tried to reconceptualize drunk driving as a public health problem, that change would begin to occur. Among Haddon's first self-appointed tasks was to get people to stop using the word *accident* to describe an event caused when someone got drunk, chose to drive, and crashed his or her car.

Returning to the story of Margaret Mitchell can convey some of the barriers to controlling drunk driving during the postwar era. Gravitt did wind up going to jail. The local prosecutor had originally asked for a murder charge. However, the grand jury returned only an indictment for involuntary manslaughter because it believed that Gravitt's acts were "strictly unintentional." In November 1949, a jury convicted him of this charge, for which the penalty was 12 to 18 months in prison with the possibility of early parole. Gravitt eventually served 10 months and 20 days for killing Margaret Mitchell. Not only was this a lenient sentence, but the judge did not even bother to revoke Gravitt's license when he let him return home for several days to get his affairs in order prior to his imprisonment. Sure enough, Gravitt was involved in another crash while driving his personal car, this time hitting a truck. Ironically, he was hospitalized for his injuries at Grady Memorial, where his earlier victim had spent her last days.[2]

Despite Gravitt's repeatedly bad behavior, there was also a remarkable degree of sympathy for him. One crucial issue was that—as was often the case in drunk driving–related fatalities—the victim was not the drunk driver himself. Thus, while Margaret Mitchell was dead, Hugh Gravitt was very much alive. For example, an editorial in the November 19, 1949, *Atlanta Journal* stated: "For Gravitt as a person we have the utmost sympathy. He surely did not intend to kill anyone and tragedy will haunt him as long as he lives."[3] This characterization was promoted by Gravitt's lawyer, who claimed that the police were victimizing his client by falsely asserting that he must have been drunk at the time of the crash. Gravitt firmly stuck to his story that he had drunk only one beer four hours prior to hitting Mitchell.[4]

For his part, Gravitt did all the right things. When Mitchell was lying in a coma, he told the press that he was praying for her recovery and "would give anything" if it could have been him, rather than Mitchell, in front of his car. Gravitt's mother-in-law was quoted as saying, "We are Christian people praying for her every minute." Most remarkably, however, Gravitt and his wife actually showed up at Grady Memorial Hospital on August 15, 1949, after he'd been released on bail. They brought both red roses and a calling card, on which had been written "Mr. and Mrs. Hugh Gravitt—Came by to see family."[5]

Although the family apparently declined the offer, the Gravitts' gesture spoke volumes about public understandings of drunk driving crashes in this era. Rather than laying low because of shame and guilt, Gravitt treated the event primarily as unfortunate and accidental. Mitchell was, he might have said, in the wrong place at the wrong time. This fatalistic strain, no doubt informed by Christian beliefs common to mid-century America, came through in letters sent to John

Marsh. "Well we all have to go some way and some time," wrote one Atlanta woman. "We don't understand why she had to go the way she did, but God knows and does everything for the best." A woman from Buena Vista, Georgia, agreed, noting that "death comes when it will" and that there was "no need to weep or wonder about God's way."[6]

Marsh himself said little publicly about what had happened, but what he said appeared fairly mild. If more strict ordinances were passed as a result of his wife's death, Marsh told one newspaper, "I feel it's not a bit too soon." More interesting was a quote by Marsh that appeared in a column by Edna Cain Daniel in the August 22, 1949, *Atlanta Journal*. "It was an accident," he said, "that did not have to happen." To her credit, columnist Daniel pointed out to her readers that Marsh's ambiguous statement exemplified her own "confused gropings" about what had occurred. Although it was common to attribute such events to "inscrutable fate," she wrote, the fault instead rested with "the stupid things, neglect, careless disregard, the violent, dull, meaningless ways of our communal life."[7]

While central to understanding popular conceptions of automobile crashes, the tendency to view them as acts of God was far from the only reason that they were tolerated. Whether in Atlanta or elsewhere, whether you were a police officer, a prosecutor, or a judge, it was simply easier to look the other way. Gravitt's twenty-two previous arrests, with their minor or nonexistent penalties, proved this, as did the judge's inexplicable decision to let Gravitt continue to drive while awaiting his prison sentence. And the public, for the most part, did not seem to mind. "Public pressure, let us admit," wrote the *Atlanta Journal*, "is generally on the side of leniency." The *Atlanta Constitution* agreed, noting that the public had specifically voted for judges less inclined to enforce Atlanta's traffic laws.[8]

The lack of public revulsion at Gravitt was even more striking given that he had killed one of Atlanta's—and the South's—most beloved citizens. And if anything, as time passed, there was even more sympathy for Gravitt. Writing in 1989, the renowned *Atlanta Constitution* columnist Celestine Sibley took up his cause. She was one of the few people in 1949, she wrote, who believed that the crash was not Gravitt's fault. Sibley believed that Mitchell, seeing the speeding car approaching, had inadvertently dashed into its path while Marsh, staying still, had lived. Even at this late date, her 1989 column read, "it would be good to have a book that exonerates the taxi driver." Sibley also later remarked that Mitchell, who was her friend, would not have wanted Gravitt to go to prison.

Another Atlanta journalist, Gary Pomerantz, tracked down a remorseful 71-year-old Gravitt in 1991, penning another sympathetic piece.[9]

Rather remarkably, with the passage of time, Mitchell had become the guilty party. Gravitt, the recidivist driver who was speeding in a crowded area, driving on the wrong side of the street and possibly intoxicated, had become the victim. No wonder it was so difficult—whether in 1949 or even 1989—to see reckless drivers as culpable.[10]

Atlanta was no different from the rest of the country in its ambivalence about arresting and prosecuting drunk drivers. For one thing, the problem was potentially enormous. The percentage of drivers on the road at any given time who had been drinking was high, with estimates from 10 to 20 percent on weekend nights. Attempting to apprehend all these drivers was hardly an option for local police departments, which were often poorly staffed and funded. Even if the police became more aggressive, local courts could not handle large influxes of potential defendants. Not only was it much easier to allow such individuals to plead to lesser offenses, it was more lucrative as well. These lesser convictions often carried fines, payable to the local government. In contrast, keeping drunk drivers in jail or holding trials cost money.

The preference for fines was clear in Los Angeles, according to Bill Dredge's 1949 drunk driving series. The December 7, 1949, article told the story of "Joe Xes," another recidivist who had been arrested at least six times between 1944, when he was driving at 60 miles per hour and weaving all over Pico Street, to June 1949, when another driver deliberately pinned Joe's car to the curb to prevent him from driving while inebriated. In 1948, Joe had taken his sister and her son, age 16, on a car chase through heavy traffic. When stopped, Joe "freely admitted he was drunk, had been arrested many times before for the same offense and had no driver's license." In all these instances, save one five-day jail sentence, Joe was released after paying fines ranging from $10 to $300.[11]

Different drivers inspired different approaches. Heavy drinkers, often known to the police, might be driven home and told to sleep it off. Sometimes, the police just dropped the driver's car keys down a nearby sewer, ensuring that he could not drive home but doing no more. Social drinkers pulled over for swerving might be admonished and told to "be more careful" before being allowed to drive themselves home. One reason given by police for such leniency was that those they arrested were ultimately freed by judges anyway. Drunk drivers always had a plethora of excuses. For example, those who performed poorly on tests of balance pled overwork, lameness, or side effects from medications. "It is the rare exception," a Chicago traffic judge noted sarcastically, "when a defendant is not either doped up with pills or patent medicine, overtired, sick or crippled." Another favorite excuse: "But judge, I only had two beers."[12]

Other accused drivers offered extenuating circumstances, arguing they should not have their licenses revoked or go to jail because they needed to drive to make a living. Thus, any substantial punishment would deprive their wives and children of support. Defense lawyers and character witnesses attested to the accused's high tolerance for alcohol, outstanding citizenship, or supposedly pristine driving records and attempted to poke holes in the testimony of the arresting officers. At least in Chicago, these strategies seemed to work, leading the *Chicago Tribune* to criticize local judges for "getting sentimental over drunks." A New York police sergeant reported that while he had testified in roughly two hundred cases, only one of these drunk drivers had been sent to jail. Juries, he added, were no better, preferring to give drunk drivers "another chance," in part because they, too, had on occasion driven after drinking. These acquittals were consistent with survey data, which revealed that while Americans overwhelmingly viewed drunk driving as wrong, over half balked at voluntary blood alcohol content testing and mandatory license suspension.[13]

The ability to produce evidence of elevated blood alcohol levels potentially helped the prosecution but was far from foolproof. For one thing, most areas of the country did not have easily available testing devices. In addition, the Drunkometer was a relatively large machine, which fit in a box the size of a small suitcase. Whereas it was theoretically portable, testing was often done back at the police station after the driver's BAC had gone down. Finally, lawyers quickly learned that they could challenge the scientific basis of BAC findings, arguing that certain diseases and pills caused spurious readings, that the police officers had performed the test incorrectly, or that subjective sobriety tests were more accurate than numbers. Indeed, in the very first case tried using Harger's machine, in which Harger appeared as an expert witness for the prosecution, the defense lawyer insisted on being tested himself, right in the courtroom, and then challenged the results. Another clever strategy was to ask the police officer to explain the complicated science behind the Drunkometer, something that was rarely done to satisfaction. According to one critic, these various defense strategies experienced "waves of popularity" across the country; once prosecutors learned how to foil them, new ones were introduced. How-to books on beating drunk driving charges were decades away, but the strategies were already there.[14]

At times, there was outright corruption. According to Daniel Patrick Moynihan, the future US senator who became involved in anti–drunk driving publicity in the 1950s, it had been commonplace in Chicago for decades for drivers to place a five-dollar bill next to their driver's license and registration card in case of apprehension by a police officer. At most, such individuals were charged with "hazardous driving"; others were simply sent on their way, having paid their "fine." Phone calls to district attorneys and judges also at times helped to generate lesser sentences or findings of "not guilty."[15]

The problem of controlling drunk driving spoke, in part, to its characterization as more of a police and legal matter than a public health issue. This is not to say that these two categories were mutually exclusive. For example, the "medical police" of the eighteenth and nineteenth centuries used the strong arm of the law to enforce public health measures, such as sanitary ordinances or quarantining of infectious individuals. But no public consensus existed that driving drunk was an urgent public health matter, one that threatened American lives. The court system—or at least certain individuals working within the system—did what could be done.

This tolerance for allowing dangerous drivers on the road stood in marked contradistinction to the way in which American society dealt with more traditional public health problems. For example, during this same post–World War II era, the discovery of antimicrobials that could successfully treat tuberculosis led health officials to embark on an aggressive campaign to control the disease among its last reservoir, skid row alcoholics. With a supportive or indifferent populace, these officials misused powers of quarantine in their zeal to achieve cures. As a result, noninfectious individuals who represented little or no threat to the public were forcibly detained for months or even years.[16] In addition, health officials continued to receive wide latitude to detain individuals suspected to be at risk of transmitting other infections, such as polio and typhoid fever. Meanwhile, drunk drivers, who often posed a much greater risk of harm, were permitted to drink and drive with very few repercussions.

Beyond the limits of both legal and public health approaches, another less obvious factor was promoting a tolerance for drunk driving: suburbanization and the growth of automobile culture. The United States underwent major demographic shifts after World War II. As soldiers returned from fighting, went to college via the GI Bill, got jobs, and had families, they increasingly chose to live not in cities but in the suburbs. These included planned developments, such as Levittown on New York's Long Island, or villages and towns that expanded in all directions from cities such as Detroit, Cleveland, and Chicago. Although some commuters did take the train or bus to and from work when such services were available, many others preferred to drive.

This propensity for driving was helped by a flourishing postwar economy, which enabled Americans to purchase cars at an unprecedented rate. Between 1950 and 1970, the number of cars on the nation's roads increased by almost 250 percent, from just over 40 million to just under 90 million. The healthy economy also encouraged young baby-boom families to travel more, often on driving vacations. Meanwhile, in the 1950s, the Eisenhower administration dramatically expanded a highway construction program that had begun in the interwar years, leading to massive growth of the country's interstate system. Sensing the new business opportunities, entrepreneurs opened motels, fast food restaurants, and gas stations along these thoroughfares. Suburban families readily took to their cars to patronize shopping centers, drive-in restaurants, and drive-in movies, which peaked in popularity in the 1950s and 1960s.

Providing convenient access to so many different places so easily, the automobile became an icon of the postwar era. It represented a pathway out of an earlier era, which had been marked by the "age-old bonds of locality." No longer forced to spend their entire lives in crowded urban neighborhoods or on farms, people with cars had personal mobility, "an enlargement of life's opportunities and boundaries."[17] Moynihan termed the automobile a "central symbol of potency and power, the equivalent of the sword, or the horse or the spear of earlier ages." As early as 1934, one California man had written: "I say that today men and women love their liberty to drive an automobile almost more than they love anything else in modern life." Postwar fiction, such as Jack Kerouac's *On the Road* and John Updike's *Rabbit* novels, pushed this notion even further, equating the ability to drive with the search for life's meaning.[18] Driving, seen as a privilege in the early twentieth century, was becoming much more of a right.

General Motors, Ford, Chrysler, and other smaller automobile manufacturers took advantage of these cultural shifts, designing flashier, larger, and faster cars and placing alluring advertisements in newspapers and magazines. Cars suddenly came in dazzling colors, wrote historian Mark S. Foster in *A Nation on Wheels*, while "engines became bigger, faster and stronger." "The American people want good cars, good looking cars, fast cars, cars with power and styling, and that's the kind of cars we build," stated Henry Ford II during his years as chairman of Ford Motor Company. If Cadillacs, with their gaudy tail fins, were the choice of wealthy suburbanites, young men turned their cars into dragsters and raced them on approved tracks and unapproved highways. One of the best-known films of the era, the 1955 classic *Rebel without a Cause*, features a daredevil car race in which the contestants drive their cars toward a cliff. The winner ditches his car last. The automobile, Pat Moynihan opined, was "a prime agent of risk-taking in a society that still values risk-taking, but does not provide many outlets."[19]

Alcohol was not an essential component of this new fascination with automobiles, but many drivers partook. After all, when they exited the new highways and took smaller roads to cities, small towns, and resorts, they could increasingly find bars and liquor stores (then known as package stores), which sold alcohol. Meanwhile, the liquor industry, which had exhibited conservatism immediately after repeal and continued to voluntarily refrain from putting commercials on television and radio, became bolder in its print advertising, spending more than $110 million annually by the mid-1950s. These ads often equated drinking with the good life and masculinity.

Many consumers took these themes very seriously, such as the mother who wished that her teetotaler son would drink, thereby becoming "a man, not a sissy." Another indicator of the growing respectability of alcohol was the failure of multiple legislative efforts between 1946 and 1958, at both state and federal levels, to ban alcohol advertising. In 1958, the *Saturday Evening Post*, the nation's second-largest magazine by circulation, announced that it was reversing its longtime policy of not accepting liquor advertisements. The *Post*'s decision was all about the bottom line: it was estimated that the magazine could earn at least $7 million annually working with its new client. None of this was accidental. The Distilled Spirits Institute, Licensed Beverage Industries (LBI) (a pro-alcohol public relations organization founded in 1946), and other alcohol manufacturers actively donated money to sympathetic politicians and helped create position statements and policies for voluntary organizations like the National Council on Alcoholism. These documents consistently characterized the problem of drunk driving as one fostered by alcoholism as opposed to alcohol.[20]

Liquor sales increased throughout the postwar era, but the product that really experienced a boom was beer. The push to sell more beer had actually begun in the late 1930s, when the United States Brewers' Association formed the United Brewers Industrial Foundation and hired public relations whiz Edward L. Bernays to promote its product. Bernays recruited academics to write booklets with titles like *Beer in the American Home* and *It's Smart to Serve Beer*. Among the arguments these publications made was that beer was less an intoxicating beverage than a "liquid food." "Beer," read one representative entry, "combines the value of tea and coffee, which act as stimulants, with that of milk, which is merely a food."[21] These authors, coached by the beer industry, also characterized beer as a "safe" beverage, in contrast to hard liquor, owing to its lower alcohol content. It took roughly 12 ounces of beer (or 5 ounces of wine) to equal the alcohol content of a 1.5-ounce shot of whiskey. Playing up its purported safety, beer manufacturers advertised more aggressively and boldly, not only in print publications but also on the airwaves. In addition, by the 1950s, television personalities, including talk show host Steve Allen, often conspicuously and enthusiastically drank beer on the air. "Such smacking of lips!" remarked one television critic sarcastically, "such full-bodied enthusiasm!"[22]

Beer, moreover, had become the predominant drink for young American males in their teens, twenties, and thirties, the exact age groups with the highest rates of alcohol-related fatalities. Again, one would be hard pressed to find advertisements from this era that specifically advocated drinking beer and driving, but these ads most surely equated the beverage with social success, happiness, and consumer goods such as cars. Among the slogans used by the beer industry were "A bottle or two of beer will cheer you up" and "Drinking beer is a part of gracious living." Schaefer beer of New York was well known for a radio and television jingle that specifically promoted drinking multiple beers at one sitting: "Schaefer is the one beer to have when you're having more than one." Not surprisingly, perhaps, Seliger and Shupe's 1953 anti–drunk driving pamphlet had a separate section devoted to "the truth about beer." Beer, they warned, "contains a narcotic," "can and does intoxicate," and "may make an automobile driver a killer."[23] As usual, such warnings went unheeded.

The tension between calls for better control of drunk driving, on the one hand, and efforts to temper such measures, on the other, became apparent over the issue of involuntary BAC testing. Some jurisdictions, trying to put teeth in their laws, had begun to ask physicians to draw blood BACs from individuals too drunk or injured to give consent. Yet as Tucson, Arizona, police chief Bernard Garmire reported, rather than appreciating the benefits of such a policy to the public, jurors often looked "askance" and voted to acquit obviously drunk drivers, owing to a belief that the police had overstepped their bounds.[24] Even the American Medical Association opposed the practice, fearing that it would make physicians vulnerable to lawsuits charging assault and battery.

The issue was so contentious that it made it to the United States Supreme

Court in a 1957 New Mexico case, *Breithaupt v. Abram*. Breithaupt was unconscious in an emergency room after being involved in an automobile crash in which three people died. At the request of a highway patrolman who suspected that Breithaupt was intoxicated and had caused the crash, a physician drew a blood alcohol level, which came back at 0.17%, making the driver legally drunk. Breithaupt was convicted of voluntary manslaughter, but his lawyers appealed all the way to the Supreme Court, arguing that taking the blood from an unconscious man denied him due process.

By a 6-3 vote, the high court upheld the lower court's verdict. At first glance, the ruling seemed to be a ringing endorsement of the nascent crusade against drunk driving. "The increasing slaughter on our highways, most of which should be avoidable," Justice Tom C. Clark's majority opinion remarked, "now reaches the astounding figures only heard of on the battlefield." But this public health perspective, which one group of police commentators termed "a sharp turn in judicial interpretation," was once again mitigated by the more traditional view of drunk driving as a criminal justice issue.

This became clear in the two dissenting opinions, both of which invoked judicial precedent to argue that taking blood from Breithaupt had violated the petitioner's due process. The Warren Court, of course, would make its name by protecting the rights of individuals under arrest or suspected of having committed a crime. But the dissents also foreshadowed an even more virulent libertarian objection to anti–drunk driving efforts, which would become prominent in the 1990s. In calling for a "libertarian approach," which should have disallowed the BAC test, Justice William O. Douglas, joined by Justice Hugo L. Black, stated that Breithaupt's body had been "invaded and assaulted by the police, who are supposed to be the citizen's protector." Those who fashioned the Constitution, he added, "put certain rights out of the reach of the police."[25]

The Supreme Court would be even more deeply split when it ruled on the 1966 case *Schmerber v. California*. In this instance, the five-justice majority upheld the notion that obtaining blood alcohol samples without consent was constitutional, again underscoring the importance of protecting the public's health. Four justices, Douglas, Black, Abe Fortas, and Chief Justice Earl Warren, dissented, mostly on the grounds that involuntary blood collection violated the Fifth Amendment's prohibition against self-incrimination. It might be argued that this libertarian viewpoint, when applied to cases in which the accused turned out to have a high BAC, came remarkably close to declaring drunk driving a constitutional right for those who were drunk enough to have passed out.[26] It is no wonder that public health officials promoting better highway safety feared continuing legal challenges to these efforts.

As arguments persisted about how aggressively drunk drivers should be pursued, several organizations involved in anti–drunk driving efforts quietly began to craft a less-restrictive message. Specifically, the LBI, the National Safety Council, and other groups had concluded that promoting the slogan "If you drink, don't drive" had been "largely wasted and unproductive." Such messages, according to LBI President Thomas J. Donovan, were "scare tactics" that should be "studiously avoided."[27] Gradually, the LBI would adopt the more ambiguous "Know your limits," which implied that some drinking before driving was acceptable behavior. This slogan, however, would land the group in hot water in 1970.

In addition to introducing its new message, the Licensed Beverage Industries also influenced the drunk driving debate by funding research. In the 1940s, for example, it gave several grants to the National Safety Council to study the Drunkometer and other ways to assess intoxication after car crashes. Although alcohol industry funding raised few eyebrows at the time, such financial remuneration potentially threatened the objectivity of NSC policy statements on issues such as proper BACs, law enforcement, and advertising. The LBI would also partially fund what was probably the most famous drunk driving research paper, the 1964 "Grand Rapids Study," by Robert F. Borkenstein, an Indiana University researcher and inventor of the Breathalyzer, which would eventually replace Harger's Drunkometer as the main way to test BAC.[28]

The unassuming and diminutive Borkenstein had taken an interesting pathway into the study of drunk driving. He was born in Fort Wayne, Indiana, in 1912 to a building contractor and his wife, both of whom came from German families. Finishing high school at the beginning of the Depression, Borkenstein was unable to attend college. He instead worked as a photographic technician, which mostly involved developing pictures, but he also made innovative discoveries in the field of color printing that would later earn him a visit to England to meet an admiring Queen Elizabeth II. In 1936, the Indiana State Police Laboratory hired Borkenstein as a police photographer, a job that exposed him to the carnage associated with drunk driving crashes. When he left the police laboratory in 1958 to become chairman of the Department of Police Science at Indiana University, he had reached the position of chief of laboratory services, helping to establish one of the first forensic laboratories in the United States.

Along the way, Borkenstein, a natural and brilliant inventor, also broke new ground in the development of speed-measuring devices and lie detectors.

Borkenstein's interest in measuring BAC began in 1937, when Rolla Harger sought the assistance of the police laboratory in field-testing his Drunkometer. Over the next seventeen years, Borkenstein, building on his work with color photography, conceptualized a device that would improve on the earlier one. Then, in February 1954, during his annual two-week vacation, he built it in the basement of his home. The Breathalyzer, in Borkenstein's own words, was "so amazingly simple—two photo cells, two filters, a device for collecting a breath sample, about six wires." The most important advances produced by the Breathalyzer were its small size and portability—it was easily carried and operated by police officers—and its reliability. If operated properly, the results were accurate and replicable. The breath sample passed through an ampule containing acid dichromate, a yellow reagent, which changed colors depending on the amount of alcohol present in the exhaled air. The reading was automatically expressed in blood alcohol units.

The invention of the Breathalyzer was only the first step in its eventual acceptance as the standard technology for measuring BAC. Borkenstein patented the device, which was first manufactured by a small business in Indianapolis and later by larger companies. Improvements were made in the technology over time. At both Indiana University and across the country, Borkenstein taught police, lawyers, and other interested people how to use the device properly. Eventually, Breathalyzers and their related kin became standard equipment throughout the United States, Canada, and Australia.[29]

Historians of technology have written extensively about the complicated ways in which new technologies are introduced and adopted. The Breathalyzer was no exception. Yes, it generated seemingly reliable data about blood alcohol levels, but would these automatically be accepted by people involved in drunk driving enforcement and, if so, would it lead to change? Borkenstein first publicly demonstrated the Breathalyzer at the National Safety Congress in Chicago in October 1954. There it received positive reviews as a device that was easy to use and gave uniform results.

More interesting, however, were the less formal ways that experts "studied" the Breathalyzer. For one thing, it was possible to take the machine to cocktail parties held in conjunction with scientific meetings and do some personal "experimentation." At a seminar on drunk driving in Louisville in 1956, for example, attendees watched one colleague become drunk at a BAC of roughly 0.08%.

At a level of only 0.04%, a colleague later recalled, this person had been "obviously incapable of properly operating an automobile." Nevertheless, those attending the conference agreed that obtaining a conviction on such an individual, had he actually been driving, would have been "very difficult." A salesman who volunteered to participate in a demonstration at Fordham University in 1959 took twice as long to make driving-related decisions with a BAC of 0.14%, which was legal in New York at the time.[30] Such findings could hardly have come as a surprise to people like Herman Heise, who had been preaching the dangers of two drinks for twenty years and now had even better proof. But translating such information into policies and laws with teeth would remain elusive.

Indeed, Borkenstein himself was an oenophile and enjoyed drinking alcohol. When he and his wife, Marjorie, hosted parties, at which Borkenstein prepared German delicacies from recipes handed down from his mother, he often made a special punch that contained alcohol. This fact is worth underscoring because it reminds us that Borkenstein never saw the Breathalyzer as an instrument to discourage drinking but rather as one that could help individuals monitor their alcohol intake. Many anti–drunk driving activists who would emerge in the coming decades were also drinkers, a point that belies periodic characterizations of them as neoprohibitionists.

Of course, some fans of the Breathalyzer were teetotalers and saw Borkenstein's innovation as a golden opportunity. One such individual was William N. Plymat, an insurance company president from the Midwest. As a teenager in Minnesota in the waning years of Prohibition, Plymat had formed a "student sobriety society" to discourage drinking. He achieved some fame from this initiative and was a featured speaker at a July 4, 1932, rally of dry forces in Des Moines, Iowa, later dubbed "the last gasp of Prohibition." After law school, Plymat moved to Iowa and became involved in the insurance industry. When he founded his own company, the Preferred Risk Mutual Insurance Company, in 1947, Plymat insured only nondrinkers, a policy he believed would enable him to offer competitive rates and still make significant profits.

Plymat always liked to say that "it is a sin to run out of ideas," and by the mid-1950s the highly successful executive had become engrossed in drunk driving, which he believed was poorly regulated, and had given testimony on the issue before Congress. He also began to attend national conferences on the subject. One such meeting was the Symposium on Alcohol and Road Traffic, chaired by Robert Borkenstein and held at Indiana University in December 1958. During the question-and-answer session following the panel on law enforcement, Plymat stood up and criticized the infamous intermediate BAC zone between 0.05% and 0.15% used by most jurisdictions. Because 0.15% had become the default value for DWI prosecutions, significantly impaired drivers were routinely not charged. Plymat then asked the audience how it would respond if there were a similar intermediate zone for speeding in which driving between 60 and 80 miles per hour did not mean guilt but "would be some evidence to be taken into account." "If I came to you with this proposal," Plymat speculated, "you would laugh me out of this place."[31]

What was Plymat's solution? He proposed an "intermediate offense" making it illegal to drive with a BAC of over 0.05%, which would automatically result in a $25 to $50 fine. As long as the BAC did not reach 0.15%, such individuals would not be charged with drunk driving, merely with "driving after drinking" and having a blood alcohol level that was known to cause impairment. A major advantage of such a plan, Plymat concluded, was that drinkers—especially social drinkers—could be told that having any more than two drinks was likely to put them over 0.05% and thus at risk of punishment. The audience applauded as Plymat sat down.

Plymat's timing was good. In 1950, physician and researcher Leonard Goldberg of Sweden's Karolinska Institute had done a controlled study of thirty-seven "expert" drivers given enough alcohol to raise their BACs to 0.05% and then asked to drive on a controlled track. Mirroring what Heise had shown in the 1930s, he found that this BAC "caused a deterioration of between 25 and 30 percent in driving performance of expert drivers." Goldberg noted that his data likely represented an underestimate of impairment among the general public as he had used skilled drivers who were asked to complete a series of specific tasks. Then, in 1958, researchers from the University of Washington in Seattle reported that drivers "primed with Martinis, Manhattans or whiskey" all showed "measurable objective impairment of the functions tested in the simulated driving test" at or slightly above a 0.05% BAC. "Current law," these authors concluded, "is thus too lenient." Or, as a *Los Angeles Times* reporter covering this story asked, "Haven't you seen someone bombed on less than six [drinks]?"[32] Over time, data would continue to show that even mildly elevated BACs led to decreased reaction time, tracking, information processing, psychomotor performance, and visual functioning.

Aware of these data, having heard Plymat's plea, and armed with Borkenstein's impressive new Breathalyzer, a seven-man ad hoc committee, chaired by Rolla

Harger and including Herman Heise, was formed to draft a statement by the end of the 1958 Indiana University conference. It took an all-night session, which indicates how tricky and contentious drunk driving enforcement could be, even when all the individuals on the committee were basically in agreement that the current situation was dangerous and unacceptable.

Ultimately, the statement fell far short of what Plymat had proposed. But it was nevertheless an important public attestation that the existing laws did not jibe with the emerging science and that legal BACs needed to be made lower: "As a result of the material presented at this Symposium, it is the opinion of this Committee that a blood alcohol concentration of 0.05% will definitely impair the driving ability of some individuals and, as the blood alcohol concentration increases, a progressively higher proportion of such individuals are so affected, until at a blood alcohol concentration of 0.10%, all individuals are definitely impaired." The National Safety Council and the American Medical Association, the two organizations that had helped promulgate the ambiguous 0.05% to 0.15% range, endorsed this statement, as did the Association of Chiefs of Police, and legislators in Utah and Illinois soon introduced bills making 0.05% an intermediate offense. Even Henry Newman, the California physician so concerned about not convicting people who could apparently drive well with high BACs, agreed that lowering the legal BAC made sense.[33]

The Breathalyzer represented a major technological advance and was a major reason that Borkenstein would be showered with honors during his long career, including being elected into the Safety and Health Hall of Fame International and being the first recipient of the National Safety Council's Robert F. Borkenstein Award. But the improved science itself created no immediate change in the prosecution of drunk driving cases in the United States. Like the Drunkometer, the Breathalyzer was not infallible, and defense lawyers pounced on its supposed flaws as well as the competency of police officers who used the device. To Borkenstein's dismay, some actually constructed their arguments after attending the courses on alcohol and highway safety that Borkenstein, toxicologist Robert B. Forney Sr., toxicologist and chemist Kurt M. Dubowski, and other colleagues held at Indiana University beginning in 1958. In addition, because of the Fourth Amendment's protections against unreasonable search and seizure, breath testing could only legally be done if the police officer had "probable cause" for testing—usually that the driver had committed a traffic violation or been involved in a crash. It would take a much broader cultural transformation—one that saw automobile crashes not as inevitable but as preventable—to enable the

Breathalyzer and BAC laws to more effectively punish and deter drunk driving. This cultural change began with a group of state government employees in Albany, New York, headed by William Haddon Jr.

As the sociologist Constance A. Nathanson has shown, the manner in which certain issues become public health problems is not inevitable but rather is determined by social processes.[34] This was surely true of drunk driving in the 1950s and 1960s. The impetus for Haddon's work began with demographic shifts in the causes of death in the United States. Whereas tuberculosis and other infectious diseases topped mortality lists at the turn of the twentieth century, chronic diseases such as cancer and heart disease had taken over by the 1930s. Demographers had also begun to pay closer attention to causes of morbidity and mortality that were not strictly diseases. Thus, it was reported in the 1940s that accidents were the leading cause of death among individuals up to age 37 and that automobile crashes made up the largest single fraction of these. It should be noted that the per capita death rate from car crashes in the United States was among the lowest in the developed world and that rates had been decreasing since the 1920s. Nevertheless, the toll resulting from such crashes—roughly 50,000 annually by the 1960s—was distressingly high.

Because anti–drunk driving efforts had always been centered in the worlds of the police and the courts, the first step had to be making the lowering of automobile crashes part of a public health program. New York State Health Commissioner Herman E. Hilleboe had begun to do this in the late 1940s and, by 1954, the state's Department of Health had formed a Driver Research Center and made Haddon the director. Haddon was born in Orange, New Jersey, in 1926 and served in the Army Air Forces at the end of World War II. He then attended, in succession, the Massachusetts Institute of Technology, Harvard Medical School, and the Harvard School of Public Health, where he studied epidemiology with John E. Gordon, author of a seminal paper entitled *The Epidemiology of Accidents.* A staunch advocate of public health measures to prevent disease and injury, Haddon was a natural for the New York position.

That Haddon entered the field of crash prevention through medicine and public health is crucial to understanding how he approached the problem. Most of the other experts on drunk driving, such as Borkenstein, Richard Holcomb, Robert L. Donigan, and Franklin Kreml, of the Northwestern Traffic Institute, had become interested in the subject through law and traffic enforcement. Although these experiences provided them with excellent firsthand knowledge of the problem, they were insiders, comfortable working within the parameters and expectations established by the National Safety Council. Haddon's background led him to develop an alternative, epidemiologically based model of drunk driving control to improve safety on the roads. It also made him an outsider willing to challenge dogma and tradition.

Haddon's first gripe with the existing paradigm was its lack of a firm scientific basis. Police departments collected data about crashes, but most of it was anecdotal. And, Haddon believed, there had been almost no research at all into whether various legal deterrents to drunk driving actually worked. With his training in public health methods, he knew how to design research studies that could potentially generate more definitive answers. His first major investigation, published in the prestigious *Journal of the American Medical Association* in April 1959, looked at the role played by alcohol in single-car accidents in New York's Westchester County between 1949 and 1957. Haddon found that half of the drivers had been legally intoxicated, with a BAC of 0.15% or more, and that another 20 percent had been in the 0.05%–0.14% range.[35]

This study was crucial because it helped to cement the notion that alcohol was responsible for an extremely high percentage of automobile crashes, a point originally posited by Heise, Holcomb, and other researchers in the 1930s. Despite these earlier studies, some commentators had continued to claim that alcohol was responsible for only about 5 percent of crashes. Haddon believed that this figure was a dramatic underestimate of the problem, and his Westchester study corroborated this theory.

So did a 1962 controlled study by James R. McCarroll and Haddon, published in the *Journal of Chronic Diseases*, which compared the BACs of New York City drivers killed in nighttime automobile accidents with a control group of drivers who safely passed by the same sites. The authors found that 73 percent of drivers killed had been drinking compared to 26 percent (itself a high figure) of those who passed safely. As might be expected, of the former group, nearly half had extremely high BACs of at least 0.25%, whereas none of the drinkers in the other group had a level that high.[36]

Another way to demonstrate the role played by alcohol in car crashes was to look at pedestrian deaths. In a 1961 study, Haddon compared 50 such individuals, most of whom had been killed at night, with a control group of 200 others who had walked past the same locations (four at each crash site). Again, there was a high baseline rate of drinking—33 percent among the controls—but it was 74 percent among those killed. And while those who died often had very high BACs, others were at 0.05% or lower. These findings and other research emerging at this time, such as a 1956 Delaware study finding that 59 percent of crash-related deaths involved alcohol and data from the Cleveland coroner's office reporting that 40–60 percent of all crash victims had alcohol in their blood, convinced Haddon that the problem of drunk driving was enormous and, despite the efforts of groups like the NSC, underpublicized. "Why," Haddon asked, "should we continue to let a tiny fraction of drivers, those who are problem drinkers, and drive after drinking heavily—kill tens of thousands of people every year, many of their victims innocent men, women and children?"[37]

As Haddon grew increasingly interested in drunk driving, he acquired an interesting ally at the New York State Department of Health: Daniel Patrick Moynihan. Born in 1927 to an Irish Catholic family, Moynihan had an uneventful childhood until his father walked out in 1937. This event plunged the family into poverty, and Moynihan, his mother, and siblings lived in several different low-rent Manhattan apartments and in Westchester County. At different times, Moynihan shined shoes, sold newspapers, and mixed drinks at a seedy Hell's Kitchen bar that his mother ran in the 1940s. Always a precocious child and a great reader, Moynihan attended Middlebury College, the City College of New York, and the London School of Economics, but he was adrift until he entered politics, eventually working in a series of capacities for New York State governor W. Averell Harriman, from 1954 to 1958.

Moynihan and Haddon first met at a meeting of the Governor's Traffic Safety Policy Coordinating Committee, and Moynihan was immediately struck by Haddon's impressive knowledge about automobile crashes. The two formed a working and personal friendship despite their vastly different personalities: Moynihan was outgoing, funny, upbeat, and fond of quoting the classics. Haddon, with his military crew cut and bow ties, was a workaholic, uninterested in the perquisites of public office or in playing the political game. Even his most ardent admirers admitted that Haddon had a nasty side and an intolerance for what he believed was inferior research. The two men stayed in close touch after Nelson A. Rockefeller defeated Harriman in 1958, putting Moynihan out of a job.[38]

An intellectual with a wonk's penchant for statistics and a growing interest in politics and public policy, Moynihan was especially impressed with Haddon's ability to place traffic safety in the larger context of public health. Specifically, Haddon had come to deplore the use of the word *accident*, which he believed made automobile crashes sound inevitable and, by implication, not preventable. After all, if the National Safety Council could predict the number of people likely to die in car crashes over a holiday weekend, how accidental were such deaths? In the past, Haddon liked to argue, society viewed infections, plagues, and famines, whether caused by God or nature, as out of man's hands. Thanks to public health successes, such as cleaning up polluted water, screening for tuberculosis, and vaccinating children against polio, that situation had thankfully changed. This left accidents, according to Haddon, as "the only remaining source of human morbidity and mortality still substantially viewed by educated and uneducated alike in extrarational terms."[39]

Prevention in public health traditionally emphasizes the environment and the product, and Haddon did both.[40] In the case of the former, he focused on the inside of vehicles that crashed and the roadways where crashes occurred. One of Haddon's heroes was Hugh De Haven, a Canadian engineer known as the "father of crash survivability." De Haven had been the only survivor of a Royal Canadian Flying Corps plane crash during World War I. He ultimately concluded that the deaths from his crash—and others in the air and on the ground—had as much to do with the trauma that occurred within the vehicle as with the impact of the crash itself, a phenomenon later termed the *second collision*. This finding led De Haven to advocate for the removal of sharp and otherwise dangerous items within cockpits and cars as well as immobile objects on the sides of roads that might impale skidding cars and their occupants. He eventually conceptualized the notion of "packaging people": creating such safe traveling environments that bodies might withstand almost any type of crash. Haddon himself became known for the concept of the matrix, which involved studying the driver, the vehicle, and the roadway during three time intervals: the precrash period, the crash itself, and the postcrash period. This approach provided a roadmap for preventing crashes and limiting trauma when they occurred.[41]

When it came to the product, Haddon, and a very simpatico Moynihan, focused on American cars, which, they believed, were unsafe. The major villain here was the auto industry, which had long claimed that safety "doesn't sell" and was "bad for business" and had thus refused to discuss safety issues with insurance companies and other interested parties.[42] As Henry Ford II once said, "We could build a tank that would creep over the highways and you could bang 'em into each other and nobody would ever get a scratch . . . but nobody would buy it either." After a visit to Detroit, in which General Motors executives politely deflected his concerns about safety, Haddon remarked that it was "an incredible instance of the blind leading the blind leading the blind."[43]

How did this state of affairs persist? Based on his research, Haddon blamed not only Detroit's greed but also the traffic safety establishment, which he had concluded was the *problem* rather than part of the solution. Not one to mince words, at least among his colleagues, he paraphrased H. L. Mencken in 1961: "No one will ever lose money underestimating the intelligence of American safety experts. With few exceptions, a dull and stupid bunch."[44] Haddon directed special enmity toward the National Safety Council, which billed itself as having saved over one million lives. He believed that the NSC relied on poor data, had not updated its thinking about drunk driving or traffic safety in decades, and most distressingly, was in bed with automobile manufacturers. When he was feeling charitable, Haddon charged the group with having "automatically applied group attitudes."[45] When he was angrier, the NSC was arrogant and incompetent. Another organization that scored low points was the American Automobile Association. It opposed new "implied consent" laws, which mandated that drivers undergo BAC testing if stopped for possible drunk driving, because of concerns that such laws forced drivers to incriminate themselves. Haddon also disliked the President's Committee on Traffic Safety, an advisory group with an executive director actually paid by the automobile industry. Thanks to the passive nature of these organizations, Detroit pretty much did what it wanted.[46]

But Haddon was a scientist and a government official, so he chose his words much more carefully in public. He met with automobile industry representatives and did research in conjunction with the NSC. This is where Moynihan came in, helping to air some of Haddon's more pointed arguments. Although he moved to Syracuse University to obtain a PhD degree in 1959, Moynihan embarked on a brief career as a journalist at the same time. One of his articles, which appeared in the April 30, 1959, edition of the *Reporter*, a liberal investigative magazine, was entitled "Epidemic on the Highways" and argued that automobile crashes were one of the country's foremost public health problems. Moynihan was extremely frank, arguing that drunk driving and other laws promoting automobile safety "have about as much scientific validity as wrapping a dirty sock around the neck to cure a cold." He singled out the NSC for incompetence, stating that it underestimated by two-thirds the annual number of automobile-related injuries and seriously misled the American public about what was a "disastrous epidemic" on the highways. Elsewhere Moynihan called the NSC a "flunky organization" and charged the automobile industry with "brute greed and moral imbecility" for ignoring safety concerns.[47]

In one sense, Moynihan was a strange ally for Haddon's anti–drunk driving efforts. Moynihan was a regular drinker, both at work and at home, a habit that would draw increased scrutiny and occasional disapproval during his later years as a US Senator. In late 1959, newspapers paraphrased a research study from Haddon's group as having concluded that drivers should have no more than two drinks before taking the wheel. By this point, Haddon was working for the new governor, Nelson Rockefeller. From Syracuse, Moynihan wrote to his former colleague: "I do hope, however, that you are not responsible for the notion of the 'two-drink range.' Do you realize this makes a man like me practically an outlaw? If that damfool Baptist governor of ours doesn't stop he's going to have half of the population of the state hiding in their homemade bomb shelters and the other half in State Police uniforms looking for them."[48] Moynihan was pontificating and joking in his characteristic manner, but Haddon took him seriously enough to have scribbled "Papers wrong, is 4–5 drinks minimum" in the margin of the letter.

A major reason that Haddon remained comfortable with the collaboration was that while Moynihan surely drank, he did not drive afterward, again making the point that fighting drunk driving did not necessarily mean fighting alcohol. As Moynihan's wife, Elizabeth, aptly noted about her husband many years later, "He hasn't been arrested for drunk driving or fallen into the fountain at the Plaza."[49] Among the drunk driving control measures strongly favored by Haddon was one that originated in Scandinavia: having sober persons (later termed *designated drivers*) drive intoxicated ones home. Moynihan was likely an early beneficiary.

Slowly, with a sympathetic governor in Rockefeller, Haddon's work began to bear fruit in New York. In 1953, the state had actually been the first to pass an implied consent law stipulating that refusal to undergo BAC testing permitted local officials to automatically revoke a driver's license. In some states, refusal of testing became admissible evidence—raising a presumption of intoxication—during trials. Haddon frequently voiced his concerns about the 0.05% to 0.15% "twilight zone," which had received scrutiny at the 1958 Indiana University meeting, in which a driver "had enough alcohol to impair his driving ability but yet not enough to be adjudged drunk." In 1960, Rockefeller partially addressed this concern by signing a law that made driving with a BAC of 0.10% or higher a driving infraction in New York State. First time offenders, if convicted, received a 60-day mandatory license suspension, second time offenders a 120-day suspension, and third time offenders, license revocation. Within five years, as a result of this law, New York was suspending the licenses of more than 3,000 drivers annually.[50]

In part due to Haddon's work, momentum to strengthen drunk driving laws increased elsewhere. In 1960, the NSC's Committee on Alcohol and Drugs made changes to two of the three levels of impairment it had set in the 1930s. It recommended that the old intermediate zone become 0.05% to 0.10% and the level indicating that a driver was under the influence of alcohol intoxication become 0.10% instead of 0.15%. The Uniform Vehicle Code, which provided suggested guidelines for traffic laws in all fifty states, was amended to include this change in 1962. But it was up to individual states to pass laws to reflect this change, and as of 1964, only two states had done so. Without visible national leadership on this issue, there were simply too many factors interfering with change: an indifferent public, a lax legal system, and antagonistic automobile and beverage industries.

But what if one could generate more definitive data about the actual risk that alcohol consumption caused? Here Robert Borkenstein, inventor of the Breath-alyzer, stepped in. In 1962 and 1963, now based at Indiana University, he carried out the famous Grand Rapids Study, collecting data on 6,589 of the 9,353 drivers involved in car crashes in Grand Rapids, Michigan, during a twelve-month period. As Haddon had done in his studies, Borkenstein included a control group, in this case 8,008 drivers who had driven safely by similar locations. Using this very large sample size, he was able to correlate risk to specific BACs. For example, an increased risk of crashes began at a BAC of 0.04%. At 0.08%, a driver was nearly twice as likely to crash; at 0.10%, crashes were six times as likely and at 0.15%, ten times more likely. In addition, Borkenstein found that crashes involving drivers who had BACs of over 0.08% were more severe in terms of injury and damage.[51]

An incidental finding from the study—that having one or two drinks might actually *lower* the chance of a crash—initially got more publicity than Borkenstein's much more ominous and important results. The notion that drinking perhaps relaxed drivers and thus improved their concentration was not a surprising one in a society that always managed to put a positive spin on drinking and driving. Partial funding of Borkenstein's work by the Licensed Beverage Industries probably contributed to the exaggerated attention given to the small amount of counterintuitive data the study produced. Eventually, however, the study's powerful evidence associating increasingly high BACs with increasingly high risk became its lasting legacy.

By 1965, the longstanding national inertia about both drunk driving and traffic safety was finally coming to an end. That year, Senator Abraham Ribicoff, chairman of the Senate Subcommittee on Executive Reorganization, held

William Haddon Jr. (in bow tie), Undersecretary of Commerce for Transportation
Alan S. Boyd, and President Lyndon B. Johnson after the signing of the Highway
Safety Act in October 1966. Courtesy of Gene Haddon

hearings; the next year, the Institute of Medicine issued a report with the provoca-
tive title *Accidental Death and Disability: The Neglected Disease of Modern Society.*
These developments, in turn, led President Lyndon B. Johnson, in September
1966, to sign into law the National Safety Act and the Highway Safety Act.
Johnson also named William Haddon to be the first head of the newly formed
National Traffic Safety Agency, which later became the National Highway
Safety Bureau and eventually the National Highway Traffic Safety Administration (NHTSA). Haddon was an ideal choice as America's first traffic czar due to
his broad interest in making cars and highways safer. Although Johnson chose
Haddon, another critic of Detroit, Ralph Nader, had made many of the same
arguments in a series of articles and in his highly influential 1965 book, *Unsafe
at Any Speed.* Even though they agreed on many points, Haddon, the careful
scientist, and Nader, the zealous activist, had very different approaches and an
uneasy relationship.[52]

In addition to creating a traffic safety infrastructure, the newly created Department of Transportation, which housed Haddon's agency, promulgated new federal standards regarding alcohol and highway safety. The DOT urged individual states to implement a series of measures using grant funding from the Highway Safety Act's Section 402 program. These initiatives included improved chemical testing procedures, such as mandatory use of BACs in fatal crashes; laws setting acceptable DWI levels at 0.10% as opposed to 0.15%; and the institution of implied consent laws similar to New York State's 1953 version.[53]

By 1968, Haddon and his colleague A. Benjamin Kelley had completed the first comprehensive document on the problem of drinking and driving in the United States.[54] The 182-page report reviewed the history of drunk driving, efforts to control it, relevant research on the topic, and plans to combat the problem. Among the most important pieces of information included were that alcohol was involved in 800,000 crashes annually, which caused 25,000 deaths. In addition, the authors painstakingly reviewed data by Haddon and others that demonstrated the high percentage of car crashes—multiple-vehicle, single-vehicle, fatal, nonfatal, or involving pedestrians—in which alcohol evidently played a key role. Kelley and Haddon also reported that roughly two-thirds of alcohol-related traffic fatalities involved "alcoholics and other problem drinkers," mostly men. Such individuals were not deterred by the usual sanctions. Beyond stricter laws, the authors argued that better treatment for alcoholism had to be offered to these recidivists. In this manner, sociologist Joseph R. Gusfield commented, they continued to emphasize the post-repeal notion of alcoholism as a disease (substance abuse) while concurrently reviving the Prohibition era concerns about the dangers of alcohol (abusive substance).[55] The publication of such a document under government auspices was an explicit attempt by Kelley, Haddon, and their DOT colleagues to advance their emerging notion of drunk driving as a major public health problem, one that had been sorely neglected when compared to other causes of death.

From its title to its content, the *1968 Alcohol and Highway Safety Report* reflected the mindset of its authors. First and foremost, it was a document that emphasized the existing science, called for much more research into the actual rates and causes of drunk driving, and offered potential solutions to the problems drunk driving created. Second, it viewed control efforts within the context of Haddon's "matrix," only one part of a larger public health program to "package" drivers, passengers, pedestrians, and bicyclists to "reduce injury and death in crashes, whether those protected are responsible or innocent."[56]

This final phrase was key. Although Kelley and Haddon's report addressed a "tragic . . . loss in life, limb and property damage" and called for "an all-out drive to reduce the contribution of alcohol to highway death, injury and property damage," it was remarkably free of moralistic language, anger, blame, or calls for drinkers to demonstrate personal responsibility. The authors surely favored helping the police and courts to better deter drunk driving, but, like the researchers who saw alcoholism as a disease, they also acknowledged how hard it was to change individual behaviors. "Those who have been drinking, especially heavily," they wrote, "are probably far less likely to follow sensible safety practices directed either at crash avoidance, or at the reduction of crash injuries."[57] To William Haddon, what needed to be done was to use science to figure out the best ways to save lives and then force Washington and Detroit to cooperate.

Just as Haddon's report was being issued, J. Marse Grant was beginning work on a book on drunk driving, *Whiskey at the Wheel*, which would be published in 1970. Grant was the editor of the *Biblical Recorder*, a Baptist newspaper published in Raleigh, North Carolina. As memories of Prohibition faded, Baptists, as much as any other group, kept alive the old arguments about the evils of alcohol, especially when drunk to excess. In contrast to scientists like Haddon and Borkenstein, Grant was more than happy to identify victims and perpetrators. To Grant, drunk driving was a game of "Russian roulette," in which the "surest loser is the innocent driver or passenger." Those people who drove after drinking were "potential killers," while those who actually killed people were murderers. Grant quoted a Louisiana man who had told him about a husband, wife, and teenage daughter killed by a drunk driver in what was termed an "accident." "If the man had been drunk and had blown off their heads with a shotgun," Grant's correspondent wrote, "we certainly would call it murder and insist upon punishment and control." Other culprits were those who manufactured and marketed alcohol: "Until it presents strong and convincing evidence to vindicate itself, the liquor industry stands condemned for the major part it plays in this nation's highway carnage."[58]

What was also notable about *Whiskey at the Wheel* was the inclusion of specific stories, most of which Grant had collected by publishing an author's query in dozens of religious newspapers across the country. In one case, a 4-year-old girl saw her mother beheaded at the hands of a drunk driver. In Iowa, a 39-year-old farmer driving his tractor was killed by a drunk driver, leaving a widow and six children. In Dallas, a man with numerous prior DWI arrests, who had been stopped for drunk driving the day before and released to his relatives to sober up, crossed the median and drove his pickup truck into an oncoming car, killing himself and two other people.[59]

This recounting of tragic and poignant stories, accompanied by a large helping of moral indignation, gripped readers in a way that statistics, even devastating ones, could not. This same type of presentation would be used to great effect by anti–drunk driving activists in the 1980s. Grant anticipated other aspects of future activism as well. "No testimony is more powerful," he presciently wrote, "than that which comes from a heartbroken mother whose lovely daughter lost her life because of a drunken driver."[60] Chapter 9 of Grant's book was entitled "When Are We Going to Get Mad?" But while Grant's book generated considerable attention within Baptist churches, the general public did not notice. Ten years later, when the messenger was an actual mad mother, it would.

CHAPTER THREE

The MADD Mothers Take Charge

In thinking about the rise of MADD and drunk driving activism after 1980, it is tempting to ask why no one aside from J. Marse Grant had previously thought about using the tragic stories of victims—particularly children—to attract public attention and further the cause. This question is, of course, ahistorical. Events occur in a particular historical context. It was not until 1980 that the political and cultural climate was conducive to the angry, moralistic, and media-driven campaign that would, for a brief time, make drunk driving one of the country's preeminent social issues.

The first salvo was fired in Schenectady, New York, in 1978, when journalist Doris Aiken, appalled at the deaths of two children she knew, began Remove Intoxicated Drivers (RID), a grassroots organization devoted to getting drunk drivers off the road. Two years later, Candy Lightner, a California realtor, and Cindi Lamb, a manager for Tupperware in Maryland, both of whom had experienced personal tragedies involving their own children, joined forces as leaders of Mothers Against Drunk Drivers (MADD). Other organizations would form as well, but MADD became the centerpiece for an activism campaign that figuratively dropped a bomb in the previously sedate worlds of drunk driving policy and research. That these new activists were women, mothers, and nonprofessionals in the field made all the difference.

The early, heady days of this new crusade would peak in 1982, when President Ronald Reagan condemned the "slaughter" caused by drunk driving and appointed a presidential commission to study the subject. Driving while intoxicated, wrote *Newsweek*, was a "socially accepted form of murder."[1] True, there would be jostling of the various players and interest groups from the start, and this conflict would intensify over the next decade. But early on, MADD's powerful and seemingly uncontestable message made it among the best-known and best-loved charities in America.

Perhaps the most perceptive insight into drunk driving circa 1970 comes not from MADD but from *Mad—Mad* magazine, that is. In its 1970 collection *Sing Along with Mad*, among the song spoofs was one entitled *Deck the Bar*, to be sung to the tune of *Deck the Halls*.[2] Like any good satire, the spoof contained elements of both hyperbole and truth. Not everyone celebrated Christmas by driving drunk, but lots of people did:

Deck the Bars with Xmas drinking
Fa-la-la-la-la-la-la-la-la!
See the people all get stinking
Fa-la-la-la-la-la-la-la-la!
Though their brains are half corroded
Fa-la-la-la-la-la-la-la-la,
Still, they try to drive home loaded
Fa-la-la-la-la-la-la-la-la!
See the busy intersection
Fa-la-la-la-la-la-la-la-la!
See them come from all directions
Fa-la-la-la-la-la-la-la-la!
See the carnage as they're meeting
Fa-la-la-la-la-la-la-la-la.
What a novel Xmas greeting
Fa-la-la-la-la-la-la-la-la!

Drunk driving was also seen as inevitable. As one man candidly remarked, "People are going to drink and people are going to drive. And if you've gotten to a bar, there is only one way to leave and that's by your car. I don't think there is anything that can be done about it. There's no way that you can help it."[3]

But also in 1970, a controversy emerged that demonstrated the growing fragility of the coalition—the National Safety Council (NSC), academic researchers, and the alcohol industry—that had essentially called the shots about drunk driving prevention since the end of Prohibition. It arose from an advertisement in national magazines that seemed to suggest that it was acceptable to drive after having had up to three drinks on an empty stomach.

The ad was the brainchild of the Licensed Beverage Industries, one of the industry's public relations groups. In the years after its founding in 1946, the LBI had generally been cautious in its pronouncements about drinking and driving. But by 1970, due in part to Robert Borkenstein's data ostensibly showing that low BACs were not harmful, it was actively pushing its new slogan "Know your limits" to social drinkers. The full-page ad, which appeared in *Time* and *Newsweek* in July 1970, was careful to state that abstinence before driving was always best. But the reality was that drinking "continues to be socially acceptable" and that "millions of Americans drink moderately and drive safely." In the ad, the LBI provided a "simple, factual" chart to enable social drinkers to do so.[4]

That the LBI anticipated no firestorm over the advertisement is unsurprising. The copy merely put into print what had become the existing state of affairs regarding drinking and driving in the United States. Indeed, prior to running the ad, the LBI had contacted members of the NSC and the AMA (American Medical Association) to get their approvals, a point that was mentioned in the text. But there was something about stating so openly that it was acceptable to drink and drive—and to assist people in doing so—that made the message especially provocative. It was as if a long-kept secret, that drinking and driving was actually legal, had been outed. As a result, the longstanding discrepancy between impairment and legal intoxication would finally receive public scrutiny.

The accompanying chart, which was prepared by physiologist Dr. Leon A. Greenberg, of the Rutgers University Center of Alcohol Studies (the Yale program had shifted locations), advised that persons who weighed 120 pounds or more could drive immediately after imbibing two one-and-a-half ounce shots of whiskey. Similarly, those weighing at least 160 pounds could drive safely after three shots. Finally, if you weighed 200 pounds it was acceptable to have four shots provided that you waited thirty minutes after the final drink. Although the advertisement did not say so, most people following these instructions would have had BACs less than, but close to, 0.10%, so they would have been just under the legal limit.

The LBI's message particularly infuriated William Plymat, the Iowa insurance company president and former Prohibitionist who had proposed a 0.05% BAC at the 1958 conference in Indianapolis owing to his insistent concern that social drinkers—not only alcoholics—contributed significantly to the drunk driving problem. Plymat rapidly sent off a series of letters indicating his displeasure, first to the NSC and the AMA. Having rethought their earlier bad decisions, both said they agreed with Plymat and contacted the LBI to complain. In October 1970, Plymat followed up with a more extensive missive to the Federal Trade Commission (FTC), which was in charge of monitoring misleading advertisements. Plymat listed numerous studies that had found evidence of impairment at BACs of 0.05% or lower. True, from a strictly legal perspective, maybe those who followed the LBI's advice would not be driving while intoxicated, but that missed the point. "If one drinks up to a point just beneath the level at which he could normally be convicted of drunk driving," Plymat explained, making the same argument he had been making for decades, "he is a dangerous driver on the road."[5]

But the LBI did not relent. That same month it ran another version of the advertisement in *Publishers' Auxiliary*. The NSC and AMA were no longer mentioned but now the Department of Transportation (DOT) was, and Plymat quickly wrote to John A. Volpe, the Secretary of Transportation. Plymat supplemented his earlier criticism by mentioning a recent study from Chicago that found 80 percent of 400 people arrested for drunk driving fit the category of social drinker as opposed to alcoholic. "I would like to point out," he told Volpe, "that the LBI chart in their [*sic*] ad indicates *legal limits*, not the point at which substantial impairment begins."[6]

To what degree had the LBI deliberately obscured drunk driving data—conflating a legally unimpaired state with the ability to drive safely—to promote the sales of its products? It was not Plymat's style to speculate on this, but Julian A. Waller, a professor of community medicine at the University of Vermont and an author, along with Kelley and Haddon, of the 1968 report, was glad to do so. "The industry representatives are hardly naïve," he wrote to the FTC. "Therefore, I can only consider their present advertising to represent an intentional attempt to mislead the public. The time has come to call their bluff."[7] The *Christian Science Monitor* agreed, accusing the liquor industry of playing "Dr. Jekyll and Mr. Hyde," portraying an image of concern but opposing drunk driving legislation that might interfere with sales of its product.[8]

The DOT acted in November 1970. Robert B. Voas, who worked with Volpe, sent a letter to LBI president Thomas J. Donovan saying that the chart did "present a problem" because there was an important difference between being "safe from breaking the law" and "safe from having an automobile crash." Donovan, in turn, promised Volpe that the ad would not run again. Then, in February 1971, at a speech given to the LBI, Volpe surprised even Plymat by publicly criticizing the advertisement for ignoring the fact that the legal drinking limit was a "far cry" from the safe drinking limit. "The man who thinks he can safely drive with a blood alcohol content of up to 0.10 per cent," Volpe warned, "is the man who will jump a median strip to hit your car—or will speed through a crosswalk to kill your son or daughter."[9]

Volpe's concerns mirrored those of Dr. Max Hayman, a psychiatrist at the University of California at Los Angeles Medical Center and author of "The Myth of Social Drinking," an article that had appeared in the November 1967 issue of the *American Journal of Psychiatry*. Hayman believed that the supposed distinction between social drinking and alcoholism was "nebulous or nonexistent." This point mattered, he argued, because the concept of social drinking led to rationalizations and denials of real problems when drinkers missed work, got into fights, or were arrested for DWI. Hayman cited data showing that most social drinkers did, at times, go over a 0.05% BAC, the generally accepted level for impairment. To suggest that drinking only led to problems among full-fledged alcoholics, he concluded, was a myth.[10]

Perhaps it was the news that nearly 60,000 people had requested copies of Leon Greenberg's chart that had finally made Volpe angry. But in private, the Department of Transportation still was ambivalent about putting too much focus on social drinkers for fear that it would deflect attention—and support—from its efforts to get problem drinkers off the road. Yes, many Americans drove after drinking, one of Volpe's associates, James E. Wilson, explained to Plymat, but they did so in moderation. "Only by such understandings," he added, "can we gain support for strong measures directed at the relatively small minority who are the chief culprits."[11] Debates over this calculus—tolerating drinking and driving to gain support for the elimination of drunk driving—would emerge again, with much more rancor, in the MADD era.

Just as this controversy was dying down, another one arose. In 1970 on New Year's Eve, symbolically, President Richard M. Nixon had signed into law the Comprehensive Alcohol Abuse and Alcoholism Prevention, Treatment and Rehabilitation Act. As a result, among other things, the National Institute on Alcohol Abuse and Alcoholism (NIAAA) came into being. The NIAAA's first head was Morris E. Chafetz, a psychiatrist and alcoholism expert at Harvard Medical School and the prestigious Massachusetts General Hospital, who was a passionate devotee of the notion of alcoholism as a disease. This meant that he drew a firm distinction between drinkers who had a dangerous tendency toward alcoholism and those who were not at risk—and thus could safely drink. In fact, for the latter group, he was a fervent supporter of alcohol use. In his 1965 book,

Liquor: The Servant of Man, he wrote that alcohol was a "lovely substance" and a "gift of God" that caused no "permanent direct damage" to the body. Chafetz even wrote that there was no problem with teenage drinking as long as it was done in moderation.[12]

Even if these beliefs had some scientific validity, they made Chafetz a curious choice to head the NIAAA. Although the alcoholism model still held a lot of sway, it was gradually being replaced by a public health model, which sought to prevent "alcohol problems" throughout the population, not just among a subset of the heaviest drinkers. Chafetz's ardent advocacy of responsible drinking, even before driving, reminded activists of the recent LBI advertisement controversy and raised the question as to whether the new NIAAA head was too closely tied to industry. By characterizing alcoholism as a psychological problem that affected "a small maladjusted minority," William Plymat told Clark Mollenhoff, the Washington Bureau Chief of the *Des Moines Register*, Chafetz held opinions that were "completely consistent" with the desires of the LBI and thus "conducive to increasing the sale and consumption of alcoholic beverages." Indeed, the LBI had published a brochure to publicize Chafetz's 1965 book, and after he established the Health Education Foundation in 1976, funders would include the United States Brewers Association, Anheuser-Busch, and the Miller Brewing Company.[13]

This disagreement spilled over at a conference, "Public Information Programs on Alcohol and Highway Safety," held at the University of Michigan in November 1971. Among the speakers was the LBI's Thomas J. Donovan, who characterized driving after moderate drinking as both inevitable and acceptable. Predictably, Chafetz concurred with Donovan's emphasis on alcoholism as opposed to alcohol but objected to what he saw as the anti–drunk driving movement's law-and-order approach, which tossed alcoholic drivers into jail and "pass[ed] moralistic judgments against them." Taking the opposite side was *New York Times* travel columnist Paul J. C. Friedlander, who objected that some speakers were treating drunk drivers with "soft kid gloves." He then rhetorically asked how many conference attendees were actually willing to face a drunk driver on their way home from the meeting. In his closing remarks, Chafetz again criticized those in favor of punishing alcoholics, reminding them they were "talking about *people* and we seem to forget that." This was too much for conference attendee Willard Y. Howell, director of the National Highway Traffic Safety Administration's (NHTSA) office of alcohol countermeasures, who got into a heated argument over what he saw as Chafetz's lack of concern for the victims of drunk driving. Robert Borkenstein later characterized the episode as a "fiasco." Friedlander was so stunned by the animus at the conference that he wrote three *New York Times* articles about it. Once again, it was clear that a serious rift existed between those who saw drinking and driving as absolutely morally wrong and those who tried to carve out exceptions or conceptualize the problem somewhat differently.[14]

The Chafetz era at NIAAA lasted five years. Chafetz's successor, Ernest P. Noble, a basic scientist, immediately urged the NIAAA to abandon the notion of responsible drinking, which a fellow critic would later term "a seductive slogan . . . designed to teach and encourage everyone to drink."[15] "The more you drink, whether as an individual or as a society," Noble stated, "the more problems you will have." Noble also confronted the beverage industry for what he believed were inappropriate products directed at youth, for example, Hereford Cows, milkshakes with a 20 percent alcohol content. In 1976, Senator William D. Hathaway of Maine held hearings on "media images of alcohol," which he said portrayed alcohol as "glamorous, friendly, healthy, adventuresome [and] sexy." Among the issues before the committee were increased taxes on alcohol and warning labels on liquor bottles, both of which Chafetz opposed. These issues, which the sociologist Carolyn L. Wiener called "little prohibitions," would receive growing scrutiny in the 1980s.[16]

In the case of drunk driving, the 1968 report was followed by an uptick in both federal and local activity. These efforts largely followed the Scandinavian model, as Norway, Sweden, and to a lesser degree, Denmark and Finland remained the acknowledged world leaders in the field. These countries relied largely on public education and legal deterrents: per se laws with low BACs and, most important, tougher and more consistent punishments to discourage people from drinking and driving. Norway and Sweden had each established a BAC of 0.05% decades earlier; in both countries, the concept of what would eventually be termed a *designated driver* was widely accepted. Another model for the United States was England, where the 1967 British Road Safety Act led to widespread condemnation of what the British called "drink driving" and the establishment of a per se law criminalizing BACs greater than 0.08%. In the first months that the law was in place, fatalities and serious injuries dropped by as much as two-thirds. The English preferred the term *drink driving* to *drunk driving*, believing that the latter condemned only drivers who were obviously intoxicated and thus ignored others with significant impairment.[17]

The new federal initiative, run by NHTSA and called the Alcohol Safety

Action Projects (ASAP), received $88 million of federal funds between 1969 and 1976. The money went to thirty-five communities to establish and evaluate "comprehensive, multifaceted countermeasure programs designed to reduce the incidence of alcohol as a causal factor in motor vehicle crashes."[18] For the most part, the programs stuck to the traditional law-and-order model, training police in identifying, arresting, and helping to prosecute drunk drivers. Specific initiatives included administrative license suspension, which involved immediate revocation of drivers licenses for a high BAC, and sobriety checkpoints—breath and sobriety testing of arbitrarily stopped drivers who appeared inebriated on questioning. To enhance the visibility of the ASAP, NHTSA released a spate of public service announcements in newspapers and on television stations across the country. Among the slogans used were: "Talk a problem drinker out of driving," "Today your friendly neighbor may kill you," and "How many people will somebody's cocktail party kill tonight?" Most of these announcements featured ordinary-looking people who, by implication, were problem drinkers and in denial, although a 1979 spot that showed heavy alcohol use in the Star Wars Cantina reminded viewers that, even in other galaxies, "Friends don't let friends drive drunk." NHTSA also recruited celebrities, such as the actor Dana Andrews, who told radio listeners that when he used to drive drunk, "I was about as good a driver as my two-year-old grandson." Concurrent spots put out by Chafetz's NIAAA reminded readers and viewers that "if you need a drink to be social . . . that's not social drinking."[19]

Although the ASAP program was organized by NHTSA, William Haddon played no role. Frustrated by what he believed was DOT's unwillingness to confront the auto industry, he had resigned as head of NHTSA in 1969. Haddon was soon named head of the Insurance Institute for Highway Safety, which, using his epidemiological approach to crash reduction, became a distinguished research organization and a progressive force in safety reform.

The ASAP projects varied in their success, and researchers ultimately disagreed about whether increasing arrests and penalties had prevented mortality. Although the number of DWI arrests increased by as much as 100 percent in the various ASAP sites, the number of total fatal crashes stayed the same or possibly increased. A concrete legacy of the ASAPs was mandating educational programs for DWI offenders as a probation requirement. In addition, the need to evaluate the ASAP data led to the creation of the national Fatality Analysis Reporting System (FARS) in 1975.[20]

In 1978, the Department of Transportation issued *Alcohol and Highway Safety*

1978: A Review of the State of Knowledge, which updated Kelley and Haddon's report from a decade earlier. Among the topics covered was the department's own ASAP, which it conceded had done little to clarify the effectiveness of various control measures. That there was a "problem of major proportions," which had not abated despite a decade's worth of research and implementation, was clear. The authors, systems analyst Ralph K. Jones and University of Michigan lawyer and researcher Kent B. Joscelyn, confirmed earlier work estimating that nearly half of all fatally injured drivers had BACs of at least 0.10%. Other risk factors were being male, a beer drinker, a nighttime and weekend driver, and having a history of prior DWIs. Alcohol-related crashes, according to Jones and Joscelyn, cost American society roughly $6 billion in 1975 alone. And, they noted, the probability of being arrested while driving with a BAC of greater than 0.10% was extremely small, roughly 1 out of 2,000 trips.[21]

Still, Jones and Joscelyn were remarkably cautious in their conclusions. Pending additional research findings, they wrote, "There is no apparent justification for implementing new, large-scale operational programs." At one point, the authors even called into question the significance of decades-old data linking alcohol with erratic driving. "It is impossible to state conclusively," they wrote, "that impairment of the ability to perform critical driving tasks by alcohol has caused any given fraction of crashes involving alcoholics or problem drinkers."[22]

If the federal government was essentially throwing up its hands, the American public was not even doing that. NHTSA, the National Safety Council, and other interested organizations had publicized the figure of 25,000 annual deaths and the ASAP initiatives, and specific cases of drunk driving, either involving celebrities or fatalities, continued to make the newspapers and evening news. But Americans remained relatively uninterested in drunk driving. Sensing this ennui, Jones and Joscelyn acknowledged the need to "explore new approaches to provide new direction and new blood."[23] The federal government, however, just did not seem to know how to do it.

Fortunately, Doris Aiken did. On December 5, 1977, while preparing dinner for her family, she glanced at a headline in her local newspaper. Two local teenagers, Karen and Timothy Morris, whom she knew distantly, had been hit by a drunk driver in her city of Schenectady, New York. The driver, whose BAC was 0.19%, almost double the legal limit of 0.10%, had been clutching a can of beer between his knees as he drove. One of the children had died at the scene and the other was mortally wounded. This event fueled what would become Aiken's thirty-plus-year crusade to save the lives of other children—and adults—from people who had knowingly gotten behind the wheels of their cars despite being impaired by liquor. When Doris Aiken wrote her autobiography, she called it *My Life as a Pit Bull*.

Before exploring the formation of Aiken's group, Remove Intoxicated Drivers, and the other organizations that followed, it is worth revisiting what transpired after drunk driving crashes just prior to the activist era. In one sense, it is not easy to recount these stories, which were rarely published, especially before 1980. But the victims themselves and family members still recall what happened, and at times, they documented their experiences. Like all anecdotes, these accounts, by definition, tell only one side of the story and may have been crafted over time to create "idealized victims." As such, these stories may not be representative of drunk driving in general. Nevertheless, the common language of helplessness, frustration, and anger, occurring at a particular historical moment, lend them considerable credibility. As we will see, most victims and family members were passive bystanders, excluded from the legal process. When they spoke up, one woman told Aiken, they were accused of being "teetotalers" or "wanting revenge."[24] The message to these suffering families could not have been clearer: We're sorry, but now shut up and get on with your lives.

When Janet S. Besse of Syracuse, New York, was hit head on by a drunk driver in October 1966, her "greatest shock" was that the driver received only a $10 fine for "failure to keep right" and a 30-day license suspension. The police had not bothered to charge the driver with DWI, Besse wrote, because "it was too late and too much trouble." Besse tried to interest judges, lawyers, the local district attorney, and the New York State Police in her story, but they all "slammed doors in [her] face."[25] Thirteen years later, she was one of the first victims to join RID.

Two places that ordinary citizens could tell their stories to the public in the 1970s were in letters to the editor and by writing to the syndicated columnist Ann Landers. In September 1973, victims did both. Richard J. Warren of Van Nuys, California, told the *Los Angeles Times* the horrifying story of how a drunk driver had killed his wife and two small children. "My wife," he wrote, "was lowered into her grave beside my daughter on the day that would have been our daughter's fifth birthday." Most people, Warren said, just "shook their heads" over drunk driving accidents, seemingly much more concerned about "saving giraffes, otters and Arctic crabs."[26] Ann Landers reprinted a letter from an Oklahoma newspaper written by a drunk driving victim who had suffered a fractured skull, a broken collarbone, nine broken ribs, and a collapsed lung. His treatments included thirty-nine blood transfusions, removal of his spleen, and permanent kidney dialysis; he had not been able to return to work. The drunk driver's only punishments, the man reported, were a $100 fine and mandatory driving school. "I have not heard one word from the drunk who hit me," he concluded. "He has never said so much as 'I'm sorry.'"[27]

Three years earlier, 21-year-old Edward Rohr was a passenger in a van in Wyoming, New York, that was sideswiped by a car being driven by a man who had been drinking for five hours in a nearby bar. The van turned over and burst into flames; Rohr burned to death. His parents, Bob and Penny, asked to attend the trial but were told it would jeopardize the case. Nevertheless, the court assessed only a $35 fine. Ironically, Bob Rohr recently recalled, the courts viewed cases involving death to be less worthy of compensation than those that resulted in severe physical handicaps. He went to the New York legislature to try to get the laws reformed, he said, but was a "voice crying in the wilderness with nobody interested."[28]

That same year Katherine du Treil was a 20-year-old living with her father and two younger siblings. Her mother had died some years before. One evening, her father was killed by an underage drunk driver. Du Treil suddenly became the family breadwinner. As was common at the time, the local prosecutors termed the death an "accident." "The young man that ran over my father two times with his car," she recalled thirty-five years later, "was never even issued a traffic citation."[29]

John Turk was the 17-year-old son of a nurse who worked for surgeon Ralph F. Hudson in Eau Claire, Wisconsin. Turk was riding his bicycle when he was killed by a drunk driver with a BAC of 0.20%. The driver pled no contest, according to Hudson, and the judge gave him the customary slap on the wrist—probation. Hudson paraphrased the judge's reasoning: "After all, it wasn't intentional and was an accident. We can't bring John back—and the defendant has suffered and will continue to suffer." Turk had often told his mother that he wanted to be a physician, "like Dr. Hudson."[30]

Robert M. Carney became a prosecutor in Schenectady County, New York, in the late 1970s. There was generally "acceptance" or "passivity" on the part of victims' families, he recalls. Activism was only beginning to emerge. Most jurors, meanwhile, "sympathized with the defendant, thinking there but for the grace of God go I."[31]

In 1977, Susan Wright, a 28-year-old divorced mother, got the *Los Angeles Times* to chronicle the aftermath of the third instance in which a drunk driver had hit her car. Wright had told the prosecutor's office that she wanted to testify at the trial and thereby prevent the reduction of charges—for a third time. After all, the third offender's Breathalyzer readings had registered over 0.15%, and Los Angeles had just announced a crackdown on drunk drivers. Nevertheless, according to Wright, during a supposed continuance in the trial, charges were quietly reduced. The drunk driver pled guilty to speeding and making an illegal left turn and only had to pay a $50 fine.[32]

Doris Argotsinger was a 57-year-old woman returning from church in up-state New York in May 1980 when she was hit and killed by a car carrying two teenage girls. According to Susan Goodemote, her granddaughter, the district attorney in Gloversville, New York, had run for office promising no plea-bargaining for drunk drivers, but "it was a lie." The driver did not even lose her license. After encountering the perpetrators soon thereafter, Goodemote wrote, "The thing that really hurts me is to see the two girls that killed her out drinking beer. I have seen both of these girls and it makes me sick to think it didn't affect them."[33]

Stewart Rosenkrantz was riding his bicycle in Fort Lauderdale, Florida, in July 1981 when he was struck from behind by a driver in a pickup truck whose BAC turned out to be 0.18%. The bicycle wedged in the grill of the truck, and Rosenkrantz was thrown to the ground. He wound up paralyzed by a spinal cord injury, which also left him incontinent and impotent. The driver pled no contest, according to Rosenkrantz, and received a 90-day license suspension, a $175 fine, and mandatory attendance at a driving school. "But what about the victims?" Rosenkrantz fumed. "If the victim dies, we seem to have had the attitude 'Well, we can't bring them back and anyway it was just an accident' and we don't make the drivers pay."[34]

A North Carolina couple wrote about the death of their son at the hands of a drunk driver. The local district attorney allowed the driver to plea-bargain to the least possible charge, losing her license for only a month. But what was as upsetting to these parents was "the lack of compassion for the surviving family of the deceased." The highway trooper never contacted the parents to tell them what had happened, and they learned from a newspaper article—not from the district attorney's office—that their son's case had not gone to trial but had been pled out. "This does prove," they concluded, "that death by motor vehicle is excusable."[35]

The degree to which drunk driving was part of the culture was nicely demonstrated when Carlton E. Turner, who favored aggressive, punitive measures as Ronald Reagan's first "drug czar," was asked his opinion about the value of appointing a presidential commission on drunk driving. Here Turner was passive, opposing the idea because of the well-known reluctance of police officers and other local officials to arrest or punish prominent people suspected of DWI.[36]

These stories were not particular to the 1970s and early 1980s, but for the first time they began to have traction. In addition to the challenges to the auto industry by Nader, Haddon, and colleagues, other venerable institutions were coming under fire. Grassroots movements challenged Jim Crow laws in the South, the continuing bloodshed in Vietnam, and male domination of society. Good examples of the era's feminism were the efforts of women to regain control of the childbirth process and to challenge male obstetricians and breast cancer surgeons who routinely excluded them from medical decision-making. By the mid-1970s, a consumerist movement had emerged, urging Americans to question authority and the status quo, whether purchasing a house, choosing a lawyer, buying food, or, thanks to Nader and Haddon, buying a car.

Doris Aiken had never previously had a personal connection to a drunk driving crash and had not given the topic special thought. A 51-year-old journalist from Schenectady, New York, she was married to William Aiken, an engineer, and had three children. But as a member of her Unitarian church's social action group, an abortion rights activist, and host of *Forum*, a local television news program that featured issues such as prison sentencing, women's rights, and homosexuality, Aiken was herself immersed in these changing trends in American society. Thus, it is not surprising that the headline in her local newspaper jumped out at her that evening as it might not have ten, or even five, years previously. Aiken first did what any journalist would do: she made some phone calls. The first was to the local district attorney. She asked him if the driver had lost his license or his freedom. As Aiken later recounted, he first chuckled and then said "No, we don't take away licenses or put people in jail." And then, in language that drunk driving victims knew all too well, he added: "This is an accident. He didn't mean to do it and probably feels very bad about it. You shouldn't get involved in this."[37] Aiken did better than Bonnie Morris, the bereaved mother of the two dead children. According to Aiken, the district attorney had not even returned her phone calls.

The dismissive remarks "jolted" Aiken into action. What she did next was pure grassroots. She asked her church for $50 to print stationary with a letterhead announcing the formation of an organization seeking justice in the Morris case. Aiken next used her media connections to invite interested people to a community meeting. Roughly twenty people showed up, including a reporter, a member of the local alcoholism council, a city court judge, and several church members. There were no victims or family members. The first speaker was the judge, who issued a well-meaning warning. "You people should be aware," he said, "that you might be treading on drunk drivers' rights by calling the D.A. or publishing letters."[38]

Of course, for Aiken and the thousands of victims she would come to represent, concern for the rights of drunk drivers was not something they needed to heed but was itself the problem. As far back as 1937, when the American Medical Association and the National Safety Council set 0.15% as the legal limit for drunk driving, legislators and health officials had been bending over backward to make sure that any drinkers who could conceivably navigate the roads after several drinks did not have that option taken away. Meanwhile, the vast majority of people who drank and then drove, and who were certainly impaired, benefited from these purposely lax statutes.

Interestingly, Aiken knew none of this history when she embarked on her crusade. She did not even know of the work of William Haddon and Pat Moynihan, although they did most of their seminal research and writing on drunk driving in nearby Albany. Nor had she heard of the ASAP projects. This ignorance, however, may have been a blessing in disguise. Rather than merely pushing for standard reform measures, such as lowering the acceptable BAC, Aiken initially focused on what happened locally—specifically, plea-bargaining and sentence reduction—which she anticipated would happen in the Morris case. The idea was to follow and then publicize what occurred in specific DWI court cases. At the meeting, attendees decided to form a "court-watching group." They also planned to find a pro bono lawyer to take on the Morris case and ensure that the driver would at least serve some time in jail.

There was dissent in the room, as Aiken recalled in her autobiography. One speaker opined that New York would never change its plea-bargaining laws because the defense lawyers who represented drunk drivers were such a strong lobbying group. Plea-bargaining, according to Aiken, was a quick way for lawyers to make a buck, whereas going to trial required money and time. The alcoholism activist wrote a letter to the local paper suggesting that more punitive measures against alcoholics were inappropriate because such individuals were diseased. She also objected to another idea raised at the meeting—publishing the names of drunk drivers in newspapers—because it would further lower the esteem of those cited.[39] But the word spread and the small group, now named

Remove Intoxicated Drivers, began to grow in membership, especially after its first press conference, held in February 1978. Herself a member of the press, Aiken knew how crucial media attention would be for her fledgling group to thrive.

Many of those who ultimately became RID activists were victims, either having been in a drunk driving crash themselves or having a personal connection to one. Of course, the term *victim* was far from straightforward, especially when people died in crashes. As far back as Barbee Hook and Hugh Gravitt, the perceived victim was often the drunk driver himself, condemned to live with guilt the rest of his life. Aiken and her colleagues sought to turn this idea on its head. Without minimizing the seriousness of alcoholism or the psychological ramifications of inadvertently killing someone, they argued that justice was almost never served in drunk driving cases. Society needed to care more about the "real" victims lying in hospital beds and cemeteries and, as importantly, the *potential* victims of crashes when chronic drunk drivers were continually allowed back on the street.

Essential to the enterprise, Aiken soon concluded, was pressure. "Pressure is the only tactic that mattered," she wrote, "and only if that pressure were perceived to come from voters." Aiken's self-characterization as a pit bull was not far from the mark. A colleague called her "unarguably stubborn, intractable and uncompromising." As RID grew, it relied on court watching, relentless letters and phone calls to legislators and judges, constant lobbying in Albany and other state capitals, and press conferences, often outing what members believed were outrageous injustices being perpetrated on individuals and families who had already suffered enough. "RID-NYS has collected a group of cases where the [Department of Motor Vehicles] took from 6 weeks to 15 months to suspend or revoke drivers who refused the chemical breath test and who were driving legally all that time in spite of deplorable driving records and previous DWI convictions," Aiken wrote to the New York State Department of Motor Vehicles commissioner. "We hope we will not have to bring public attention to the poor record of the DMV in this area." "Last year," she told *Time* magazine in 1981, "each drunk driver in New York paid, on the average, a $12 fine, while those who killed a deer out of season had to pay $1,500."[40]

By 1983, RID had more than 130 chapters in thirty states. But it was in New York, Aiken's home state, that the earliest successes occurred. Persistence and outrage, the group soon learned, could produce substantial results. In 1979, forty bills pertaining to drunk driving were introduced into the New York State

Memorial and balloon lift-off for drunk driving victim Michele Martin held by RID on Mother's Day, 1983, Capitol building steps, Albany, New York. Courtesy of Doris Aiken

legislature. None passed. One legislative aide told Aiken, "You can't legislate morality; people like to drink and love their cars in America."[41] But in 1980 and 1981, thirteen bills passed. It was clearly RID's doing. In addition to its usual strategies, RID generated report cards of the state legislators regarding their voting records on drunk driving legislation. And then there was the vigil. For eleven straight days, in October 1981, RID representatives, including numerous members of the clergy, stood vigil outside the voting hall of the state legislature holding pictures, placards, and a twenty-foot scroll listing the names of those killed by drunk drivers in the Albany area during the previous eighteen months.

Among the new laws signed by Governor Mario Cuomo were ones that prevented plea-bargaining in DWI cases, immediately revoked the drivers licenses of second-time offenders, and earmarked fees collected from drunk driving cases for the purchase of Breathalyzers, the payment of overtime costs for police officers, and the funding of other anti–drunk driving enforcement measures. RID also strongly pushed for the regular use of sobriety checkpoints for drivers at locations and times when the likelihood of finding intoxicated drivers was highest. Another early success of RID in New York was the ouster of veteran judges who were lenient on drunk drivers. In one instance, in Schodack, New York, a retired police officer ran against a veteran Republican judge known as "Let 'em go Snow." RID generated a list of cases in which Snow had gone easy on the defendant, such as the man with a BAC of 0.33% who permanently maimed a victim and left the scene of the crash but received only a suspended jail sentence as punishment. Although no Democrat had won a local race there since 1924, Snow was defeated, thanks to the sudden rise of activism.[42]

On a smaller scale, RID also sought to empower all individuals involved in drunk driving crashes. In the early 1980s, RID published a manual entitled *The Drunk Driver: Victim's Rights*, which was basically a how-to guide to try to achieve justice. Among the advice offered was: asking the officer to perform breath tests; finding out where the offending driver had his last drink; obtaining the accident report; hiring a lawyer specializing in negligence cases; contacting the Department of Motor Vehicles to obtain the record of the offending driver; personally discussing the case with the local district attorney; speaking in court at the time of sentencing; and possibly bringing lawsuits against the intoxicated driver and the establishment at which he had been drinking.

In practice, Doris Aiken or other RID members often assisted victims in achieving these tasks. "You will receive letters from other RID members in Florida, who are watching this case closely, as an indicator and example of the aggressiveness and seriousness of your office," Aiken wrote to a district attorney on behalf of a Florida family that had lost a son to a drunk driver. "We want the license of the offender NOW, and the swift resolution with the harshest punishment including some recommendations from your office to the judge and to the parents."[43]

Aiken constantly received letters of thanks from those whom RID had helped. "With RID's assistance and my pleading, the District attorney impounded the cars involved and found the evidence necessary to bring the charges and the plea to criminally negligent homicide by the alcohol impaired offender," wrote a woman from Clifton Park, New York, who had lost a daughter. "Without RID's assistance and my persistence, we wouldn't have had a case." Also appreciative was the Morris family, whose two dead children had originally inspired Aiken. Belying the indifference of the district attorney to whom Aiken had originally spoken, the perpetrator was convicted of criminally negligent homicide and sent to jail for six months. At least it was something.[44]

Meanwhile, in Unionville, Maryland, Cindi Lamb went out to shop on the morning of November 10, 1979. She took along her five-month-old daughter, Laura, and strapped her into a car seat in the family pickup truck. As Lamb drove through Mount Pleasant, Maryland, her truck suddenly collided with a swerving car, ultimately ending up against an embankment. It turned out the car, driven by a 37-year-old mechanic, Russell J. Newcomer Jr., had been going 70 miles per hour on a slick road and had crossed the midline into oncoming traffic. Lamb's truck was actually the second vehicle that Newcomer hit, but it would be the most damaged. Lamb, who was thrown through the windshield, wound up with twelve broken bones, but it was Laura who was most severely hurt, ripped from her car seat when the straps snapped. Ultimately, an injury to her spinal cord left her paralyzed from the shoulders down. This devastating and tragic event, noted the local paper, the *Weekly Courier*, "shattered" the "idyllic" lives of Cindi and her husband, Alan Lamb, as they faced a series of demanding medical and emotional challenges.[45]

Newcomer was drunk, having imbibed two pints of Canadian Mist whisky beginning at 9 a.m. Apparently no BAC was obtained. Moreover, Newcomer was a recidivist, with more than thirty traffic violations, including three arrests for DWI. He was also on probation for armed robbery at the time of the crash. Whereas Doris Aiken had a history of political activism, the Lambs had none at all. Alan Lamb was an engineer, and Cindi was a manager for Tupperware; they were raising Laura and an older boy. But, like Aiken, they could not merely accept what had happened as an accident, especially because Newcomer's past behaviors had made another crash utterly predictable.

As they were tending to Laura's needs, the Lambs began writing to state legislators about the state's lax DWI enforcement, which was among the worst in the nation. Met with indifference, the Lambs gradually gravitated toward the media as a channel for publicizing their concerns. Several local papers had covered the tragedy, for good reason. What made the Lamb case especially newsworthy was that there was an infant victim—and one who was especially compelling. Despite her condition, Laura Lamb was a very happy baby and extremely photogenic. Cindi Lamb was always fearful of exploiting her daughter and actually declined many media requests, but she chose to stay involved. She thought to herself that one day Laura might ask her, "Why am I in this chair and what did you do about it?" Lamb said she could not bear to say that she had done nothing. As a result, Laura became a local media icon. Cindi later recalled, "People would look at her and ask, 'What have we done?'"[46]

Laura Lamb, the adorable drunk driving victim who was for a time the face of the movement. Courtesy of Bill Bronrott and Cindi Lamb

There was national attention, too. On September 23, 1980, the *Washington Post* covered state legislative hearings held in Annapolis, Maryland, at which Laura Lamb appeared and her mother spoke. "I remember the last time Laura felt a hug," Cindi Lamb told the assembled legislators. "I remember the last time Laura moved her fingers and hands and feet and legs. Now, she doesn't feel any kisses, doesn't feel any hugs, doesn't feel anything." Two days later the newspaper published an editorial entitled "Why Laura Lamb Can't Move." The piece retold the story of Laura's injury and then, noting that Maryland was one of few states that still had a 0.15% BAC for legal intoxication, took state lawmaker Joseph E. Owens to task for stonewalling more progressive legislation.[47]

Laura Lamb was featured on television in Washington, DC, as well. Sandy Golden, a reporter for the CBS television affiliate there, had read about the Lambs and subsequently did a five-part series on the family and the subject of drunken driving. Shortly thereafter, incensed by the apathy among the public and legislators, Golden actually quit his job and began to work full time on the issue of drunk driving. Newcomer's sentence was reason enough for Golden's decision. The judge gave the drunk driver only two years in prison, in part because he believed that internment would have little deterrent effect on Newcomer's future behavior. Even Newcomer admitted that a longer punishment would have been more appropriate. He actually wound up serving five years because the DWI was a violation of his parole.[48]

A third drunk driving activist emerged in 1980 from a story that was perhaps even more distressing and alarming than those of Aiken and Lamb. This time the victim was 13-year-old Cari Lightner, an identical twin of Serena, who loved to talk on the phone, cook, imitate people, and play basketball and softball. On May 13, 1980, while Cari was walking to a carnival on a suburban street in Fair Oaks, California, a hit-and-run drunk driver killed her, throwing her body 125 feet. Ironically, the Lightner family had been involved in two prior crashes. A drunk driver had rear-ended Lightner's mother's car when the twins were 18 months old and in the back seat. Then Travis, the twins' younger brother, had been hit by a car in 1975, suffering brain trauma and other severe injuries. He would require multiple operations.

Cari's parents, Candy and Steve Lightner, were divorced. As they grieved and went ahead with funeral preparations, details of the crash began to emerge. The driver, quickly apprehended by the police, was a 46-year-old cannery worker named Clarence William Busch. Not only had Busch been drunk, Candy Lightner learned from a highway patrolman working on the case, but he had four prior DWI arrests and had only served a total of forty-eight hours in jail. Even more appalling, the latest arrest had occurred just two days prior to Cari's death; the police had let Busch go home to await trial without even taking away his license! When Lightner asked the patrolman whether Busch was likely to go to prison, he was frank. "Lady, you'll be lucky if he sees any time in jail at all, much less prison," he said. "That's the way the system works."[49]

Candy Lightner was not a political person. A 33-year-old real estate agent raising three children, she was not even a registered voter. But she, too, would undergo a transformation as she grew angrier and angrier. The night that she learned about Busch, Lightner and some friends and family decided to go to dinner at a local restaurant. She later wrote: "I was furious. I got in the car and I gave this information to my friends. All the way to the restaurant I couldn't concentrate on anything they were saying because I was so angry that this could happen in a civilized society. My friends felt the same way; nobody could believe that that's the way the laws worked. I was fuming. I felt enraged and helpless."

While waiting at the bar for a table, Lightner and her sister Kathy discussed ways that Lightner could deal with this anger. Finally, Candy announced that she wanted to start an organization to alert the public. Her friend Leslie then blurted out a name for the group. "And you are going to call it Mothers Against Drunk Drivers," she said.[50]

Lightner later liked to point out that the idea for MADD started in the bar of a restaurant. Over the years, she, Cindi Lamb, Doris Aiken, and other drunk driving activists would be termed neoprohibitionists by their critics, but all of them drank—Lamb, heavily at times. They just did not drink and drive. Lamb later wrote: "I love beer; always have, always will. So what? I'm not hurting anyone, and I'm not driving, so what's the big deal, right?"[51]

Lightner then began the process of making connections, first with Steve Blankenship, who was an aide to the California attorney general. Soon she was publicizing Mothers Against Drunk Drivers, also known as MADD, telling Cari's story to anyone who would listen, including local politicians, judges, and district attorneys. They were supportive to varying degrees, but there was one group that Lightner soon realized she could always count on: the media. This became eminently clear when Lightner delivered her first public speech about her daughter's death, to a traffic safety conference in Oregon, where her story was unknown. She began talking about a 13-year-old, freckle-faced, auburn-haired girl. She ended by describing that girl's death at the hands of a drunk driver with several previous convictions. This is Lightner's description of what happened next: "So when I said, 'That little girl was my daughter,' the audience gasped. The press jumped up and ran out the door to call the photographers. Pandemonium broke out."[52]

Lightner's story of a needless, horrific drunk driving death was similar to so many others. For decades no one had seemed to care. But now, when NHTSA announced that drunk driving crashes killed someone every twenty-three minutes and were the leading cause of death of people under 34, including children, it struck a chord. There were mothers like Lightner—lots of them—who were outraged and insistent on change.[53]

Very few people could have done what Candy Lightner did. Once she made MADD her cause, it "became a twenty-four-hour-a-day, seven-day-a-week job." Cindi Lamb, herself a formidable woman, termed Lightner "tough as nails."[54] Typical was Lightner's decision to appear every single day at the office of California governor Jerry Brown until he agreed to appoint a task force on drunk driving. Lightner later realized that one of the reasons she so immersed herself in the MADD cause was to avoid the painful grieving over her daughter's death. She quickly became a media darling, appearing on the *Today* show, the *Phil Donahue Show*, and *60 Minutes*. She cultivated the press and it cultivated her. Lightner was attractive, photogenic, and able to cry in public, fiercely debate opponents, and supply pithy sound bites, qualities that were movingly and effectively featured in a 1983 made-for-television movie, *The Candy Lightner Story*, starring Mariette Hartley. "Prisoners have a union and a paid lobbyist," Lightner tells the California legislature in a scene from the film. "What do we have? We, the innocent victims."

Lightner, whom the sociologist Frank J. Weed termed the "MADD Queen" in an article on charismatic reformers, would be the main reason that MADD would undergo enormous growth, having more than 300 chapters and 600,000 volunteers and donors nationwide by 1985. MADD received over $1 million from NHTSA and the insurance industry in 1981 and, by 1985, had a $12 million annual budget. Its successful campaign to put red ribbons on car antennas further enhanced its visibility. By the 1990s, several surveys listed MADD as America's favorite charity.[55]

Sandy Golden also played a role in the success of MADD. It was he who engineered a news conference with Lightner, Cindi Lamb, and Maryland congressman Michael D. Barnes in the summer of 1980. Lamb had agreed to begin a MADD chapter in Maryland and worked closely with Lightner for a time. Barnes, thanks to a highly motivated aide named Bill Bronrott, was extremely outspoken as well, terming drunk driving a "neglected national disgrace" and a "holocaust on our highways." Another high-profile event took place in October 1980. This time Lightner, Cindi Lamb, Laura Lamb, Barnes, California representative Robert T. Matsui (from Lightner's district), Rhode Island senator Claiborne Pell, and NHTSA head Joan Claybrook gathered in a Capitol Hill hearing room. Press coverage was considerable. Both mothers, unable to hold back tears, told their stories, emphasizing how the drunk drivers in question had received trivial punishments for multiple previous drunk driving offenses. Cindi Lamb once again vividly described Laura's condition: "Laura feels absolutely nothing from her shoulders down. No kisses, no hugs. Laura doesn't laugh when I tickle her motionless feet. Laura can't play patty-cake."[56] The MADD mothers also announced a nationwide petition drive to urge President Jimmy Carter to appoint a blue-ribbon panel to combat drunk driving.

As mothers, fathers, and other individuals joined RID and MADD, press coverage of drunk driving, particularly tragic accidents involving innocent victims,

A historic group photo taken just prior to the October 1, 1980, news conference that put MADD on the national map. *Left to right*, Candy Lightner, Representative Robert Matsui of California, Cindi Lamb (with Laura Lamb), Senator Claiborne Pell of Rhode Island, and Representative Michael D. Barnes of Maryland. Courtesy Bill Bronrott. Photo by Keith Jewell increased dramatically—by more than 800 percent, according to one index of newspaper articles. Typical were a front-page article in the March 22, 1981, *Washington Post*, entitled "A National Outrage" and the September 13, 1982, cover of *Newsweek*, entitled "The War on Drunk Driving: Getting Tough with the Killers of 26,000 Americans a Year."[57] Like those who joined RID, MADD members did educational outreach in communities, at schools, and in churches. They sent out press releases, attended conferences, and held public vigils. MADD also emphasized the importance of bartenders, party hosts, friends, and family in preventing obviously drunk people from driving. This intervention was captured by the slogan "Friends don't let friends drive drunk," originally introduced by the Department of Transportation and the Ad Council and also promulgated by the Licensed Beverage Industry. As the 1980s progressed, MADD would court celebrity endorsements from the likes of Phil Donahue, Betty Ford, Carol Burnett, and Bob Barker and produce moving and often graphic public service announcements showing the carnage caused by drunk driving crashes. Typical examples depicted teenagers in wheelchairs or drivers who had killed their friends. MADD also spearheaded a campaign encouraging the placement of roadside crosses at the sites of fatal car crashes involving alcohol. These served both as a memorial to the deceased but also as a political statement condemning such acts of violence.[58]

As had been the case in New York, however, much of MADD's early energy was focused on changing drunk driving laws. In Maryland in 1981, thanks to Bronrott, Barnes, Cindi Lamb, and Tom and Dot Sexton, whose 15-year-old son, Tommy, had been killed by a drunk driver in 1980, Governor Harry Hughes signed six bills, which included provisions to lower the legal BAC, to allow portable breath testing, and to raise the penalty for refusing such a test. In addition, the state announced a new program to pay troopers to work overtime at nights and on weekends, when drunk drivers were most often on the roads. As a result of these efforts, the arrest rate for DWI in Maryland more than doubled. In California, Lightner's efforts yielded tough new laws, including either two days in jail or a 90-day license restriction for a first drunk driving conviction and mandatory imprisonment of up to four years for repeat offenders. (Clarence Busch ultimately served one and a half years for Cari's death.) Other new measures in California sought to discourage plea-bargaining and close loopholes that invalidated Breathalyzer testing.[59]

To say that Lightner was a breath of fresh air in the world of anti–drunk driving activism would be a huge understatement. For years, those in the field had mused about the need for new energy but had themselves been unable to provide it. The data about what to do was there, recalls James C. Fell, then at NHTSA, but we "couldn't get the public's attention, couldn't get Congress's attention, couldn't get anyone's attention." "I have appealed for an 'outraged minority' in our field for many years," Robert Borkenstein told Lightner. Scientific research, he admitted, was "but a skeleton needing flesh and blood—and emotions."[60]

Lightner was careful to stay in touch with Borkenstein and other veterans in the field, both as a way to increase her knowledge and to pay homage to those who had preceded her. She told Borkenstein about one seminar of defense attorneys that she had attended, undercover. These meetings, she wrote, "are nothing more than an opportunity to beat their chests, tell everyone how successful they are at abusing the law, finding loopholes and getting their clients off scot-free." She closed the letter by thanking Borkenstein for their correspondence, adding "You are such a sweet man, Bob." Borkenstein, obviously impressed and charmed, wrote back: "It was such a coincidence being called 'sweet' by Candy on St. Valentine's Day."[61]

Perhaps the pinnacle of drunk driving activism in the 1980s was reached on April 14, 1982, the day that President Ronald Reagan stood in the White House Rose Garden and announced that "Americans are outraged that such slaughter can take place on our highways." The genesis for this event again began with the ubiquitous Sandy Golden, who drafted a petition calling for a presidential commission on drunk driving and asked Michael Barnes and Utah representative James V. Hansen to try to get everyone in Congress to sign it. Eventually, 340 members did so. In addition, MADD had obtained more than 200,000 signatures from members of the public urging that such a commission be formed. At the Rose Garden event, Reagan announced the formation of a highly diverse thirty-person Presidential Commission on Drunk Driving, to be headed by former Secretary of Transportation John Volpe.

Commission members included many familiar names, including Candy Lightner and Doris Aiken, both of whom attended the ceremony. Aiken scored the big publicity coup of the event, pinning a "RID" button on the president's suit, something she was not supposed to do.[62] Others on the commission included Senators Robert Dole and Claiborne Pell, Ann Landers, the actor Dick Van Patten, and Morris Chafetz, who had become the president of the Health Education Foundation. Reflecting the ongoing efforts of the alcohol industry to advocate responsible drinking, those named included Henry B. King, of the United

States Brewers Association, and Frederick A. Meister Jr., of the Distilled Spirits Council, a trade association that had formed in 1973 from the merger of the Licensed Beverage Industries, the Distilled Spirits Institute, and the Bourbon Institute. V. J. "Jim" Adduci, of the Motor Vehicle Manufacturers Association, represented the automobile industry. Another member was 71-year-old William Plymat, wearing his hat as executive director of the American Council on Alcohol Problems, which was the successor group to the old Anti-Saloon League. Plymat's presence provided a symbolic link to an earlier momentous occasion in the history of alcohol control, Prohibition, which had been repealed one-half century earlier.

The momentum continued into the fall, when, on October 25, President Reagan signed the first federal drunk driving legislation, a bill that provided $75 million of highway funding for states that passed four laws: (1) setting a 0.10% per se BAC; (2) administrative license revocation; (3) mandatory jail time or community service for repeat offenders; and (4) better enforcement of drunk driving laws. The states took the bait, and many went further. By 1984, all fifty states had lowered their legal BACs to 0.10%. In sum, between 1981 and 1986, 729 new state laws went on the books. Surveys, such as one showing that 77 percent of respondents favored mandatory prison sentences, indicated the public's support of the anti–drunk driving crusade.[63]

When the Presidential Commission issued its final report in December 1983, the breadth of its recommendations reflected the diversity of the panel. It seemed as if everyone's pet program had been included. In addition to supporting the 0.10% BAC legal limit and stricter punishments, the commission recommended stronger "dram shop" laws, increasing the liability of establishments that served alcohol to intoxicated customers; the prohibition of open alcohol containers in motor vehicles; sobriety checkpoints to detect drunk drivers; uniform implied consent statutes for BAC testing; greater use of victim impact statements of the sort favored by RID and MADD, in which survivors or their surviving relatives could detail for sentencing judges the often devastating impact of crashes on families; and the publication of the names of individuals arrested for and convicted of driving while intoxicated.[64]

Some localities had already begun to publish the names of offenders. This type of publicity indicated the ubiquity of a problem that was otherwise invisible unless one happened to witness a drunk driving arrest or crash. During a one-week period in October 1981, for example, the *Cedar Rapids* (Iowa) *Gazette* published six different articles listing thirty-eight persons who had been arrested for DWI in Cedar Rapids alone. The age range of the offenders, who included thirty-five men and three women, was from 19 to 65, although most were males in their twenties. A RID member in St. Louis, commenting on the publication of names in the *St. Louis Globe-Democrat*, noted "a few grumblings about the list being a violation of civil rights," but "999 out of 1000 people view the listings in a positive manner." "I was glad to see my neighbor's name on the list," noted another St. Louis resident. "He's drunk all the time, but hasn't killed anyone yet." William Plymat liked to tell the story of a woman who told him she had stopped driving drunk because her local paper printed not only the names and addresses of those arrested but also their ages—and she refused to let anyone know that she was 69.[65]

Finally, in July 1984, Ronald Reagan reluctantly signed the Minimum Legal Drinking Age Law, also favored by his Presidential Commission, which sought to force states to pass laws prohibiting the sale of alcohol to individuals younger than 21. Subsequent to the 1971 passage of the Twenty-Sixth Amendment, which lowered the voting age from 21 to 18, more than half of the states also lowered the legal drinking age to 18 or 19. But when data demonstrated higher numbers of alcohol-related crashes among young drivers in these states, Senator Frank Lautenberg and Representative James J. Howard, both from New Jersey, sponsored a bill to raise the drinking age back to 21. Once again, states needed to comply or lose millions of dollars of federal highway construction funding.[66]

Passage was far from assured. Much of the alcohol industry opposed the bill, as did Morris Chafetz, who had originally joined his fellow commission members in support of the measure but who much preferred approaches that discouraged drunkenness as opposed to making alcohol unavailable. However, RID and MADD, as well as the National Parent Teacher Association and other groups, heavily lobbied the congressmen, including delivering thousands of petitions. Even *Car and Driver* magazine, a longtime proponent of drivers' rights, lent its support. Although reluctant to intrude on states' rights, Reagan eventually signed the bill to "help persuade state legislators to act in the national interest to save our children's lives." NHTSA would later report that this legislation saved up to 900 lives annually.[67]

Ronald Reagan's involvement with anti–drunk driving activism underscores another reason the movement initially proved so phenomenally successful: it united both progressives and conservatives. The activism clearly emerged from the consumerist, feminist, and rights-based movements of the 1970s, but it was also congruent with Reagan-era efforts to fix social issues through the criminal justice system, which author and law professor Jonathan Simon has termed "governing through crime." It is no coincidence that in addition to appointing a task force on drunk driving, Reagan also appointed a task force on crime, which, using familiar language, termed the neglect of crime a "national disgrace." Specific efforts to address crime rates included a "War on Drugs," culminating in the federal Anti-Drug Abuse Act of 1986, which sought to increase both the interdiction of drugs and punishments for drug-related crimes. This effort had actually begun with the formation of a sort of cousin group to MADD, Families in Action (later the National Federation of Parents for Drug-Free Youth), consisting of parents concerned that their children were being exposed to cocaine and other dangerous drugs. This movement inspired Nancy Reagan's "Just say no" antidrug message. Other examples of social problems that were increasingly prosecuted in the 1980s included domestic violence and the use of alcohol or drugs by pregnant women.[68]

In his 1988 history of MADD, Northeastern University sociologist Craig Reinarman argued that the organization's agenda was "in harmony with the morality, policy ideologies, and social-control strategies of the Reagan administration and a renascent right." Individuals involved in drunk driving control have disputed this assessment, seeing their efforts as largely apolitical. However, it is reasonable to conclude that the initial focus of MADD on punishing and deterring individual drunk drivers—as opposed, for example, to taking on the alcohol industry—was an approach more suited to the conservative end of the political spectrum. So, too, was the emphasis on victims' rights. Just like Reagan's vilified "welfare mothers," drunk drivers had abused the system for far too long. The real victims, ordinary law-abiding Americans who paid their taxes or were hit by drunk drivers, deserved to be recognized and even rewarded.[69] As one Virginia woman upset about the lax punishment of drunk drivers asked, "When will the victim and his family ever be considered the 'good guys'"?[70] That time had come.

By 1985, the media was trumpeting the success of the anti–drunk driving movement, particularly MADD, which had become the largest and most visible organization. As *Time* magazine reported, deaths attributed to drunk driving had declined by 32 percent since 1980, from roughly 25,000 to 17,000 annually. Innovations were emerging throughout the country, including special drunk driving task forces in Miami and Los Angeles, the banning of happy hours, restrictions on beer at sporting events and on college campuses, and nonalcoholic graduation parties for high school students, often sponsored by chapters of Students

Against Drunk Drivers, another organization that had emerged.[71] Both RID and MADD continued to instruct thousands of victims and their families about how to assert their rights both before and during prosecution of alcohol-related crashes.

—―—

Writing in 1982, the historian David F. Musto termed the changes caused by RID and MADD "the most significant shift against alcohol since Prohibition's repeal in 1933." A good measure of how mores about alcohol changed during the 1980s is the portrayal of inebriation on television and in the movies. The British actor Dudley Moore charmed audiences playing a lovable drunk in the 1981 movie *Arthur*, but the 1988 sequel flopped, with the *Washington Post* deriding it as "about as funny as the plight of an alcoholic." "If *Arthur 2* has any significance," the reviewer wrote, "it's to herald—unwittingly—the death of the Happy Drunk in the movies." Drunk driving was far out of favor as well. Foster Brooks, the comedian who had played the drunken airline pilot on television, liked to joke about being a charter member of the "DWI Hall of Fame." But such a quip was no longer funny when competing with images of actual children killed by intoxicated drivers, and indeed, Brooks quietly phased out his drunken persona in the mid-1980s.[72]

Thus, it was a seminal moment when one of America's premier entertainers, *Tonight Show* host Johnny Carson, was charged with drunk driving in the early hours of Sunday, February 28, 1982. Carson had been out to dinner and had a BAC of 0.16%, considerably higher than the California limit of 0.10%. When he recorded his first show after the incident, on Tuesday, March 2, he could not resist making a joke. As sidekick Ed McMahon announced "Here's Johnny," Carson appeared with an actor dressed as a policeman, who reluctantly let Carson out on stage by himself. The audience roared and Carson asked the audience members to be his character witnesses.

But that is where the joke ended. Carson quickly turned serious and announced: "I regret the incident and I'll tell you one thing—you will never see me do that again." And apparently Carson, who died in 2005, never did.[73]

The measure of a successful social movement is not only its early triumphs but its durability and universality. Just how large and devoted was the anti–drunk driving constituency? Did the movement's emphasis on morality, deterrence, and punishment ensure continued progress or internal schisms?

CHAPTER FOUR

The Movement Matures and Splinters

It took decades to generate a meaningful attack on drunk driving in the United States, but maintaining the movement's energy and reputation in the 1980s and early 1990s was nearly as tall a task. Within five years of its founding, MADD was in turmoil, and neither Cindi Lamb nor Candy Lightner was still involved. Critics charged that the successor group to the President's Commission, the National Commission Against Drunk Driving, had so many agendas and conflicts of interest that it was largely useless.

Meanwhile, issues that had seemed so black and white just a few years earlier now routinely generated controversy. MADD members, in particular, were criticized on several fronts, ranging from supposed poor financial management to being co-opted by industry. Such arguments were inevitable, perhaps, but another was not. When a group of academics, in the spirit of William Haddon, examined epidemiological and other data regarding drunk driving, they wound up questioning the validity of almost every claim made by the morally outraged MADD mothers.

Help would come from an unlikely source: US Surgeon General C. Everett Koop, who convened a workshop on drunk driving in 1988. Building on earlier efforts by a consumer advocacy group in Washington, DC, Koop tried to expand the movement's focus from a law-and-order approach to one that embraced a broader public health agenda. But the conference generated enormous opposition from the alcohol, broadcasting, and hospitality industries, which even tried to have it halted. Ultimately, the achievements of the workshop were modest, leaving drunk driving activists to forge ahead with conflicting and uncertain goals.

Cracks in the efforts to make drunk driving a preeminent public health issue had actually begun much earlier. When Ben Kelley and William Haddon originally generated the figure of 25,000 annual deaths due to alcohol-related crashes for their 1968 report, they came under fire. The number was, of course, an estimate. Studies reviewed by the authors had found that in roughly one-half of fatal crashes, at least one driver had been drinking and had a BAC of at least 0.10%. Because approximately 50,000 Americans died annually in car crashes, use of the 25,000 figure made sense when trying to quantify the damage done specifically by drunk driving.

Among the first persons to question this figure was, surprisingly, an insider. Richard Zylman had actually begun his career and gotten interested in drunk driving as a state trooper in Wisconsin. He later moved to Indiana University, where he worked closely with Robert Borkenstein before moving to New Jersey and becoming a researcher at the Rutgers University Center of Alcohol Studies. Despite his ongoing interest in preventing drunk driving fatalities, he could not let go his reservations about how Kelley and Haddon had arrived at their numbers. In a forty-page paper published in the journal *Accident Analysis and Prevention* in 1974, Zylman painstakingly reviewed the studies and statistical assumptions used to arrive at the 25,000 number. He pointed out that the presence of one driver or pedestrian with a BAC of 0.10% did not prove that that individual—or his or her BAC—was necessarily the cause of the crash. In practice, things were much more complicated and depended on whether the event was a single- or multivehicle accident, the degree of impairment that drivers actually had, and, especially, which driver had driven recklessly. Sober drivers, Zylman argued, could be responsible for fatal crashes in which other drivers, passengers, or pedestrians might have been drinking. In such cases, automatically indicting alcohol as causative was misleading.[1]

Zylman went on to make his own calculations about annual deaths using 1972 as an example, being careful to use very precise language. He concluded that out of 56,000 motor vehicle deaths that year, 20,650, or 36 percent, "may have involved alcohol in some causal fashion," thus lowering the standard figure of 50 percent.[2] While Zylman was critical of the "semantic gymnastics" used by those seeking to publicize the issue of drunk driving, he was hardly questioning the larger cause. Rather, using more accurate statistics would give the whole enterprise more credibility.

Much of the confusion about impaired driving, Zylman believed, arose because it was seen primarily as a moral problem. "While I agree that offenses such as drunken driving should be regarded as crimes against society," he told attendees of a conference on the prevention of alcohol problems in 1974, "I do not agree that drunken driving should be regarded as a moral issue."[3] Doing so sacrificed objectivity.

Two other researchers interested in how the moral indignation that surrounded drunk driving influenced the "facts" were two accomplished sociologists, Joseph R. Gusfield, of the University of California at San Diego, and H. Laurence Ross, of the State University of New York at Buffalo and later the University of New Mexico. Thirty years later, their work expertly shows how the basic tenets of drunk driving research and policy were at times based on faulty premises.

Sociology in the 1980s had taken a turn to what was called "social constructionism," the notion that facts took shape from a complicated mixture of the observations, attitudes, and conclusions of the individuals who studied them. The most extreme proponents of this theory suggested that there was no such thing as objective reality, just different constructions of it. But most sociologists working in this area did not go that far. Rather, they believed that studying the assumptions that underlay supposed "facts" was as important as or more important than the data themselves.

Gusfield was a masterful practitioner of this type of thinking. His original research interest was Prohibition. His first book, entitled *Symbolic Crusade: Status Politics and the American Temperance Movement*, published in 1963, argued that Prohibition had less to do with the issue of alcohol than with how a certain group of Americans used moral reform to try to preserve its status in a changing society. Gusfield got involved in the world of drunk driving when he was asked to conduct a study of sentencing practices for intoxicated drivers in the San Diego County court system. Chosen because of his expertise in alcoholism, he would again wind up focusing on issues of moralism.

Having concluded that everyone involved in sentencing drunk drivers shared the same assumptions, Gusfield, increasingly interested in social construction, asked a stimulating question: Why is it that driving an automobile under the influence of alcohol is a public problem at all?[4] This line of inquiry ultimately led to his major work on drunk driving, *The Culture of Public Problems: Drinking-Driving and the Symbolic Order*, published in 1981. Even the title of the book displayed Gusfield's careful attention to language, as he noted that the term *drinking driving* more exactly characterized the broad nature of what was being studied in the field. The term *drunk driving*, in contrast, had automatic negative connotations and also incorporated the potentially misleading assumption that it was "drunkenness" per se that drivers needed to avoid.[5]

Gusfield's book is full of what he terms "fictions," "façade[s] of certain and ascertained generalization and fact" from which ambiguity and doubt have been "removed." One of these was the BAC, which, as was well known, caused different levels of impairment in different individuals. The increasing reliance on BACs to determine whether or not a driver was under the influence of alcohol was ironic, therefore, since it measured "alcohol in the blood" rather than "the effect of alcohol on driving ability." That is, a "physiological-chemical condition" was being mistaken for a behavioral one. Gusfield readily acknowledged that throwing out BACs for this reason was out of the question, but the information being obtained was nevertheless "created knowledge."[6]

An even larger problem was the "fiction of association," a point that Zylman had also raised. Studies of alcohol and driving, Gusfield argued, wrongly assumed that the involvement of a drinking driver or pedestrian proved that inebriation was the cause of the crash. After all, 50 percent or more of crashes did not involve alcohol but were the result of night driving, fatigue, inattention at the wheel, slippery roads, speeding, or other factors that investigators had not yet even discovered. These factors could easily be at play as well in cases in which someone had been drinking. Indeed, Gusfield added, the causes of most car crashes were probably multifactorial. So why should one assume that in crashes involving alcohol, the drinking driver was the culprit? The problem was that "association is converted into causation," something another critic termed a "malevolent assumption."[7]

So why had drunk driving become the traffic violation of such overriding concern to Americans (and Europeans)? What was occurring, according to Gusfield, was not an objective assessment of the situation but rather a "drama of morality and order in the explanation of auto accidents and deaths."[8] Because of cultural beliefs about excessive alcohol use and drunkenness, as well as the tendency of Americans to blame individual behaviors instead of the social factors that promote such behaviors, a mythical figure known as the "killer drunk" who "threatens 'innocent' individuals" had emerged.[9] Even though many other factors led to car crashes, many people drank and drove without causing harm, and intoxicated drivers most often killed themselves as opposed to others, the nefarious drunk driver had become the overwhelming villain in the world of traffic safety.

What did Gusfield himself think about this situation? At times it was hard to tell. At a 1974 conference he expressed disappointment at the lack of public out-cry about alcohol-related fatalities. Recalling the infamous anti-alcohol activist, he joked, "Carrie Nation, where are you now that we need you?"[10] But by the early 1980s, Gusfield was much more interested in demonstrating the multiple constructions of facts than judging among them. For example, because it raised questions about the National Safety Council's timeworn moralistic and legalistic approach to drunk drivers, he spoke approvingly of the new epidemiology-based traffic safety paradigm being proposed by William Haddon. But, he cautioned, the "unsafe car" hypothesis was no less a social construct than the earlier "unsafe drivers" hypothesis. Another time, to drive home the point about the social con-struction of facts, he even made the seemingly outrageous statement that "pub-lic discussion has seldom included a pro-DUI position." Ultimately, Gusfield concluded, moral judgments and interest-group politics would always dictate the strategies of social movements such as anti–drunk driving activism. Such movements were crucial "public symbols," even if their tenets and strategies had inadequate scientific validity.[11]

Ross surely agreed with Gusfield, but he was more of a traditional sociologist than a social constructionist. Ross, who had gotten his PhD degree in sociology at Harvard, had come to the study of drunk driving through other research in law and criminology. For example, a book on out-of-court law settlements ex-amined how social processes led to "law in action" that often violated formal legal rules and statutes. Ross's best-known work in drunk driving had an inter-national flavor. He had researched both the 1967 British Road Safety Act as well as the ongoing efforts of Scandinavian countries to control drunk driving. Spe-cifically, Ross called into question what had always been a reflexive belief of workers in the field: that deterrence, if implemented wisely and broadly enough, would lower drunk driving rates as well as injuries and deaths. He was especially skeptical about increasing the severity of punishment through strategies such as imprisonment, which he believed had no deterrent value. Indeed, there was even the possibility that harsh punishments that seemed to "exceed established levels of fairness" might, paradoxically, discourage the prosecution of drunk drivers.[12]

In some ways, Ross wrote, the 1967 British initiative was the most success-ful deterrence-based measure ever launched against drunk driving. The act drew directly on the Scandinavian model. It criminalized driving with a BAC higher than 0.08% and allowed police to perform a breath test on anyone stopped for a traffic violation or involved in an accident. Those who flunked the test or refused to take it automatically lost their licenses for a year and were subject to various fines and prison sentences. The act was accompanied by an enormous publicity push, which both emphasized the new 0.08% level and also strongly discouraged drinking to just below this limit. Drunk driving, announced England's Minister of Transport, "is a problem posed by a thoughtless, anti-social minority."[13] Publicity efforts had actually been enhanced when civil libertarian groups raised a series of objections.

Ross and others evaluating the results of the act found a dramatic decline—of as much as 66 percent—in the number of serious injuries and fatalities that occurred during the heaviest hours of drinking. But the achievement was fleeting. Within six to twelve months, the decline had largely reversed. This research and other studies he conducted led Ross to conclude that it was possible for deterrence-based measures to work temporarily, presumably by scaring a percentage of the population into behaving. But over time, as publicity died down, attention turned elsewhere, and, most important, the perceived chance of being apprehended decreased, old habits returned. This notion of "perceived risk" became Ross's mantra: "You can scare people for a while, but it's hard to keep it up." "The spirit of gambling applies," Robert Borkenstein concurred, "and as soon as the driving public finds that the odds are in their [*sic*] favor the suppressing effect of the countermeasures disappears at least in substantial part."[14] It is not surprising that a well-known drunk driving documentary from this era was entitled *Until I Get Caught.*

Ross even took on Norway and Sweden. These were the two countries that had, decades earlier, passed per se laws setting acceptable BACs at low levels, between 0.05% and 0.08%. They were also more likely to use prison as routine punishment—indeed, almost always in Norway for BACs over 0.05%. Scandinavian researchers, such as Norway's Johannes Andenaes and Leonard Goldberg, of Sweden's Karolinska Institute, routinely reported on drunk driving–control measures at international conferences, where participants agreed that these countries represented the gold standard.

In a paper published in the *Journal of Legal Studies* in 1975, Ross carefully and persuasively challenged this accepted orthodoxy. Having spent three months in the two countries doing research, he found that there was "little solid support" for the "widespread belief in the deterrent effect of the Swedish and Norwegian laws." The existing arguments in the literature, he added, were "inconclusive." That a country like Norway had fewer drunk driving crashes reflected not the efficacy of the laws but "a politically powerful and moralistic temperance movement," which, in turn, had promoted high taxes on alcoholic beverages, better knowledge of drunk driving laws, more enthusiastic support of such laws, and greater use of sober drivers and taxis from parties and bars.[15] Punishments might be morally satisfying, but they did not have a deterrent effect—either in Scandinavia or in the United States. Provocative as always, Ross entitled his paper "The Scandinavian Myth," ensuring pointed criticism, both to his face and behind his back, from those who believed otherwise.

It turned out that Ross would spend years attempting to clarify what he had meant by the word *myth*. All he had said, he explained in his 1984 book *Deterring the Drinking Driver*, was that there was no scientifically acceptable proof that the strong-armed legal approach actually served as an effective deterrent to drunk driving and, by extension, reduced fatalities. "I did not claim," he stated, "to have disproved the general preventive effectiveness of the Scandinavian approach to drinking-and-driving law."[16] Still, between his work in Great Britain and Scandinavia, it would be reasonable to conclude that Ross retained a high degree of skepticism that deterrence programs, especially those that stressed punishment, were worth the effort.

In his book, Ross approvingly quoted former Secretary of the Treasury Henry Morgenthau, who had said that "the genuine intellectual must be the 'enemy of the people' who tells the world things it either does not want to hear or cannot understand." Ross was not an enemy of drunk driving control. After all, his research focused on the discovery and promotion of strategies that would *really* work, not just those that people thought were effective. But some people thought Ross was not particularly helpful to the movement. One MADD representative called him "the drunk driver's best friend." Asked to blurb Ross's 1984 book, Candy Lightner was lukewarm at best. "Although I disagree with some of Dr. Ross' findings based on his studies," she wrote, "I feel his work has been thoroughly researched and documented."[17]

Ross's most pointed criticism of drunk driving–control efforts occurred in 1986, when he coauthored an article in the *Nation* with New York University law professor Graham Hughes. The authors began by citing the recent efforts by MADD, RID, SADD, and other groups to crack down on intoxicated drivers, including increased public education, stepped-up police activity, and harsher punishments. Because deterrence-based programs had only evanescent effects,

Ross and Hughes explained, it followed that such scare tactics had a relatively small impact—especially on alcoholics and problem drinkers. Ultimately, the authors concluded, the current push against drunk driving was "misguided." More logical, they believed, would be a focus on public health strategies, such as better control of liquor sales and wider use of technological innovations that protected drivers whether they were drunk or not—for example, seat belts and air bags. But such innovations inspired little enthusiasm among the anti–drunk driving crowd.

What about the 32 percent decline in alcohol-related fatalities that groups like MADD and RID understandably took credit for? Some critics pointed to similar decreases that had occurred in other countries without activist organizations, arguing that these American groups may have played a smaller role than had generally been assumed. Ross and Hughes agreed, arguing that the lowered death rate was due not to anti–drunk driving efforts but rather to "a variety of causes: the reduced speed limit, safer cars, better roads with lighting [and] improvements in medical techniques and in the delivery of emergency medical services."[18]

Not surprisingly, activists were outraged by the article. One, Thomas M. Stout, a member of RID's advisory board, replied to the *Nation*, terming the piece a "counsel of despair." Stout pushed back on a number of points, arguing that RID's efforts had absolutely helped lower drunk driving fatalities in New York and elsewhere and that interventions like checkpoints and mandatory breath testing were reasonable ways for society to protect itself. Hughes replied to this letter, not backing down a bit. The anti–drunk driving activists, he wrote, were diverting attention from road and car safety and "prefer expensive retribution to the economical prevention of fatal accidents."[19]

In later years, Ross would go even further, suggesting that because heavy drinking was so rooted in the social fabric of contemporary American life and because mass transit was sorely lacking, a program of subsidized taxi rides to and from bars and restaurants was needed. A few such entities existed in specific communities, such as the industry-funded Washington (DC) Regional Alcohol Program's Sober Ride project, but Ross wished to see them expanded, ideally paid for by a surtax on individual drinks served in bars. He encouraged alcohol manufacturers and taxi companies throughout the country to fund such programs as both goodwill gestures and business efforts, but he found no takers. Part of the concern, admittedly, was that subsidized rides might promote binge drinking. And, even though such a notion bothered many anti–drunk driving activists,

Ross also continued to advocate for broader traffic safety initiatives that would help "impaired drivers . . . navigate safely," such as cutting down roadside trees, installing better reflective markers, paying for better emergency medical services, forcing carmakers to install air bags, and mandating the use of seat belts. He even offered the potentially incendiary suggestion that Laura Lamb, truly one of the icons of the movement, might not have been properly belted into her car seat, thereby increasing the likelihood of injury when Russell Newcomer hit her mother's truck.[20]

The debate here nicely demonstrated a perpetual challenge of activist movements: balancing fervor for a cause with justification from the available scientific data. How much scientific "proof" is necessary for activists to forge ahead with seemingly just and moral agendas? Successful public health movements to control infectious diseases, prevent smoking-related lung cancers, and remove lead from paint, to name just a few, relied on suggestive—not definitive—data. This strategy has been termed the "precautionary principle." Waiting for the science, in retrospect, would have cost lives.

Doris Aiken and Candy Lightner pursued a similar strategy for drunk driving. They identified what they believed was a serious public health threat that had received inadequate attention for decades and was killing thousands of Americans annually, even if no one really knew exactly how many. They told and retold countless moving stories about needless drunk driving deaths and the new laws they had helped to pass that would prevent future similar tragedies. Yet here were academics and scientists, ostensibly on their side, calling into question their celebrated anecdotes and asking them to justify everything they were advocating.

In the *Nation* piece, Ross and Hughes even objected to a recent US Supreme Court decision that refusal of a breath test could be used as evidence that a driver was intoxicated, stating that such reasoning violated the Fifth Amendment. The next year, in an article on MADD mothers, Ross opined that "committed parties tend to see research results in light of their [preexisting] commitments."[21] That people working in the field of drunk driving could be so contrary was both baffling and frustrating to the activists. Ross, of course, simply thought he was doing his job.

Gusfield raised hackles as well. In his 1981 book, he amusedly related an anecdote about a conference he had attended in Berkeley, California, in 1974 on the prevention of drinking problems. Exasperated by the "sociological constructivism" and "epidemiological relativism" presented by Gusfield and others, the noted British alcohol researcher Griffith Edwards lashed out, accusing them, in Gusfield's words, of "having our fingers in our ears so that we needn't hear the suffering." Like Ross, Gusfield demurred. Perhaps his perspective might be seen as anarchistic or nihilistic, but its value was in demonstrating how knowledge may be wrongly characterized as "certain, definitive and accurate." Science, he warned, "possesses a rhetoric as well as a rationale."[22]

Laurence Ross was not the only person to take aim at MADD. In *My Life as a Pit Bull*, Doris Aiken describes a competitive relationship between her organization, RID, and Candy Lightner's MADD. Aiken wrote that Lightner had been "furious" when Aiken beat her to the punch and pinned a RID button on President Ronald Reagan in 1982. She said that Lightner told her that the next time, she would not be behind the velvet rope. And Lightner was correct. When Reagan signed the Minimum Drinking Age Law in 1984, Lightner was standing right next to him and Transportation Secretary Elizabeth Hanford Dole. A picture of them appeared in the front section of the *New York Times*. "With her bright red dress and black blonde-streaked hair dominating the scene," Aiken grumbled, "she graciously accepted all the credit for passage of the 21 drinking age bill."[23]

Cindi Lamb, Lightner's colleague at MADD, agreed that Candy "was not warm or nurturing." However, Lightner's personality was just right when the toes of journalists, legislators, and critics needed to be stepped on: "Candy was pushy but [the movement] would not have gotten off the ground without this." This jostling for attention is hardly particular to drunk driving activism but is characteristic, to some degree, of all successful reformers. As the psychiatrist Willard Gaylin has memorably written, "I'm not sure I'd want Carry Nation, Florence Nightingale, Ralph Nader or, for that matter, Jesus, as a roommate." Lightner herself later told a reporter, "I'm a very strong and independent woman; I think it makes it difficult to develop relationships."[24]

By the mid-1980s, MADD had arguably become an embarrassment. Several groups that monitored the practices of charitable agencies had concluded that it spent too much money on administration and fundraising and not enough on its programs. Some people who ran local MADD chapters agreed, believing that the organization was top-heavy and did not involve enough victims and family members at the national level. MADD members in California and other states left to join RID or form new organizations. Lightner, whom her secretary called "unstable" and "demanding," was better suited for raising hell than for management. Finally, in October 1985, MADD's executive committee removed Lightner as chairman and chief executive officer. Lightner, who had not even been paid during her first years with MADD, had been looking for a raise, but the committee had given her a contract that would have made her more a figurehead than a leader. In what Lightner termed a "hostile" interaction, she declined the contract, thus terminating her association with MADD. Lightner believed that the coup had been carried out by men within MADD uncomfortable with a female leader. She was understandably emotional, writing to a fellow activist that she had lost one baby to DWI and had now lost another baby, MADD.[25]

Another rift within anti–drunk driving activism emerged at about this time. Despite Ross's skepticism, the overwhelming focus of efforts to this point had been to use education, moral suasion, and tougher laws to discourage driving after drinking. There was, however, another possible strategy, one that again drew on the public health model of focusing on the product. In Haddon's era, the product had been the automobile, but by the 1980s, manufacturers routinely incorporated equipment that enhanced safety. The product under scrutiny in the 1980s was alcohol, and the plan was to lower alcohol sales as a way to decrease drinking among individuals apt to drive drunk. Three specific proposals existed: (1) removing ads for beer and wine from television; (2) putting labels on alcohol products warning about health risks and drunk driving; and (3) increasing taxes on intoxicating beverages. These strategies drew on the successful efforts of antismoking activists to limit cigarette sales, beginning in the 1960s. In the case of advertising, the Federal Communications Commission had in 1967 invoked the Fairness Doctrine, mandating radio and television stations to broadcast a percentage of anti-tobacco messages in conjunction with cigarette advertising. In the case of taxes, federal excise taxes on alcohol products, corrected for inflation, had substantially *decreased* since 1951. The tax on beer, the main beverage responsible for drunk driving, was especially low, at roughly five cents per drink. These low rates persisted despite data showing that, in addition to helping to pay for the costs of excess drinking to society, increasing alcohol taxes would reduce highway fatality rates among youths. The Presidential Commission had considered, but rejected, a federal "nickel a drink" tax to pay for anti–drunk driving enforcement efforts.[26]

The main organization seeking to interfere with the marketing and sales of alcohol was the Center for Science in the Public Interest, based in Washington, which had been founded in 1971. Advocating for "nutrition and health, food safety, alcohol policy and sound science," the CSPI embodied several activist movements of the era: consumerism, environmentalism, and a public health approach to social problems that favored governmental action based on good scientific research. It was also left of center, opposing "industry's powerful influence on public opinion and public policies."[27]

The CSPI's effort to get alcohol off the airwaves was hardly the first. In the 1930s, the Woman's Christian Temperance Union had opposed radio commercials promoting alcohol and, in the 1950s, congressmen sympathetic to the old dry notion that alcohol corrupted the morals of America's youth had introduced various pieces of legislation to restrict or ban alcohol advertisements. Neither campaign succeeded, as industry argued that such efforts violated the constitutional rights of beverage manufacturers. The CSPI reopened the issue in a 1983 book, *The Booze Merchants: The Inebriating of America*, co-written by Michael Jacobson, Robert Atkins, and George Hacker. Like other critics of the alcohol industry, Hacker, a lawyer who headed the CSPI's Alcohol Policies Project, did drink. But he had been hit twice by drunk drivers and was alarmed by the damage that drinking—including social drinking—could cause. Interestingly, *The Booze Merchants* came out fifty years after the repeal of Prohibition and, like the anti–drunk driving crusade, was part of what was being billed as the "new temperance movement." Prohibition had cast a long shadow, making Americans reluctant to criticize or interfere with the purchasing of alcohol. But with alcohol sales and problems of alcohol overuse—such as drunk driving, cirrhosis, and fetal alcohol syndrome—on the rise, such an agenda had once again become fair game.[28]

The Booze Merchants focused primarily on the issue of advertising, and its thesis was straightforward: the alcohol industry was using irresponsible advertising to "purposely push . . . its product to alcoholics, young people and new users."[29] One indisputable fact was that the amount of alcohol being consumed in the United States had been on the rise since the 1930s. For example, annual consumption of wine had risen from 50 million gallons at the end of Prohibition to over 500 million gallons by 1980. Between 1970 and 1980 alone, per capita consumption of alcohol had increased by 15 percent, with the largest increases being in beer, 31 percent, and wine, 65 percent. During the same period of time, advertising expenditures by the alcoholic beverage industry increased by more than 200 percent. By 1984, Anheuser-Busch, the manufacturer of Budweiser beer and eight other brands, would spend $245 million annually on advertising, including $122 million on network sports events. As of 1988, the overall total spent on advertising by the alcohol industry was $1.4 billion, which would increase to $2.2 billion by 2005.[30] Of note, the liquor industry continued to voluntarily restrict its advertising to newspapers and magazines.

Was there a correlation between money spent on marketing and alcohol sales? The alcohol industry downplayed any connection, stating, as did cigarette manufacturers, that advertising only aimed at getting existing smokers to switch brands. Admitting that there was not a lot of conclusive data, Jacobson, Atkins, and Hacker disagreed, arguing that the ads specifically targeted inappropriate groups. First among these were heavy drinkers, who were generally young male beer drinkers. Advertisements aimed at this demographic equated drunkenness with having a good time. For example, Budweiser drinkers were encouraged to take "big swallows" and "empty your schooner sooner." Cuervo tequila print ads urged drinkers to "bust loose." Ads like these often showed people involved in activities—such as hang-gliding and white-water rafting—that would be dangerous if mixed with drinking. Drivers showed up as well. A television advertisement for a new product known as Harley Davidson Wine Coolers showed motorcyclists stopping their bikes and rehydrating with wine. Other ads liberally used sexual themes and often featured scantily clad women.[31]

Even more worrisome, according to the CSPI and fellow critics, was the apparent marketing to youth. Beer manufacturers, in particular, advertised heavily in college newspapers, even in states where the drinking age was 21. They also sponsored sports events, concerts, and parties on or near campuses. On television, advertisements routinely appeared on programs, such as football games and *Saturday Night Live*, watched by a younger audience. Favored magazines included *Rolling Stone* and *National Lampoon*. The *Booze Merchants* argued that alcohol manufacturers were consciously focusing on this population, seeking "entry-level" drinkers who might develop a loyalty to their specific product. "Kids from the age of 2 or 3," Hacker stated, "are bombarded with messages that glorify drinking by associating it with glamour and athletic success." "Lite Beer is like quarterbacks," one advertisement stated. "We can't wait to knock 'em down."[32]

With respect to potential new drinkers, Jacobson and his coauthors mentioned two populations that overlapped: light drinkers and women. One way to reach these customers was to offer products lower in calories, such as light beers, which usually had about 75 percent of the alcohol content of regular beer. A second strategy was to expand the range of sweeter beverages, which did not taste like alcohol. These included a series of fruity liqueurs, sweet wines, and the spiked milkshakes that Ernest Noble, at the National Institute on Alcohol Abuse and Alcoholism, had opposed. An advertisement for 43 Liqueur, for example, featured a drink called a Creamsicle, named after the popular frozen treat and made with vanilla and citrus liquor, milk, and orange juice. Spots for these types of product used the same sorts of alluring imagery, including attractive models participating in exciting and risky activities.[33]

What was the relationship of these advertisements to drunk driving? Jacobson, Atkins and Hacker wrote: "As part of living a dangerous life, problem drinkers act recklessly. The best example is driving while drunk. The risk-taking ads not only appeal to such personalities, they may in fact encourage such behavior."[34] That is, the ads never told people to drive or hang-glide when drunk, but they *implied* that such a combination was not only acceptable but desirable. Marketing to youth, with less driving experience, was also a concern. If a sports event or concert was on a college campus, there might be no drunk driving. But what if it was not? If everyone drank beer at the concert, just who was driving home?

The Booze Merchants concluded by noting that, while many other countries had restricted various types of alcohol advertising, few such efforts had occurred in the United States. While calling for more research, the authors' final recommendations included a wide variety of public health strategies aimed at regulating alcohol: (1) banning commercials that depicted risky activities and were directed at heavy drinkers and youth; (2) balancing ads with public service announcements warning of the potential dangers of alcohol, including drunk driving; (3) prohibiting celebrities from appearing in ads; (4) limiting the sales of beer and wine at roadside stores, such as gas stations and supermarkets; (5) adding warning labels, which the CSPI also strongly advocated for all consumer products, to alcohol; and (6) raising federal excise taxes on alcohol to pay for educational efforts and control measures.[35]

The CSPI forged ahead on two fronts. First, it petitioned the Federal Trade Commission, asking that it prohibit the practice of targeting heavy drinkers and young people in advertisements. Second, it started Project SMART (Stop Marketing Alcohol on Radio and Television), a "nationwide grassroots petition campaign" seeking one million signatures demanding either a ban on advertising or equal time for health and safety messages about alcohol. The petition was delivered to Congress in May 1985. By the fall, a bill had been introduced into Congress by Ohio representative John F. Seiberling, whose mother, coincidentally, had introduced the two founders of Alcoholics Anonymous to each other

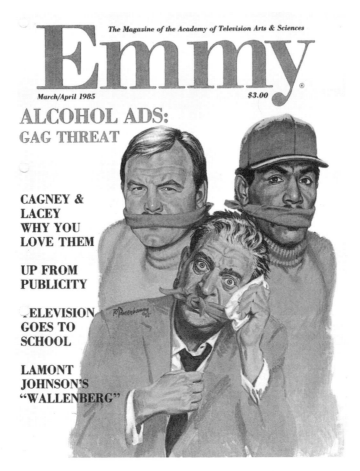

Cover of *Emmy* magazine, March–April 1985, at the height of the controversy over alcohol advertisements. This painting depicts Dick Butkus, Rodney Dangerfield, and Deacon Jones, all spokesmen for Miller Lite Beer, gagged. Courtesy of the artist, Robert Tanenbaum, and the Academy of Television Arts and Sciences

in the 1930s. However, neither Congress nor the FTC ultimately chose to act. What doomed Project SMART, the historian Pamela E. Pennock has written, was a combination of aggressive and well-financed opposition from the alcohol and broadcasting industries, a political environment favoring deregulation, and lack of definitive scientific proof of its claims. For example, four industry presidents and two vice presidents, representing brewers, vintners, and the advertising and broadcasting industries, testified at a hearing held by Senator Paula

Hawkins in February 1985. The National Association of Broadcasters (NAB) had made defeat of the initiative its "number-one top priority," including hosting members of the House Telecommunications Subcommittee at its annual meeting.[36]

Over time, a few elements of the CSPI's larger agenda would become law. These included a 19 percent increase in the federal excise tax on distilled spirits in late 1985 and, three years later, mandatory warning labels on alcohol containers stating, among other things, that alcohol consumption impaired one's ability to drive.[37]

The CSPI successfully recruited to Project SMART dozens of groups concerned with drunk driving, including the National Parent Teacher Association, the American Public Health Association, Public Citizen, the American Academy of Pediatrics, the American Medical Student Association, and the National Council on Alcoholism. Sympathetic members of the media, such as syndicated columnist Colman McCarthy, joined in, criticizing the beer industry for making commercials that equated drinking with "youthful good life and fun-time USA." "Miller and Anheuser-Busch," he scoffed, "aren't worthy of anyone's respect."[38]

Doris Aiken's RID also eagerly joined up. Although Aiken had always been among the fiercest critics of individuals who chose to drive drunk, she saved some of her enmity for elements of the beverage industry that she believed were thwarting drunk driving reform. So she had no problem joining Project SMART. Evidently, however, the move dealt a severe blow to her organization. Once RID went on the record as opposing alcohol advertisements, according to Aiken, the NAB put into place what she termed a "blackout" of the organization, meaning that she and her RID colleagues received many fewer calls from the national media, including radio and television. As a result, it became harder for RID to recruit new members and raise funds for its existing chapters. Among the programs that canceled RID appearances, Aiken said, were CBS-TV's *60 Minutes* and *Sunday Morning*.[39]

Proving Aiken's claim is difficult without written documentation of such a policy. Leslie Arries, a member of the NAB board and president of WIVB-TV in Buffalo, did tell the *Christian Science Monitor*, "You don't go all out with somebody trying to hit you over the head with a big stick." "As long as they're on Capitol Hill trying to get rid of beer and wine ads," he admitted elsewhere, "we're not going to be very friendly." In addition, a feature on Aiken written by Bard Lindeman scheduled to appear in *50 Plus* in July 1988, in which she stated that "the alcohol industry has this country by the throat," was pulled, even though

Lindeman was the editor of the magazine. An apologetic Lindeman blamed "the liquor lobby," telling Aiken that there were financial connections between the companies that advertised in *50 Plus* and the beverage industry.[40] The RID blackout, scandalous if true, apparently did not attract rebel reporters seeking to humiliate their media colleagues for what amounted to an unfair boycott of a legitimate news source.

What the blackout meant in practice was that MADD representatives became the default spokespersons for the drunk driving movement. MADD's own relationship to industry was complicated. According to Craig Reinarman's history of MADD, Lightner and the MADD board had rejected the position of one original board member that the organization should formally decline money from alcohol interests. In 1983, with Lightner still in charge, MADD accepted a $175,000 offer of support from Anheuser-Busch; it ultimately received only $50,000, which was used to hire an executive director to assist Lightner. Reinarman also reported that MADD took funding from Miller Brewing, although others disputed this. MADD was hardly the only activist group to shed the outsider mantle for more of an insider approach, choosing to work with industry and the larger power structure to create change. A good example is the breast cancer movement, which has partnered with pharmaceutical companies to sponsor Breast Cancer Awareness Month and a variety of "pink ribbon" fundraising events.[41]

One reason MADD was comfortable working with industry was a shared belief about the causes of car crashes: both groups placed the blame on the alcoholic driver as opposed to alcohol itself or to unsafe cars. "MADD's war is with the impaired driver," said MADD board member and NAB official Shaun Sheehan. "It isn't with the people who choose to drink, or with people who have driver's licenses." It is reasonable to assume that Anheuser-Busch, in addition to earning favorable publicity (it put billboards up in St. Louis saying "Anheuser-Busch Supports MADD"), also hoped its donation would encourage MADD to maintain this focus. Lightner was comfortable taking money from the "enemy" as long as there were no strings attached.[42]

Even more so than MADD, Students Against Drunk Driving was dependent on the beverage industry for its existence. The seeds for SADD had been sown in 1981 when, in response to the deaths of two students in drunk driving crashes, a Massachusetts high school teacher and hockey coach, Robert Anastas, began teaching his classes about teenage drinking and driving. The students found the topic so compelling that they started a campaign of "peers working on peers," which eventually became SADD. Anastas was the organization's first director. SADD pioneered the "Contract for Life," a document that students signed in which they pledged to call their parents for a ride if they or the person planning to drive them home had drunk too much. Like MADD, SADD went national and needed to raise funds. Anheuser-Busch became a major supporter, contributing an estimated $850,000 between 1983 and 1988. One of SADD's board members was Donald Shea, the president of the US Brewers Association. Interestingly, William Plymat, the Iowa teetotaler and insurance executive, was a devoted supporter of SADD and helped Anastas make funding connections with Shea, Anheuser-Busch, and others representing the alcohol industry. Shea and Anastas made this point when rejecting the charge that alcohol money influenced SADD's policies. Shea liked to quote Plymat's response to claims that beer money was tainted: "You're right—it tain't enough!"[43]

Not surprisingly, perhaps, when it came to supporting Project SMART, MADD (and SADD) declined. One reason, explained a MADD official, was that "the available evidence does not show a clear correlation between advertising and impaired driving." But even more, this choice represented confirmation of MADD's decision to try to create change from within the system. At the height of the Project SMART controversy in April 1985, Candy Lightner spoke at the annual meeting of the National Association of Broadcasters. She told reporters, "We will not support SMART ever," terming its organizers "callous," "biased," and "unfair." Instead, MADD intended to work with the broadcasting industry to reduce portrayals of drinking as glamorous. Lightner did warn the NAB that it needed to "clean up its act." MADD also supported increased taxes on alcohol.[44]

But opponents of MADD saw its rejection of SMART as evidence that the organization had been co-opted. For example, Doris Aiken believed that MADD was beholden to the NAB, as the two groups had worked together to produce anti–drunk driving public service announcements that carefully avoided any mention of the advertising controversy. In addition, the NAB had cosponsored certain of MADD's education programs. Moreover, critics argued, an attack that focused narrowly on impaired driving ignored a major reason that impaired driving occurred: the alcohol industry had insinuated its product into nearly all of the country's social events. Not addressing this contributing cause of drunk driving was naïve. "The rise of MADD," Reinarman concluded in his article, "has helped to eclipse competing claims about the social costs of unregulated cultural promotion of *drinking-as-intrinsic-to-social-life*."[45]

For Reinarman, MADD's decision about SMART was simply further evidence of the fundamental conservatism of the anti–drunk driving movement of the 1980s. Whereas SMART's consumerist and public health approach focused on *corporate* accountability and responsibility, MADD's primary inspiration was the moralistic victims' rights movement, which focused on *individual* accountability and responsibility. It was no surprise, he added, that the organization's original name was "Mothers Against Drunk Drivers," although it was changed to the less vindictive "Mothers Against Drunk Driving" in 1984.[46]

Politics had also entered the world of drunk driving when Ronald Reagan established the President's Commission in 1982. Because such a committee had never before existed, just who would be asked to join was not predetermined. The choice of John Volpe as chair was a logical one. Volpe had been a Republican governor of Massachusetts and had served as head of the Department of Transportation from 1969 to 1973. The imbroglio over the Licensed Beverage Industries ads, which occurred during Volpe's tenure at the DOT, had shown him to be willing to criticize the alcohol industry if necessary but also sympathetic to the notion of responsible drinking. The commission as announced included several members representing various industries.

The initial response to the commission's December 1983 report, with its calls for broad application of existing and new deterrent measures, as well as better seat belt laws and improved roadside markers, was positive. But when academics weighed in, they found the document wanting. James F. Mosher, a lawyer specializing in alcohol policy, used a story of a recent Stevie Wonder concert held at the Capitol Center outside Washington to illustrate why the recommendations were only "symbolic gestures" and thus "seriously flawed." Once again, the problems were the environment and the product. As far as the environment went, there was little public transportation serving the arena, ensuring that almost everyone left by car. And the product, alcohol, was far too available. Extra booths, set up specifically for the event, sold beer, wine, and distilled spirits. Mosher saw little checking of identification cards, suggesting that underage youth were able to make purchases. Finally, large time gaps during the program encouraged spectators to return to obtain additional drinks. As a result, "hundreds and probably thousands of drunk drivers left the concert that evening."[47]

Mosher noted several ironies, for example, that those serving alcohol wore buttons that read "Friends don't let friends drive drunk" and that the owner of the Capitol Center had won an award for his anti–drunk driving efforts. In addition, although some obviously impaired individuals leaving the concert might have been stopped for DWI, the vast majority drove home unchallenged.

What the commission's report had ignored, Mosher concluded, were "drinking situations." The circumstances of the concert—no public transportation, the extensive down time, the emphasis on heavy alcohol sales and underage drinking—all fostered drunk driving. The commission had not mentioned possible solutions to these problems: increasing taxes on alcohol; changing marketing and sponsorship policies at public events, especially those geared to young people; implementing server intervention programs; and improving transportation services.

Why had the commission not considered these more progressive strategies, many of which dovetailed with those promoted by the Center for Science in the Public Interest? Mosher hypothesized that the presence of representatives from the alcohol, insurance, and automobile industries had ensured that the report's focus remained only on changing the bad behaviors of individual drunk drivers, behaviors that were made almost inevitable by events such as the Capitol Center concert.

Not surprisingly, Laurence Ross agreed with Mosher, even going so far as to call the Presidential Commission's report "mean-spirited and unimaginative." "It is . . . not surprising," he wrote in *Accident Analysis and Prevention*, "that a law enforcement approach dominates the report and that very little is proposed that would seriously affect the interests of the industries that have created the drunk driving problem." One such strategy, a five-cent tax on alcoholic beverages, had been rejected in deference to "vested interests." Rather than mining the body of existing scientific knowledge about traffic safety for effective countermeasures, Ross concluded, the commission had once again favored punishment for punishment's sake, which was "vengeful" and even "bloodthirsty."[48]

Unfortunately, from the perspective of Mosher, Ross, and other critics, what happened next in the world of drunk driving only further cemented the hold of the law-and-order model. As part of its final recommendations, the Presidential Commission had proposed the formation of a follow-up group, to be run by the National Safety Council and funded by National Highway Traffic Safety Administration and industry, to continue its work after it ceased to exist on December 31, 1983. Thus was born the National Commission Against Drunk Driving (NCADD), which continued to advocate for certain traditional measures, such as administrative license revocation, dram shop statutes, open container laws forbidding unsealed alcohol containers in cars, and the prohibition of plea-bargaining in DWI cases. The NCADD, which was even more dominated by industry than the Presidential Commission, turned out to be so wedded to the deterrence model and other aspects of the status quo that severe disputes erupted within its ranks. The issue of co-optation of the five-year-old grassroots anti–drunk driving movement was squarely on the table.

The first sign of problems arose when Aiken, Lightner, and Plymat, the activists from the Presidential Commission, were not appointed to the new panel. Complaints led to the reinstatement of all three. But the corporate imprimatur persisted. Committee members included multiple representatives from the beverage, automobile, and broadcasting industries. Funders of the new commission, Doris Aiken recalls, included Anheuser-Busch, the Distilled Spirits Council, the NAB, and other industry sponsors.[49] John Volpe was the initial chair, but he was replaced in January 1985 by V. J. Adduci, of the Motor Vehicles Manufacturers Association.

As these developments occurred, the consensus that had characterized the early years of the Presidential Commission began to break down. For example, Candy Lightner, who had been criticized by some as too pro-industry, abstained from the vote confirming Adduci and former Arkansas governor Frank L. White as vice chair. Lightner argued that the prominence of alcohol industry representatives on the commission and the acceptance of industry money was not healthy and sent a "mixed message" to the public. Later, she went further, terming the arrangement "a direct conflict of interest." She added: "I know of no other non-profit organization in the field of highway safety which receives *one fifth* of its funding from the liquor industry [or] one whose directing board is so well represented by professionals with affiliations to liquor companies."[50] Predictably, RID's Doris Aiken agreed, terming the NCADD "a business arm to raise money for itself without creating waves that would discourage corporate donors from contributing." Whether or not one agreed that the new leadership was further evidence of co-optation, the alcohol industry's ongoing strategy of publicly admitting that its product was *potentially* harmful gave it more credibility than cigarette manufacturers, who had agreed to any governmental regulation of their product only under duress.[51]

Meanwhile, William Plymat was making one last push for the two-drink maximum 0.05% BAC, which he had first promoted in the late 1950s. For Plymat, the issue had not changed. He strongly believed that having legal levels set at 0.10%, or even 0.08%, as a few states had done, made no sense if the scientific data indicated that impairment of driving skills began for most people at 0.05%.

Also, epidemiologists now talked about the "prevention paradox," which stated that larger numbers of lower-risk individuals actually caused more harm than smaller numbers of higher-risk persons. To the extent that this was the case in drunk driving, it focused more attention on social drinkers. Plymat liberally peppered Volpe, Adduci, other commission members and Secretary of Transportation Elizabeth H. Dole with letters that included his latest slogan: "It's better not to drink and drive, but if you do, keep it under 0-5." Ralph Hudson, the Wisconsin physician and activist who himself would later serve on the NCADD, also took up Plymat's cause. "It may be a simple statement," he announced at a conference of the National Safety Council, "but to approach an alcohol impairment problem with statutes that legally allow alcohol impairment is a lousy way to approach the problem."[52]

This effort got little traction. Most states had only recently moved their BACs to 0.10%, so another drop was politically unlikely, especially with the almost certain opposition of the alcohol and hospitality industries. Ironically, there was still resistance to promoting a two-drink maximum, even though reliance on more complicated BAC calculations meant potential drivers might actually drink much more. Some commission members, like Morris Chafetz, continued to believe that focusing on BAC numbers and deterrence-based punishments was not the way to engage the public. In two op-ed pieces published in 1985, Chafetz argued that responsible alcohol use—promoted through the education of party hosts, hospitality industry employees, and drinkers themselves—remained the best way to prevent drunk driving. Chafetz did more than just write, though. In 1982, he created the Training for Intervention Procedures by Servers of Alcohol program, which would eventually train hundreds of thousands of bartenders and waiters how to serve alcohol responsibly. He also went further, making the provocative claim that because 83 percent of those killed in drunk driving crashes were either drunk drivers, drunk passengers, or drunk pedestrians, these deaths were self-destructive and a "form of suicide," something that itself should be studied.[53]

The problem, of course, was that there were no data proving that educational or psychiatric interventions lowered deaths from drunk driving more effectively than punishments did. As one respondent to Chafetz noted in the *Des Moines Register*, "logical solutions to alcoholic problems work only for the non-drinker." "There is more and more evidence emerging," wrote another correspondent, "that alcoholism is a genetically acquired illness, and that all the training in the world will not teach alcoholics to drink 'responsibly,' nor will training prevent those people who are genetically predisposed to alcoholism from becoming alcoholics."[54]

The enormously divergent views of NCADD members underscored an important point. Although activist movements are often seen as monolithic, they generally comprise multiple interest groups, often with very different agendas. The "big tent" approach can increase publicity and funding, but it may also cause splintering and inertia. This is what happened to the NCADD. In 1999, a new president, longtime government drunk driving researcher John V. Moulden, was hired. Although he tried to get the committee to reach consensus on a national anti–drunk driving agenda, industry representatives believed that he was not sufficiently sympathetic to their point of view. Moulden resigned in 2003, and the NCADD disbanded the next year.[55]

In their paper "The Rise and Fall of Social Problems: A Public Arenas Model," the sociologists Stephen Hilgartner and Charles Bosk argue that the ability of activist movements to command public attention for prolonged periods of time is limited.[56] Such was clearly the case with drunk driving. By the late 1980s, as those in the movement forged ahead with a semiunited front, the public's attention was turning elsewhere. For example, the AIDS epidemic and a related outbreak of multidrug-resistant tuberculosis were increasingly dominating health coverage. But Surgeon General C. Everett Koop would make one last push, not only keeping drunk driving on the public's radar screen but also trying to redefine it as a major public health problem.

How Koop tried to achieve these goals is a story with more than one version. The event, held from December 14–16, 1988, at Washington's Mayflower Hotel, was one in a series of surgeon general's workshops that Koop had run since 1981. These were meetings that convened experts "to identify the public health implications of major health problems demanding resolution." Koop had initially achieved fame as a pediatric surgeon at the University of Pennsylvania, where he helped to pioneer a series of lifesaving operations. He was also known for his conservative views on abortion and euthanasia, which made him an attractive surgeon general to Ronald Reagan. But Koop would surprise the president and the public by becoming an activist, particularly by taking on the cigarette companies and publicizing sex education in light of the AIDS crisis.

Resolutions passed nearly unanimously in both the House of Representatives and the Senate asking Koop to address the issue of drunk driving provided the immediate impetus for the drunk driving workshop. These resolutions, in turn, had been prompted by what was being called the worst drunk driving crash in

American history. On the night of May 14, 1988, Larry Mahoney, a 34-year-old chemical plant worker, drove the wrong way down Interstate 71 near Carrollton, Kentucky, and crashed into a school bus carrying a Kentucky church group returning home from a Cincinnati amusement park. The bus caught fire and twenty-seven of its seventy passengers—including twenty-four children—were killed, mostly from smoke inhalation, although the bodies were also burned beyond recognition. The image of children vainly scrambling to escape the flames made the story even more heart-wrenching. It was eventually learned that the bus had likely caught fire because Ford had deliberately ignored a federal law that mandated bus manufacturers to protect gas tanks,[57] but more immediately relevant was Mahoney's BAC of 0.24%, more than twice Kentucky's 0.10% legal limit. In addition, Mahoney was a repeat offender, having been convicted of DWI in 1984. At that time, he paid a $300 fine and lost his driver's license for six months.

Befitting the era and the magnitude of the crime, the Oldham County prosecutor charged Mahoney with 27 counts of murder and briefly pondered the notion of asking for the death penalty. MADD president Robert Beck concurred. "This was no accident," he said. "People intentionally drink and they intentionally drive. I'm sick and tired of people sugar-coating murder." But even Mahoney generated sympathy. Fellow residents of Carrollton raised money to pay for his bail. One called Mahoney's act a "terrible mistake" but added that he "ain't no murderer." Eventually, a jury convicted Mahoney of 27 counts of manslaughter and the judge sentenced him to 16 years in prison, of which he served 9 years and 7 months.[58] Yet while justice may have been served, that such a crash could occur after almost a decade of nonstop admonitions against drunk driving was both astonishing and frustrating. The congressional resolutions and Koop's interest followed naturally.

The protocol was the same as for previous workshops. An interagency planning committee from several cabinet-level departments, including the Department of Transportation and the Department of Health and Human Services, compiled a list of participants, who were experts in the latest scientific data regarding drunk driving. The organizers then divided these individuals into a series of panels, which met separately during the meeting, reviewing the existing research in their areas of expertise and generating a series of recommendations. The eleven panels were: pricing and availability, advertising and marketing, epidemiology and data management, education, judicial and administrative processes, law enforcement, transportation and alcohol service policies, injury control, youth and other special populations, treatment, and citizen advocacy.

The controversy emerged in late November when invitations, including the list of panel members, were sent out. Almost immediately, industry representatives began to complain, charging that they had insufficient presence on several panels, especially the one on advertising and marketing. Some of the harshest words came from Edward O. Fritts, the president and CEO of the National Association of Broadcasters, which had so strongly opposed the SMART campaign. Fritts's major complaint was "a total lack of balance" on the panels, which he believed would lead to recommendations that were "a foregone conclusion." Specifically, those excluded were a large number of groups long active in the fight against drunk driving, such as major league sports executives, alcohol manufacturers and distributors, advertising agencies, the Ad Council, television networks, and the hospitality industry. Although the NAB was included, Fritts added, opponents on its panel would likely negate its presence. He concluded by charging the workshop with politicizing "the emotional tragedy of drunk driving" and abusing the policy-setting process.[59]

Of particular concern was the advertising and marketing panel. Fritts wrote that eight of the ten panel participants were already on record as wanting to either restrict or ban alcohol advertisements. In addition, he added, the background paper for the panel had been written by Charles Atkin, of Michigan State University, who would also be drafting the panel's final recommendations. Atkin was a problematic choice, according to Fritts, because he was the author of the only study among more than fifty to find a "causal relationship between advertising and alcohol use." The NAB thus feared that an anti-advertising bias was the inevitable result of the panel's deliberations.[60]

Other industry representatives weighed in as well. Ronald R. Rumbaugh, president of the National Beer Wholesalers Association, a trade group representing thousands of beer distributors nationwide, wrote to "strongly object to the exclusion of all sectors of the alcohol beverage industry from the Drunk Driving workshop to be held December 14–16." Rumbaugh, like other correspondents, emphasized the anti–drunk driving efforts of the NBWA and its members, which included a Preventing Alcohol Abuse Education Program for schoolchildren, Anheuser-Busch's Operation Alert, and Adolph Coors's Alcohol, Drugs, Driving and You. He also claimed that the workshop organizers had declined requests from the NBWA to observe the workshop or to obtain copies of background papers. The current workshop, he concluded, "will only polarize and divide when what is needed is cooperation and broad consensus."[61]

Another series of critical letters arrived from V. J. Adduci, the head of the National Commission Against Drunk Driving. Representing a group that now had a substantial number of members from industry, Adduci felt that the workshop was giving them short shrift. He told Koop that he regretted that the NCADD had not been involved in planning the meeting agenda, given its prominence in the field. Although NCADD member John Grant had been invited to attend, Adduci wrote, "as best I can tell we are not invited to be speakers or presentors [*sic*]—it appears that we are invited only to listen to others present their views and as 'listeners' become a part of a report which may or may not reflect the position of the National Commission, which we would be representing."[62] Adduci indicated, as did the NAB's Fritts, that if the meeting proceeded without changes to the agenda, the NCADD would decline the invitation. Koop did agree to let either Adduci or Grant speak at the opening plenary, but he agreed to no other changes. As a result, neither man attended, and there was a conspicuously empty NCADD chair on the dais. Other groups that wrote letters of protest to Koop included the Distilled Spirits Council, several beer and liquor distributors from across the country, the Association of National Advertisers, and the American Association of Advertising Agencies, the executive vice president of which, John E. O' Toole, noted that although there was no proven relationship between advertising and alcohol abuse, the advertising and marketing panel "appears to be decidedly anti-alcohol and anti-alcohol advertising."[63]

Koop and his staff disagreed with the charges and sent reply letters, indicating how the process, to their minds, had been a fair one. Representative was a letter from Koop to Adduci. "We, along with the other sponsoring agencies," he wrote, "have sought and secured a balance of representatives from diverse interest groups . . . including sports, advertising, media, law enforcement, private citizens, local and state jurisdictions, and the academic, technical and scientific communities." To the charge that the alcohol industry had been excluded, he pointed to the invitation of Grant from the NCADD, the membership of which included the Distilled Spirits Council and the Beer Institute. Koop also claimed that the NCADD *had* been involved in the organizational process. Yet even though he asked the NAB and members of the advertising groups to reconsider their decision to boycott the workshop, none of the organizations sent a representative.[64]

On the opening day of the conference, Koop and his colleagues were stunned

Doris Aiken of RID speaks with Surgeon General C. Everett Koop during his workshop on drunk driving. Courtesy of Doris Aiken

to learn that the NBWA had filed a lawsuit in the United States District Court to postpone the workshop on the grounds that it and other interested groups had been excluded from participation. The NAB filed an amicus brief. The court ruled that the workshop could proceed but mandated that the surgeon general accept and consider comments from interested parties through January 31, 1989, and not issue his final recommendations until February 28, 1989. Ultimately, although such comments were received and reviewed, they were not included in the final report.

Several familiar recommendations came out of the workshop: the discouragement of plea-bargaining, the institution of a mandatory 90-day license revocation for first-time DWI offenders, and the encouragement of states to make driving illegal at a BAC of 0.08% and, by the year 2000, 0.04%. Other favored initiatives had been mentioned for years but were only now gaining force in the United States, including the promotion of community-wide designated drivers and alternative transportation programs, the training of servers of alcoholic beverages to detect and prevent inebriation, the use of sobriety checkpoints to identify intoxicated drivers before they crashed, and the study and promotion of technological solutions like interlock ignition devices, which required drivers to blow into a BAC-like device in order to start their car.[65]

Other recommendations, however, looked nothing like those normally contained in drunk driving control documents. These were:

- the elimination of alcohol advertising and promotions on college campuses
- an ad ban on alcohol endorsements by youth-oriented celebrities
- a stop to athletic-event sponsorships by alcohol-beverage makers
- an equal time provision requiring public service alcohol abuse ads to balance against alcohol product ads
- switching regulation of alcoholic beverages to the Food and Drug Administration from the Bureau of Alcohol, Tobacco, and Firearms
- raising the excise-tax rate on beer and wine to reflect inflation since 1970
- including in all alcohol ads the same information required on package warning labels as of November 1988

In order to help effect these more progressive initiatives, yet another big umbrella group, the National Coalition to Prevent Drunk Driving, was formed in 1989, under the leadership of the CSPI's George Hacker and University of Minnesota social epidemiologist Alexander C. Wagenaar.

Department of Health and Human Services substance abuse expert Robert W. Denniston, who was a workshop participant, believes that these new directions reflected Koop's earlier experiences fighting tobacco, which had taught him that industry-inspired educational messages only went so far. The surgeon general had learned that "you need more than smart kids," Denniston recalls. Koop would become even more impassioned by 1990, citing data showing that children saw 100,000 beer commercials before age 18 and calling for a total ban on broadcast beer and wine advertisements.[66] He had the support of the public in these efforts. A survey published that same year by Wagenaar and Frederick M. Streff reported that 82 percent of respondents favored raising alcohol excise taxes, 74 percent approved of restricting concurrent sales of alcohol and gasoline at service stations, and 63 percent wanted the government to limit the number of alcohol outlets.[67]

Koop was appalled at what the industry groups had done before and during his workshop. After all, he had held similar conferences on topics as sensational as domestic violence, child pornography, and children with AIDS and had never encountered any charges of politicization. Those who attended the drunk driving workshop appreciated what Koop had done. At the end of the proceedings, when Koop chastised those groups that had declined to participate, he received a standing ovation. "How could a group of people working in the United States be opposed to the outrageous slaughter of young people by drivers who are drunk?" he later asked.[68] This workshop episode revealed the fervent determination of the beverage industry, and others who profited from alcohol sales and advertising, to try to thwart efforts to characterize drunk driving as a major public health catastrophe. The problem, they continued to insist, was the individual alcoholic who was out of control, not the product itself.

Part of the reason for the frenzy surrounding the surgeon general's workshop reflected the fact that industry, owing to its early association with the National Safety Council and its promulgation of the concept of moderation, had a long history of influencing governmental recommendations about drunk driving. It was one thing for tobacco executives, who had blatantly lied about the purported safety of cigarettes, to get their comeuppance, but the alcohol, broadcasting, and hospitality industries saw themselves as good guys in the history of drunk driving control. Yet as activists looked for new directions, industry increasingly appeared as more of a roadblock than a help. If kicking Budweiser off college campuses and partially clothed women off beer commercials might save lives, perhaps it was time to do these things. Fearing that these events might actually happen, industry played hardball, even with someone as respected as Koop.

Had Koop really stacked the deck? Twenty years later, he and several other organizers say no, sticking to the claim that participants represented a broad range of interests and that the deliberations were nonpolitical and fair. But two individuals who helped plan the workshop, Robert Denniston and San Diego State University behavioral scientist David A. Sleet, recall a specific decision by Koop to exclude the alcohol industry from active involvement for fear that it would preclude consensus. "A decision had to be made," Sleet recently said. "That decision was no."[69] It is thus reasonable to conclude that Koop truly wished to produce a more progressive document, one that would challenge the status quo. After all, he believed that the alcohol lobbies in Washington had "really scary" power, deciding things "not . . . by negotiation but by fiat based on the power of the commercial interests."[70] Given this overriding aim, some of the panels, as constituted, clearly gave less prominence to certain groups who were used to having a central seat at the table.

This strategy was particularly apparent when it came to the issues of advertising and marketing. Numerous studies existed that looked at the purported connection between advertisements and alcohol abuse. Involving sociological, psychological, and epidemiological methods that were often difficult to interpret, such research was limited in its ability to prove causality. Indeed, on December 12, 1988, two days before the start of the workshop, Enoch Gordis, Director of the NIAAA, sent Koop a letter stating that there was not yet any definitive scientific research proving that alcohol advertising increased rates of drunk driving.[71] Nevertheless, the workshop's proposals went in the other direction.

Ultimately, therefore, many of the recommendations emanating from the Surgeon General's Workshop on Drunk Driving were based more on presumptions and a sense of right and wrong than on scientific data—another example of the precautionary principle. That moral judgment was at play at a scientific conference is hardly surprising given that the subject was drunk driving and that there were numerous participants, especially on the citizen advocacy panel, who had lost loved ones to drunk drivers and had hundreds of tragic stories to tell.[72]

Owning the moral high ground, however, was proving to be an increasingly difficult task. C. Everett Koop's workshop was part of a larger effort at the end of the 1980s and the beginning of the 1990s to reinvigorate the anti–drunk driving movement. Yet the more MADD, RID, NHTSA, and their allies tried to move forward, opponents pushed back even harder, vilifying individuals who had experienced terrible personal losses and a cause that had once seemed entirely unassailable. The surprise defections of two of the movement's early heroes only complicated matters more.

CHAPTER FIVE

Lawyers, Libertarians, and the Liquor Lobby Fight Back

Perhaps the state of the drunk driving movement in the early 1990s was best exemplified by a book published by then MADD president Micky Sadoff in 1991. *Get MADD Again, America!* reminded readers that while much had been accomplished in the 1980s, mortality rates were still extremely high. The initial decline in annual deaths from 25,000 to 17,000 had occurred between 1980 and 1985, but by 1991, the decrease had leveled off. Sadoff's book raised a key issue: How does one assess the achievements of a social movement like drunk driving control? Was the consistent 17,000 figure a sign of success or a reminder that not enough had been done?[1]

What had become clear by the early 1990s was that the anti–drunk driving arguments made by MADD and other groups, which had once seemed incontestable, could be challenged. Part of the negativity was again directed at MADD, which, despite championing an ostensibly unobjectionable cause, continued to be rebuked for both its administrative and its policy decisions. Meanwhile, critics, ranging from industry representatives to academics to defense lawyers, questioned the actual harm caused by drinking drivers and the statistics that activists used. An additional attack, promoted by the expanding use of the Internet, was that MADD and related activist groups were neoprohibitionist, against not only drunk driving but also drinking.

This is not to say that the movement was failing. In addition to the annual saving of thousands of lives, many other major strides had been made. By 2004, for example, all fifty states had set legal BACs at 0.08%, almost half the level originally established in the 1930s and more in line with Europe. Extensive data now existed proving that certain interventions—such as the age-21 drinking law, sobriety checkpoints, and administrative license revocation—truly lowered rates of drunk driving and mortality. But as Sadoff must have feared, the backlash had taken its toll. By the start of the twenty-first century, the annual number of arrests for drunk driving had declined by 30 percent, and much of the momentum that had emerged from C. Everett Koop's workshop had been lost.

As of the early 1990s, the anti–drunk driving crusade had become truly broad-based, including the National Commission Against Drunk Driving (NCADD), the National Highway Traffic Safety Administration (NHTSA) and other government agencies, the Distilled Spirits Council (DISCUS) and other industry groups, and the citizen-activists of RID, MADD, and SADD. But because of its name-recognition and multimillion-dollar budget, MADD had become synonymous with efforts to control DWI. So when it called for a reinvigoration of the movement, people paid attention. "Americans are *still* dying in horrifying numbers at the hands of drunk or drugged drivers," Sadoff told her readers. *Get MADD Again, America!* was a typical mix of anger, policy recommendations, and tragic stories. One such story was that of a 17-year-old male driver with a 16-year-old female passenger who were both killed in 1990, when they hit a pickup truck. The boy's BAC was 0.23% and the girl's was 0.16%. The storyteller was Donna McCary, who was driving the truck that the boy hit. She survived, although she required multiple operations for fractured bones and suffered permanent damage to her right eye. McCary, who subsequently became a MADD volunteer, expressed regret that the boy's family had never contacted her, stating: "I was innocent and yet neither my life nor my family's will ever be the same because this driver made the choice to drink and drive."[2]

The first half of Sadoff's book advocated "closing the loopholes"—expanding the use of existing measures to counter drunk driving, including administrative license revocation, sobriety checkpoints, and BAC testing in the field. MADD was also pushing to lower the nationwide BAC from 0.10% to 0.08%. But part two of the book—specifically, a discussion of underage drinking—represented a change in focus. MADD had long been concerned with the significant role played by teenagers and young adults in drunk driving crashes; its support of raising the drinking age from 18 to 21 had reflected this concern. But even though an estimated 6,660 lives had been saved by this new legislation, Sadoff wrote, "young drivers in America today continue to be disproportionately involved in traffic crashes, injuries and deaths involving alcohol or other drugs."

It was necessary, she added, both to "reduce the motivation" and "reduce the opportunity."[3]

Thus, *Get MADD Again* made the case for alcohol-free proms and parties for those under age 21, better enforcement of the age-21 drinking law, a "zero tolerance" BAC of 0.0% for anyone under 21, and, most notably, "the elimination of any alcohol advertising which promotes drinking among minors."[4] MADD, Sadoff emphasized, remained opposed to attempts to limit alcohol consumption in general, continuing to focus on drinking and driving. Nevertheless, she approvingly quoted a portion of the Koop report critical of alcohol advertisements that targeted the young and then proceeded to recommend many of the surgeon general's same prohibitions.

By 1992, MADD had "turned around 180 degrees," according to an article in the *Journal of Public Health Policy* by anthropologists Mac Marshall and Alice Oleson. The piece began with a description of a 1992 mailing from MADD that contained a letter on the topic of advertising advocating that the alcohol industry be held accountable "for its role in our drunk driving tragedy." Included in the envelope was a petition asking the Wine Institute, the Beer Institute, DISCUS, the newly formed public relations entity the Century Council, and the National Beer Wholesalers Association to "prohibit any and all promotions which would encourage illegal or irresponsible alcohol use."[5]

What had caused MADD to change its tune? Marshall and Oleson speculated that the national office may have been responding to the wishes of its local affiliates and did not want to be on record as opposing Koop's recommendations, in part because of fundraising concerns. In addition, Micky Sadoff, who, like Candy Lightner, had worked closely with the National Association of Broadcasters during her tenure as MADD president, had been replaced by Milo Kirk. Finally, the political climate had changed. The more liberal Clinton administration was in favor of "sin taxes" and other restrictions on the sales of cigarettes and alcohol.

MADD board of directors member William DeJong and assistant director of public policy Anne Russell replied to Marshall and Oleson's review of MADD's history, which, they said, was "distorted" and "riddled with errors." They agreed that MADD's policy toward alcohol advertising had changed since 1980 but characterized it more as a gradual evolution, "motivated foremost by a long-standing concern about the alcohol industry's youth-oriented marketing, but also by a growing impatience with the industry's arrogant refusal to curb its harmful advertising practices."[6] This statement was certainly among the most critical MADD had ever issued about the industry's indirect promotion of drunk driving.

But almost no one was prepared for what happened next. In two instances of seeming apostasy, both Cindi Lamb and Candy Lightner went to work for the alcohol industry. Although their work with MADD in the early years meant that both women had interacted with industry representatives, it was nothing short of jarring to see Lamb and Lightner, who had so passionately channeled their grief and anger into the formation of an idealistic social movement, go over to the "dark side."

In 1991, Lamb was hired by the National Beer Wholesalers Association, the group that had filed the lawsuit to try to postpone Koop's workshop. It was a story made for the media. A front-page article by Jill Abramson in the *Wall Street Journal* described a "rousing" speech on responsible drinking given by Lamb to the annual NBWA convention in Washington, DC. The piece listed a series of other new efforts by the alcohol industry to discourage abuse of its product by drunk drivers, underage drinkers, and others. For example, Miller Brewing Company was spending millions of dollars urging drinkers to "Know your limits," a sister campaign to Anheuser-Busch's "Know when to say when." Anheuser-Busch, which liked to say that "Good business and good citizenship must go hand in hand," had also recently given $2.5 million to the National Collegiate Athletic Association to promote alcohol awareness among college athletes. DISCUS, the trade association representing distillers, supported a program known as BACCHUS, which stood for "Boost Alcohol Consciousness Concerning the Health of University Students." Most notable, however, was the formation of the Century Council, a nonprofit organization also begun by distillers, which discouraged underage drinking and actually supported many of the initiatives favored by anti–drunk driving activists. These included administrative license revocation, stricter penalties and better treatment programs for hardcore drinkers, zero tolerance laws for those under age 21, and even lowering the legal BAC for all drivers to 0.08%.[7]

Abramson emphasized how money provided the alcohol industry with pervasive influence in Washington. For example, since 1985, twenty-six industry-related political action committees had contributed $4.7 million to congressional candidates. After Lamb's speech, wearing buttons stating "We're part of the solution," the distributors pled their case on Capitol Hill—and brought along $172,000 of campaign contributions.

Abramson's article quoted a series of critics who argued that hiring Lamb and starting new programs were simply the latest efforts of the alcohol industry to co-opt anti–drunk driving activism, "while moving the booze." "Would you want the Mafia underwriting anti-crime programs?" asked Andrew McGuire, one of MADD's early board members. Christine Lubinski, chief lobbyist for the National Council on Alcoholism, agreed, noting "a long history of industry giving groups money to buy their silence."[8] Lubinski and Lamb actually debated Lamb's decision to work for the NBWA on the *Today* show.

Lamb was not at all ashamed of her choice. As mentioned before, she was a drinker, and the notion of using alcohol in moderation—and never driving drunk—made sense to her. As to the charge that she had been bought out, she pointed out that her salary was only $34,000 annually. And while she gave an occasional high-profile presentation, most of her work was in the trenches, meeting with groups of beer distributors to discuss designated drivers, "safe ride home" programs, and other initiatives. The distributors would then go back to their communities and help develop these ideas locally. Lamb recalls there being "genuine interest" among those who attended her sessions and their wives and children.

After five years at the NBWA, however, Lamb did become discouraged. At one point she developed a coaster for drinks that correlated the amount of alcohol consumed with BACs. But, she recalls, her boss did not want her passing it out on the road. Ultimately, Lamb realized that he did not want his employee upsetting the apple cart. "This was a lobbying group, a bunch of good old boys," she recalled. "They would do just enough to keep criticism at bay, but would not sacrifice the market."[9]

It was even bigger news when Candy Lightner, who was interested in pursuing a career in lobbying, seemed to join the enemy. In November 1993, Lightner was hired by her friend Rick Berman, of Berman & Company, a Washington-based public relations firm that represented the American Beverage Institute. The ABI was a trade association that worked with restaurants that served liquor, including TGI Fridays, Steak & Ale, Outback Steakhouse, and Hooters. Berman had hired Lightner to work on its campaign to oppose efforts by state legislatures to lower the legal BAC from 0.10% to 0.08%. As of 1994, twelve states had already done so, but the vast majority had not.

Anti–drunk driving activists reacted to the news with a combination of bafflement and anger. After all, in her last days at MADD, Lightner had been very critical of what she saw as industry's influence over the NCADD. Former MADD leader Andrew McGuire weighed in again, remarking that "anyone who is serious about preventing drunk driving should not ever get in bed with the alcohol industry." (Although Lightner was technically working for the hospitality industry, the connection was clear.) "MADD Founder Switches Sides" was a typical newspaper headline.[10]

Lightner was prepared for this type of backlash. Consistent with the position that she had promulgated as head of MADD, she argued that the main drunk driving offenders had BACs far higher than 0.08%, as the man who'd killed Cari had. Focusing on catching drivers with readings between 0.08% and 0.10%, Lightner stated, would be "diluting law enforcement efforts" against "truly dangerous drivers." That is, using limited police and legal resources to track down and arrest less-impaired drivers potentially meant that drivers with high BACs received less attention. Lightner also continued to advocate harsh penalties for those convicted of DWI: automatic license revocation and stiffer penalties for those with especially high BACs and previous offenses. She said she was not at all embarrassed about her choice and resented assertions that she had become a traitor. "I haven't gone to the 'other side,'" she said. "The 'other side' is being a defense lawyer." Lightner also made the valid point that more lives would likely be saved by lowering speed limits than lowering BACs.[11]

Although she was being consistent with past statements, it was hard to deny that Lightner's new career choice had important symbolic meanings. Even if the alcohol and hospitality industries were not wolves in sheep's clothing, their reform efforts would always, first and foremost, take into account the bottom line—as Cindi Lamb was finding out.

But what about the data? Could one make a reasonable argument that paying attention to drivers with BACs under 0.10% did not make sense from either a public health or a cost-benefit perspective? Or, to put it another way, did the harm—or potential harm—caused by such drivers warrant arrests, license revocation, and possibly time in prison?

Candy Lightner was not the only person saying no. A little more than a decade into anti–drunk driving efforts, a series of academics had begun to question some of the basic premises that underlay the movement. Although these critics drew on the data and arguments of people like Joseph Gusfield and Laurence Ross, they were not insiders trying to shift the focus of activism to more effective interventions. Rather, these were ethicists, philosophers, and lawyers who raised counterintuitive, and at times jarring, arguments about a crusade that had become sacrosanct to many Americans.

Writing in *Public Affairs Quarterly* in 1989, James D. Stuart called into question the appropriateness of using deterrence as a basis for punishing drivers who had been drinking. Although courts meted out specific punishments in cases of injury or death, preventing future DWI episodes had been the prevailing philosophy behind drunk driving legislation since the 1930s. But Stuart wanted the punishment to fit the crime—no more and no less. "We need to ask what sort of punishment is *deserved* for a given offense," he wrote.[12]

This type of argument required determining how much harm was caused or risked by an individual instance of DWI. The problem in the aggregate, Stuart argued, did not matter. Here Stuart turned to the data, specifically, the familiar statistic that suggested there was a 1 in 1,000 chance that an impaired driver would be involved in a crash. The likelihood that such a crash would lead to injury or death was even smaller. (Laurence Ross estimated 1 fatality for every 330,000 impaired miles.) Thus, the overwhelming majority of impaired drivers caused no harm. Moreover, Stuart added, although drunk drivers did knowingly subject others to risk, they did not set out deliberately to harm others—in contrast, say, to someone who robs a bank.[13]

As drunk drivers neither set out to cause harm nor usually did cause harm, Stuart concluded, routine DWIs should not be considered serious criminal offenses and should not receive severe punishments. Stuart actually backed off at the end of the article, noting that there was no reason for society to tolerate DWI, especially because it had little or no social value. Thus, it was acceptable to punish it—just not severely. But his larger query remained: Even though DWI was a legitimate public health issue and harsher punishments were emotionally satisfying, were such punishments justifiable?

Another person answering no to this question was James B. Jacobs, a professor of law at New York University and author of a 1989 book on drunk driving. For Jacobs, the degree of intoxication was key. "It is essential to maintain the distinction between *drunk* driving and *drinking* driving," he wrote. Most dangerous drunk drivers, Jacobs believed, were "very heavy drinkers or moderate drinkers on a binge." Focusing attention on light drinkers, even those whose BACs were at or near the legal limit, was thus not a good use of resources. Jacobs also suggested that drinkers who could hold their liquor might be unfairly targeted by existing per se laws. That is, why was a driver with a BAC of 0.10% or more who had committed no traffic violation and was able to pass a roadside sobriety test automatically seen as culpable? Was such a person truly negligent and reckless?[14]

Philosopher and lawyer Douglas N. Husak built on these arguments in a 1994 essay in *Philosophy and Public Affairs*. Husak was responding, in part, to a 1985 article in the same journal by the bioethicist Bonnie Steinbock. Steinbock, writing at the height of anti–drunk driving activism, had argued that choosing to drive drunk demonstrated "gross recklessness" and "extreme indifference to the value of human life."[15] Just because a drunk driver might not crash did not mitigate the fact that he or she was guilty of a moral and legal transgression. Husak disagreed with this argument because, as Stuart had shown, the odds of an impaired driver causing harm were so low. Citing data similar to Stuart's— that the risk of being involved in a crash while driving drunk was 4.5/10,000 and that a fatality occurred only once every 600,000 miles driven drunk—Husak argued that drunk driving was most certainly *not* equivalent to shooting a gun in a crowded room, which had a much higher likelihood of causing harm.[16]

Husak also listed several other reasons he thought drunk driving should not be considered a serious offense: (1) many drunk drivers were probably unaware of per se laws, which automatically made high Breathalyzer readings equivalent to committing a crime; (2) drunk driving was commonplace among the population, and common behavior should not be criminalized; and (3) per se laws were necessarily arbitrary, and it did not make sense to convict someone for driving drunk when they would be set free with a slightly lower BAC. After questioning the basic tenets of how drunk driving was enforced, Husak did close with a helpful suggestion: create a crime called "aggravated drunk driving" for drivers with extremely high BACs who were exhibiting really risky behaviors. But he correctly noted that anti–drunk driving advocates were likely to oppose such a measure because it might be seen as exonerating others who drove and drank.[17]

Academics were not the only critics of anti–drunk driving orthodoxy. For decades, clever defense lawyers, often aided by sympathetic judges, had concocted strategies to get their DWI clients exonerated. These efforts included arguing that Breathalyzers were not accurate measuring devices, questioning backward extrapolations of BACs when testing was delayed, and contending that breath testing was unconstitutional. Robert Borkenstein, not surprisingly, believed that such lawyers displayed an "obvious callousness toward ethics."[18] By the early 1990s, thwarting drunk driving charges had become a cottage industry, as expert witnesses testified for defendants across the country and authors published multiple books and articles on the subject. Subsequently, the Internet would become especially hospitable to this type of advice, such as the website for "Lady DUI," Connecticut lawyer Teresa DiNardi, which bragged about successful outcomes for clients who had "admitted to being drunk on video."[19] If there was ever evidence that drunk driving was different from most, if not all, other serious public health issues, it was these publications. The earliest books, with titles such as *Winning Defenses in Drunk Driving Cases* and *Drunk Driving Defense*, were books written for lawyers by lawyers.

California lawyer Lawrence Taylor, the author of *Drunk Driving Defense*, became a national expert in fighting DWI charges, eventually founding the Drunk Driving Law Center. Among the types of advice found in Taylor's book were how to contest BAC readings, how to challenge whether there had been probable cause for sobriety testing, and how to impeach the testimony of the arresting officer. Taylor urged defense lawyers to ask their clients the following questions:

- Were there mechanical defects in the car that caused veering?
- Did they have any injuries that made them look intoxicated?
- Had they used any cough syrups, breath sprays, or mouthwashes prior to testing, or had they belched?
- Had someone else previously been tested using the same machine?
- Had breath testing been done by a different officer than the one who made the arrest?
- Had the field sobriety testing been done on a "sloping, gravel-strewn shoulder of the road"?
- Had the testing been done at night, without the benefit of adequate light?
- Would witnesses be willing to testify that the client had not been drinking or had passed the sobriety test?[20]

Having written a book of more than 700 pages, Taylor left no stone unturned in his zeal to create reasonable doubt and thus poke holes in the prosecution's case.

The second wave of books was marketed to drinkers themselves. Typical titles were *Beat the Breathalyzer: A Survival Kit for Drinking Drivers* and *Drunk Driving Defense: How to Beat the Rap.* A similar book was *How to Avoid a Drunk Driving Conviction*, published in 1993 by "Judge X," a longtime state judge who had presided over thousands of drunk driving cases. Among the pieces of advice Judge X gave to drinking drivers were to refuse to take a field sobriety test, especially if their levels were apt to be high; use Hall's Mentholyptus to hide the odor of alcohol; take the mouthpiece from their breath test and save it for their lawyer; ask that the breath, blood, or urine sample be saved; and request a repeat

breath test in the case of a belch. That the judge believed that everyone was taking drunk driving a little too seriously was evident from some of the "advice" he
gave in his book: "Don't drink and drive (you might spill your drink)" and "Beware of amateur drunk drivers, they give professionals a bad name."[21]

Aside from potential profits, why did lawyers and judges choose to write such
books? Taylor believed that in drunk driving cases, especially as a result of BAC
testing, defendants were presumed guilty instead of innocent—the exact opposite of most other offenses. He aimed to rectify things. Judge X's stated motivation was that the 0.08% BAC, becoming law in many states, was too low. Along
highways and roads across the country, he wrote, there were taverns, restaurants,
and convenience stores that sold alcohol. The drive home had become a way of
turning people who had had only a couple of drinks into criminals. "There is
such a thing as a reasonably prudent drunk driver," the judge stated, "and he or
she is the focus of this book." Judge X well knew that what he was writing was
incendiary. "I know the Mothers Against Drunk Drivers, a hundred million dollars strong, will be screaming for my anonymous head," he admitted.[22]

How should we assess these challenges to drunk driving control? The academics' sophisticated analysis of harm is a fair one, even though activists would
surely object to the inclination to exonerate people who are knowingly engaging
in a risky activity because it is not quite risky enough. With respect to the defense lawyers, not only is there a history of Supreme Court justices sympathetic
to the rights of drunk drivers, but these lawyers are doing what they are paid to
do: find loopholes in laws. Moreover, it can reasonably be argued that police
offers, prosecutors, and judges can make mistakes that unfairly penalize supposedly drunk drivers. Neither human beings nor the technologies they employ in
service to the law are infallible. Indeed, if someone breathes into a Breathalyzer
within twenty minutes of his or her last drink, the BAC will be spuriously elevated, something Borkenstein repeatedly emphasized. And, at times, police officers might "dial a drunk"—purposely elevate a suspect's BAC (which was not
possible to do on later models of the Breathalyzer).

Yet, unless one concludes that drunk driving enforcement is some kind of
farce, it appears that the sizable literature on how to beat the system was much
more likely to be used in cases of *actual* drunk driving than mistakenly identified
drunk driving. That is, defendants and their lawyers would be using the strategies in question to obfuscate *real* crimes. A good example was a man with two
prior DWIs who left a football game at Miami's Orange Bowl in 1986 and drove
the wrong way down a one-way street. The police measured his BAC at 0.14%.

The man hired a lawyer to get the breath test suppressed as evidence, and the case was ultimately dismissed.[23] Given that drunk driving still caused more than 15,000 deaths annually in the United States, manuals that impeded law enforcement officials from prosecuting such cases and attributing appropriate blame did a tremendous disservice to the cause of justice and protection of the public's health. Amazon.com lists no books on how to carry a concealed weapon, hide a diagnosis of infectious tuberculosis, or "beat the rap" for child or spousal abuse. Nor would society likely tolerate such books. But in the case of drunk driving, we do.

As the anti–drunk driving movement creaked into middle age in the mid to late 1990s, attacks only intensified. Once again MADD, because of its prominence and continuing missteps, was the favored punching bag. Criticisms that MADD's fundraising went to sustain a large bureaucracy, as opposed to grassroots anti–drunk driving efforts, persisted. "Mothers Against Drunk Drivers (MADD) is evolving from a well-intentioned lobbying group to a self-perpetuating Washington institution," wrote Eric Peters in the *National Review*. Several local MADD chapters even became embroiled in public fights with the national office over finances; some disbanded and formed chapters of RID. In addition, a few fundraising campaigns fell flat and actually cost MADD money. Finally, in 1991, MADD began an ongoing relationship with General Motors—which ultimately netted it several million dollars—again raising concerns that industry was buying the organization's silence on certain traffic safety issues.[24]

MADD also came under fire for using tragedies to emphasize the continuing high death rates from drunk driving. For example, after the tragic shootings at Columbine High School in 1999, which killed twelve students and one teacher, MADD issued a press release terming this death toll "insignificant" in comparison to that from alcohol-related crashes. And after the September 11, 2001, terrorist attack, MADD president Wendy Hamilton stated, "I'm not trying to minimize in any way what happened to our country on that day, because if anybody knows terror, I think the victims of drunk driving certainly do."[25]

Even when the tragedy in question involved drunk driving, the "proper" lessons to be drawn were not always clear. On August 31, 1997, Diana, Princess of Wales, and her companion, wealthy Egyptian film producer and socialite Dodi Fayed, were killed in a car crash in Paris. Although the details were not immediately known (and still remain controversial in some circles), Henri Paul, the driver of the Mercedes limousine in which they were traveling, was both drunk and speeding in order to avoid the paparazzi. Paul's BAC was 0.2275%, nearly four times France's legal limit of 0.065%. Paul had apparently had a liter of wine and two shots of aniseed liqueur at a hotel bar before getting into the automobile.[26]

At first glance, it is hard to criticize MADD and other activists from seeing the death of Diana—already being billed as "the most famous victim of drunken driving"—as a teachable moment.[27] Like the United States, France had an active anti–drunk driving movement, in part because consumption of alcohol, particularly wine, was so commonplace at meals. Indeed, its 0.065% BAC was among the lowest in the world. Still, Paul had exhibited the typical bravado and bad judgment of a drunk driver; bartenders had evidently continued to serve him liquor despite how much he had imbibed; and his companions had either refused to acknowledge that he was drunk or had been unable or unwilling to persuade him not to drive.

Specifically, activists in the United States saw the events in Paris as a way to reinvigorate the push for a national 0.08% BAC. Although the number of states that had adopted this level had increased to fifteen, as of 1997, the vast majority were still at 0.10%. At the national level, New York representative Nita M. Lowey and senators Michael DeWine of Ohio and Frank R. Lautenberg of New Jersey proposed familiar-sounding legislation that would restrict federal highway funding to states that did not lower their legal limit to 0.08%. In New York, state legislators produced a "Diana bill." MADD members wholeheartedly supported this effort, remarking that "it takes a tragedy to get people's attention again" and running an advertisement listing the names of 120 female drunk driving victims with the title "We've Seen Too Many Princesses Die." "Last year, more than 17,000 other innocent people were needlessly killed as a result of drunk driving," wrote North Virginia MADD executive Charles V. Pena. "They may not have been as rich, famous and glamorous as Princess Diana, but each was a real person with hopes and dreams and family."[28]

In 1997, however, as opposed to 1980, Diana's moving story only got MADD so far. Critics again pounced, arguing that her death conveyed the opposite lesson: the *pointlessness* of lowering the BAC to 0.08%. One such individual was Rick Berman, the lobbyist who had hired Candy Lightner in 1993 and was now also the general counsel of the American Beverage Institute. France, Berman noted, had tougher drunk driving laws than did the United States, yet they "did not prevent this tragedy." Princess Diana, he emphasized, "was killed by an alcohol abuser, not a social drinker." British wine writer Andrew Barr was even more direct. "The lesson of Diana's death," he wrote in his 1999 book *Drink: A*

Social History of America, "may well be that princesses should beware of consorting with aging playboy sons of paranoid and fantasist fathers who allow them to be driven through the streets of Paris in a defective vehicle at excessive speed by an untrained driver with inadequate security support."[29] The lesson was "certainly not" that the maximum permitted BAC needed to be reduced.

An important point of contention was the degree to which drivers with BACs less than 0.10% actually contributed to the drunk driving problem. No one really disputed William Haddon's old research showing that the deadliest car crashes were caused by drivers with high BACs. Annual data released by the Department of Transportation, for example, reported that between half and two-thirds of alcohol-related fatalities involved at least one driver with a BAC of 0.14% or higher.[30] But that meant there were still between 5,000 and 6,000 deaths when BACs were lower. Just how many of these were less than 0.10%?

One estimate came from sociologist Ralph W. Hingson and his colleagues at Boston University. In a 1996 article published in the *American Journal of Public Health*, they estimated that lowering the BAC to 0.08% nationwide would reduce alcohol-related traffic deaths by 16 to 18 percent and thus save 500 to 600 lives annually. They arrived at this figure by comparing death rates in the first five states to lower their BACs to 0.08% with five nearby states still at 0.10%. A 1999 study published by NHTSA reported similar findings. For example, the rate of alcohol involvement in fatal crashes declined in eight of eleven states that had adopted a 0.08% BAC. The benefits of the 0.08% BAC were independent of other anti–drunk driving initiatives but worked well in conjunction with them, particularly administrative license revocation.[31]

Such figures did not go unchallenged. Barr, for instance, said they "required a large leap of logic." He pointed out that the states that had lowered BACs had also been the most aggressive in implementing other anti–drunk driving measures. Lowered rates of injury and death, therefore, may have had other causes. Barr also pointed out that of the ten states with the lowest fatality rates, only two had moved to a 0.08% legal BAC. In addition, he made the familiar argument that crashes involving drivers with low BACs were apt to have resulted from reasons besides alcohol ingestion. Finally, Barr noted that Hingson sat on the board of MADD, which raised the same type of ethical conflict-of-interest concern that activists had long leveled at the beverage industry: Did Hingson's findings reflect MADD's agenda?[32]

How did the beverage industry react to calls for a 0.08% legal limit? In fact, manufacturers of alcoholic beverages were not always unified in their beliefs about drunk driving prevention. Whether due to sincere convictions, political expediency, or both, DISCUS and the Century Council decided to join with MADD, RID, and NHTSA in favoring 0.08%.

But other groups, representing the alcohol as well as the hospitality and automobile industries saw the pursuit of this lower legal limit as evidence of what they termed "neoprohibitionism"—the notion that activists had strayed from their original worthy goal of combating drunk driving to a campaign against alcohol. What else could explain this focus on a 0.08% BAC, which, these critics suggested, represented only a couple of drinks with a meal? Could 0.05%, or an even lower BAC, be far behind? No less so than at its conclusion in 1933, the common perception of the Prohibition experiment was that it was a complete failure, rammed down the throats of America by puritanical, Bible-thumping extremists. To the degree that the neoprohibitionist label stuck, therefore, the anti–drunk driving activists risked an enormous loss of credibility.

The most ardent organization hurling the neoprohibitionist accusation was Rick Berman's American Beverage Institute. Having Candy Lightner as the ABI's spokesperson gave the group's claims immediate credibility. "I worry that the movement I helped create has lost direction," she stated. "I think [MADD has] become far more neoprohibitionist over the years."[33] John Doyle, the director of communications for the ABI, boldly stated that his job was "to defend drinking and driving," making sure that social drinkers did not unfairly become outcasts. Not surprisingly, MADD referred to the ABI as "the junkyard dog of the alcohol industry."[34]

Other groups agreed with the ABI. One was the American Beverage Licensees, a lobbying group of beer, wine, and spirits retailers, which stated: "Some anti-alcohol activists are seeking to eliminate any drinking before driving through harsh restrictions and extreme policies. These groups are trying to change behavior—even though more than 40 million Americans drink responsibly before driving each year."[35] Meanwhile, a group called the National Motorists' Association, begun in 1982 to "represent and protect the interests of North American motorists," objected not only to the 0.08% standard but also to the use of sobriety checkpoints. "The reincarnated prohibitionist movement," stated an article on its website, "has seized upon the roadblock tactic as a means to employ fear in their [*sic*] holy war against 'Demon Rum.'" Among those who were sympathetic to such statements, Candy Lightner recalls, were legislators who themselves drank and drove.[36]

More interesting than these criticisms were those from members of the general public who objected to what historians have termed the "new temperance movement" of the 1980s and 1990s. The anti–drunk driving movement was only one of several government and private sector initiatives, derisively dubbed the "nanny state" by critics, that sought to curb freedoms with the goal of improving the health of Americans. Other campaigns discouraged tobacco advertising aimed at children, smoking in public, and drinking during pregnancy, which had recently been identified as the cause of fetal alcohol syndrome.[37] Once the inevitable libertarian backlash occurred, the public, too, began to compare current restrictions to the supposedly draconian era of Prohibition. The power of this analogy proved to be another reason that the broad-spectrum support enjoyed by the anti–drunk driving movement into early 1990s was crumbling.

For example, the editorial page of the politically conservative *Washington Times* wrote that "MADD's ongoing push to compel states to adopt ever-lower standards for being legally drunk is becoming a prohibitionist jihad driven by hysteria, not medical reality." Others who shared this opinion had, like Candy Lightner, once worked for MADD. "MADD generally attempts to mask its radical, neo-prohibitionist agenda in the veneer of sound science and sober statistics," wrote Charles Pena, who had left the organization.[38] Not only MADD was to blame. Ralph Hudson, the Wisconsin physician who got involved in anti–drunk driving activism when his nurse's son was killed, recalls being upbraided by a member of the Wisconsin Tavern League: "You know what your problem is, don't you? You're a prohibitionist and a teetotaler." Hudson was neither. One Internet critic wrote that, thanks to the Presidential Commission on Drunk Driving and the National Commission Against Drunk Driving, "American Prohibition was reborn."[39] During this same era, the cigarette industry and the National Rifle Association were also invoking the concept of individual rights in response to nanny state attacks on their products.

To what degree was the charge of neoprohibitionism accurate? It was certainly possible to find examples of activists vilifying alcohol without specifically focusing on drunk driving, an example of what MADD critic Radley Balko termed "mission creep." For example, certain MADD public service announcements compared alcohol to heroin. One magazine image depicted a beer bottle as an intravenous syringe. A television spot stated that "if you think there's no difference between heroin and alcohol, you're dead wrong." A Texas MADD official said that golf courses should ban beer drinking.[40] In 2009, when President Barack Obama held a "beer summit" at the White House to soothe racial tensions between Harvard professor Henry Louis Gates Jr. and Cambridge,

Altered World War II poster associating MADD with Prohibition. Courtesy of Frank
Kelly Rich and *Modern Drunkard Magazine*

Massachusetts, police officer James Crowley, a Delaware MADD official, Nancy Raynor, felt the choice of beverage was inappropriate. "It's a well-known fact that young people tend to mimic the actions they see of adults," she said. Raynor received considerable criticism, but RID's Doris Aiken agreed with her, declaring that "getting beer use burned into the minds of small children and their parents normalizes and encourages interest in beer drinking, even at the White House."[41]

Alcohol industry representatives also liked to make another point about anti-alcohol rhetoric: rates of alcohol consumption in America were actually down. For example, less beer was sold in 1996 than twenty years earlier, and during that same time span, there had been a 35 percent drop in spirits consumption. Even George Hacker, of the Center for Science in the Public Interest, which had initiated the Project SMART (Stop Marketing Alcohol on Radio and Television) campaign in the early 1980s, admitted that "America is a very dry country."[42]

But as long as more than 15,000 people were still dying each year in alcohol-related crashes and American drivers still took tens of millions of car rides annually within two hours of consuming alcohol, the decline in drinking provided little solace for RID, MADD, and other activist groups. And while it was possible to find statements by MADD officials that favored eliminating all drinking with driving, the organization fairly reliably stated that it did not have such a goal. In this light, the charge of neoprohibitionism is unfair. "Those who apply the neoprohibitionist label are red-baiting," Hacker told journalist Garrett Peck. "They either have a lot to hide, or their heads are buried in the sand for an appropriate response to America's most-damaging drug problem."[43]

Moreover, there was one form of alcohol use that was clearly a problem. Rates of binge drinking, usually defined as having five drinks (men) or four drinks (women) in one sitting, ranged from 18 to 58 percent for men aged 15–34 and 15 to 38 percent for women in the same age range. According to the Centers for Disease Control and Prevention (CDC), binging accounted for roughly 75 percent of all alcohol consumed in the United States. For those under age 21, an astounding 90 percent of all drinks were consumed during binging in bars or at parties. And binge drinking was directly connected to drunk driving, in large part because men aged 18–34 were the most common demographic group to both binge drink and drive drunk. Indeed, studies showed that binge drinkers were 14 times likelier to drive impaired than nonbinge drinkers.[44] The relationship of binging to driving led both RID and MADD, which had previously limited their attention to drunk driving, to add opposition to binge drinking to their official agendas in the mid-1990s.

Binge drinking led to many other bad outcomes as well, including alcohol poisoning, various crimes, and the victimization of women. It was hard to oppose binge drinking only for the drunk driving risk it caused. So, as had been the case with Project SMART and other efforts to deglamorize drinking, the campaign against binging had an anti-alcohol flavor. A representative public service announcement by MADD about binge drinking showed two empty glasses of alcohol surrounded by the words *assault, drowning, burns, rape,* and *suicide.*

While some of MADD's propaganda could thus be seen as corroborating the charge of neoprohibitionism, the fury unleashed at the organization and anti–drunk driving activism in general beginning in the mid-1990s was truly astonishing, even dwarfing the anger that had originally fueled the efforts of people like Doris Aiken and Candy Lightner. In books, in the print media, on television, and eventually on the Internet, a vitriolic backlash emerged. Although it is difficult to assess how widespread these anti-MADD sentiments were, they are striking in their persistence and their venom. Typical was "Mothers Against Drunk Driving: A Crash Course in MADD," the webpage of David J. Hanson, an emeritus professor of sociology at the State University of New York at Potsdam. Hanson provided an extremely detailed account of what he believed were MADD's offenses, ranging from its use of "junk science" to its "vengeance" to its "Prohibitionist goal." Another representative website was www.getmadd.com, which sought to combat Prohibition, "drip by drip." A typical book was Chris Overbey's *Drinking and Driving: War in America.* But perhaps the most vivid example of anti-MADD sentiments was the formation of a California group that sarcastically called itself "Drunk Drivers Against Mothers (DDAM)." Similarly, in 1996, Slayer, a controversial California heavy metal band, wrote and performed *Ddamm (Drunk Drivers against Mad Mothers):*

> Swerving through the street
> Drunk as fuck
> Searching for a open store
> I think I'm out of luck
> Maybe I'll find a mad mother on patrol
>
> Hit her car
> Smash it up
> Pull her out

Beat her up
Take her money
Run her down

Can't find any beer
It's way past two
There's just one thing
we can do

Hit her car
Smash it up
Pull her out
Beat her up
Take her money
Run her down
Drive her face out of town

Drunk drivers against mad mothers.[45]

What fueled this ferocious anger? Most of the writing conveys an avid libertarianism that characterized efforts to control drunk driving—or smoking, handgun possession, or the use of motorcycle helmets, for that matter—as endangering Americans' freedoms. For example, the getmadd website warned readers about "attempts by government and special interest groups to influence our thinking." Raising the familiar argument that the best way to control drunk driving was not by enacting stricter laws but by changing people's behaviors, the website approvingly quoted conservative New York State governor George E. Pataki: "When government accepts responsibility for people, then people no longer take responsibility for themselves." David Hanson cited dozens of articles arguing that activists were infringing on basic liberties. "MADD fails to understand that in North American systems of justice," one entry read, "accused individuals are innocent until proven guilty by the government." Author Chris Overbey called anti–drunk driving activism "a modern-day witch hunt." Libertarian columnist Llewellyn H. Rockwell Jr. called for the legalization of drunk driving. Although it is difficult to quantify the impact of these libertarian critiques, this type of sentiment has proven strong enough to get many states to repeal mandatory motorcycle helmet laws, contributing to a doubling of motorcyclist deaths between 1997 and 2008.[46]

One group of individuals especially opposed to MADD, not surprisingly, was the staff of *Modern Drunkard Magazine*. In an article called "Fighting MADD," editor Frank Kelly Rich laid out an indictment of the group. Surprisingly, perhaps, given that the magazine's slogan was "standing up for your right to get falling down drunk," the piece was well argued, offering a plethora of indictments along David Hanson's line. At one point, Rich invented an imaginary vigilante group from the Old West, "Cowboys Against Horse Thieves," which begins with a worthy mission but eventually runs out of horse thieves to hang. Eventually, in order to stay in business, the group strings up just about anybody who rides a horse. To Rich, MADD was supporting similarly ludicrous policies. MADD mothers were no longer "a well-meaning group of social advocates," he concluded, but a "fraudulent gang of liberty-squashing fascists."[47]

Beyond its criticisms of MADD, *Modern Drunkard* had additional relevance for the issue of drunk driving. To be sure, some of its policy suggestions, such as allowing drinking on the job, getting paid at work with alcohol, and keeping bars open 24/7, were tongue-in-cheek, as were its columns "Skid Row Poetry" and "Wino Wisdom." But the magazine had identified an audience that was truly aggrieved at how American society was increasingly criticizing and legally limiting a series of pleasurable leisure activities. "We're the new oppressed majority," Rich stated. "We're demonized."[48] *Modern Drunkard*'s message was clear: drinking alcohol is fun and getting drunk is one's right. That some of these heavy drinkers might endanger the lives of innocent people on the way home was nothing that the magazine endorsed. It was just less of a concern than assuring Americans the right to a "drunk."

Modern Drunkard's main audience was young men, probably not unlike the teenager who posted a picture of his totaled car on his Facebook page with the self-referential caption "SuperDude Walked Away from This."[49] But paeans to alcohol came from other demographics as well. Published in 2007, Virginia writer and essayist Barbara Holland's *The Joy of Drinking* celebrated ten thousand years of the "cheering, soothing and socializing pleasures of alcohol." To Holland, getting drunk during Prohibition, as did the likes of Ernest Hemingway, F. Scott Fitzgerald, William Faulkner, and H. L Mencken, was a "gloriously madcap and romantic fling." Unfortunately, "a great wave of Puritanism" had changed things to the point that "a couple of extra nips at a family reunion will have everyone urging you to get help."[50]

One way that MADD's critics underscored what they saw as injustices resulting from aggressive control efforts was to take a page out of MADD's own book and tell powerful stories. One that received wide circulation was that of Debra

Cartoon from *Modern Drunkard Magazine*, which celebrates the pleasure of drinking. Of course, as long as this man does not drive home, he does not threaten the lives of others. Courtesy of Frank Kelly Rich

Bolton, a 45-year-old attorney and mother of two who apparently drank one glass of wine at a Washington dinner party in May 2005. Unfortunately for her, the city was home to a new universal zero-tolerance policy, which enabled police officers to arrest anyone—including drivers over 21—with a BAC of 0.03% or higher for DWI. Driving home, Bolton neglected to put on her headlights and was pulled over. When the officers tested her and found a level of 0.03%, Holland wrote in her book, "they handcuffed her and hauled her off to the hoosegow for DUI." Bolton sat in a jail cell for several hours and later went to court four times to contest a $400 fine, which was eventually rescinded. After refusing to participate in a twelve-week alcohol-counseling program, it took her a month to get her driver's license back.[51]

In one sense, Bolton's story begs the question. Did she forget to use her headlights *because* her BAC was 0.03%, making her mildly impaired? And just as anecdotes about drunk driving tragedies might be misleadingly used for propaganda purposes, the same was possible for stories of supposed misuse of police powers. Nevertheless, incidents such as that involving Bolton, in which a "true" social drinker was victimized by the legal system, did potentially give a bad name to overall enforcement efforts.[52] Indeed, complaints by angry restaurant owners and members of the public quickly led the DC City Council to relax the zero-tolerance policy.

Discussions of supposedly inappropriate arrests often involved sobriety checkpoints, the roadblocks set up by police to test drivers who had neither driven in a dangerous manner nor broken any traffic laws. Checkpoints were of two types: random, in which police breath tested anyone they stopped, and selective, in which only those exhibiting signs of drunkenness were tested. Australia and a few European countries permitted the former, but, because of concerns about civil liberties, most countries did not. Police in the United States had always required probable cause for BAC and sobriety testing when evaluating erratic drivers, and the same concerns applied to checkpoints. The US Supreme Court had ruled in both *Michigan v. Sitz* (1990) and *Indianapolis v. Edmond* (1991) that selective—although not random—testing of drivers stopped at roadblocks was constitutional. As in *Breithaupt v. Abram*, the court's ruling was based on considerations of public health, providing an example in which public health and legal measures served complementary purposes. In practice, properly operated roadblocks caused only brief delays for sober drivers, who were quickly let go. Nevertheless, libertarians continued to loathe such impositions, believing that they violated the Fourth Amendment's prohibition against unreasonable search and seizure.[53]

Though there was true passion from libertarians who opposed anti–drunk driving laws, it should be noted that industry sought to fan the flames of this discontent. The Center for Consumer Freedom and its website, www.consumer freedom.com, which supported the "right of adults and parents to choose what they eat, drink, and how they enjoy themselves," worked hand in hand with Rick Berman and the American Beverage Institute and listed Philip Morris and Anheuser-Busch among its funders. DISCUS helped to fund David Hanson's anti-MADD website. In addition to lobbying Congress, industry also lobbied the public intensively in its efforts to preserve the status quo.[54]

Beyond libertarianism, another factor fueled the backlash against MADD: issues of gender. There were plenty of men involved with MADD, but women— mothers, in particular—had always represented its symbolic core. Meanwhile, men remained roughly twice as likely to die in alcohol-related crashes than women. These gender disparities led to resentment against female activists. For example, male critics implied that women involved in drunk driving control efforts were inappropriately overemotional. Hostility often took the form of fraternity-boy humor, taking aim at the (older) women themselves as opposed to their cause. One tasteless joke that made the rounds, for example, was that without drunks, no future MADD mothers would ever have been conceived. When Candy Lightner, long since absent from drunk driving controversies, appeared on a YouTube video to oppose underage drinking in the military, comments were boorish: "She must be a mean drunk"; "She's just mad because she never got invited to a [kegger] when she was in high school because she was too fat and ugly"; and "She is a horrid woman. What about DAMM, Drunks Against MADD Mothers?"[55]

Despite this backlash, it was entirely reasonable to characterize anti–drunk driving efforts after 1980 as a triumph. In October 2000, President Bill Clinton signed legislation that withheld highway funding from the thirty-one states that had still not adopted a 0.08% BAC. By 2004, all had complied. In the decades after 1980, the number of states with administrative license revocation had increased from three to forty-one, plus the District of Columbia. Between 1983 and 1998, all fifty states, plus the District of Columbia, had passed zero-tolerance laws for drivers under age 21.[56] These laws, combined with the new nationwide drinking age of 21, plus decades of propaganda aimed at teenagers, meant that the anti–drunk driving movement had made particularly great strides in combating DWIs and related injuries and fatalities among the young.

Moreover, research published by the most eminent institutions in the field concluded that these interventions were effective. They lowered fatalities and injuries, among both young and old. For example, a systematic literature review by Ruth A. Shults and her colleagues at the CDC and NHTSA found a roughly 7 percent reduction in deaths in states that had enacted 0.08% laws, smaller than Hingson's figure but significant nonetheless. Similarly, longtime drunk driving researchers James C. Fell and Robert B. Voas, of the Pacific Institute for Research and Evaluation, reported that a 0.08% BAC led to a 5 to 16 percent reduction in crashes, fatalities, and injuries among both heavy and social drinkers.[57]

As for research studying the effects of zero-tolerance laws for younger drinking drivers, Shults reported that six studies had shown reductions of fatal crashes ranging from 3.8 to 24 percent. The impact of new minimum legal drinking-age laws, Shults wrote, had been particularly well researched, and she drew on forty-nine studies to conclude that there was a 10 to 16 percent decline in negative alcohol-related crash outcomes, including nonfatal injuries and deaths. Moreover, once the new laws were in place, these lower figures persisted. Data compiled by NHTSA estimated that in 2008, the 21-drinking-age law saved the lives of 700 people who would have died in car crashes.[58]

Similarly, based on a review of twenty-three studies, the CDC and NHTSA researchers reported that sobriety checkpoints prevented "alcohol-impaired driving, alcohol-related crashes and associated fatal and nonfatal injuries." This finding applied to both random testing and the more selective version done in the United States. Many libertarians did not dispute these data but still considered the strategy too intrusive.[59]

Although checkpoints did directly remove some dangerous drivers from the road, their greatest value was as a general deterrent to drinking drivers who feared being caught. Thus, checkpoint programs were generally accompanied by publicity efforts. Unfortunately, at least for nonlibertarians, they remained "woefully underused" in most jurisdictions and not used at all in twelve states. This was in direct contrast to countries such as Australia, where checkpoints were so ubiquitous and expected that they rarely discovered drivers with BACs higher than 0.05%.[60]

Other interventions worked as well. For example, Paul L. Zador and colleagues at the Insurance Institute for Highway Safety found that administrative license revocation lowered alcohol-related fatal crashes by 9 percent. Meanwhile, according to the CDC's Ann Dellinger and David A. Sleet, ignition interlocks lowered episodes of DWI among recidivists by up to 65 percent and could save up to 750 lives annually if widely installed. These devices mandated that drivers blow into a Breathalyzer-type device installed in their cars prior to starting the ignition. If the machine detected the presence of any alcohol, it prevented the car from starting. Also, research showed that server intervention programs of the type championed by Morris Chafetz could effectively teach bar and restaurant workers strategies to prevent intoxication and alcohol-impaired driving among customers. These efforts worked best in countries like Australia, where officials actively publicized and prosecuted the "places of last drink," and less well in the United States, where compliance among servers and enforcement by local authorities remained variable. Owing in part to insufficient research, the jury was still out on whether designated driver programs and other similar strategies, such as serving "mocktails" and other nonalcoholic beverages at the end of parties, prevented drunk driving. Innovations in this area continued, however, such as Y Drive, a national program promoted by Candy Lightner, in which people, after a night of drinking, are driven home in their own cars.[61]

Another effective intervention dealt with the issue of drunk driving only indirectly but definitely saved lives of people in crashes: the use of restraints. As early as the late 1950s, people like William Haddon, Pat Moynihan, and Ralph Nader had concluded that the ability to change the behaviors of drinking drivers would always be limited, despite aggressive publicity campaigns and legal measures. They thus advocated making cars and highways as safe as possible. By the first decade of the twenty-first century, all states except New Hampshire had mandatory seat belt laws, and use averaged 82 percent nationwide. Because seat belts reduced fatal and nonfatal injuries, getting people to buckle up—including drinkers and those riding in their cars—saved lives. So did air bags for frontal crashes. The combination of air bag and seat belt use reduced fatalities in frontal crashes by 11 percent.[62]

Experts agreed on one final fact about drunk driving control. The more that people anticipated being stopped and arrested, the less likely they were to drive when intoxicated. As Laurence Ross had pointed out, this finding helped to explain the temporary successes of intensive crackdowns, accompanied by major publicity efforts, such as those in Great Britain in 1967 and Australia in the 1980s. Thus, in the summer of 2006, the National Highway Traffic Safety Administration announced that it was working with law enforcement officials across the country to crack down on drunken driving. It inaugurated the campaign with a series of original public service announcements depicting young men being pulled over in their cars as they sat chest-deep in beer, wine, or liquor. Yet the challenge of maintaining such intensity over long periods of time persisted. Such announcements were expensive to air, and drunk driving campaigns deflected attention from other police business.[63]

Importantly, statistics also revealed which interventions did not seem to work. For instance, as Laurence Ross had long argued, more severe punishments did not deter drunk drivers or lower rates of DWI, injury, and fatality. As early as the mid-1990s, RID and other anti–drunk driving organizations had gone on the record as discouraging draconian penalties, such as mandatory jail sentences, for first-time offenders who had not caused significant harm. And although certain prosecutors, such as Long Island's Kathleen Rice, successfully prosecuted drunk drivers for murder based on "depraved indifference to human life," most district attorneys preferred manslaughter charges when passengers, pedestrians, or other drivers died at the hands of a drunk driver.[64] While extreme penalties were satisfying from the perspective of getting revenge, juries still declined to equate drunk driving fatalities with deaths caused by guns or other weapons. The maturation of the anti–drunk driving movement meant that punishments had to make sense from both a scientific and a policy perspective. Murder charges were simply not effective deterrents.

Another intervention that did not work was the so-called do-it-yourself Breathalyzer, a variation of Robert Borkenstein's machine installed in bars and restaurants. The idea was that drinking customers could check their BACs before leaving, and those with high levels could wait an hour and have something to eat. Borkenstein had promoted these devices since 1970, but interest in their use grew in conjunction with the anti–drunk driving crusade of the early 1980s. Much to Borkenstein's chagrin, trials of these devices led to a very different sort of behavior: binge drinking, in which individuals used the Breathalyzers to compete for the highest BACs. At one bar in Washington in November 1982, patrons chanted "go, go, go" as one man blew into an "Alcohol Guard" and registered a 0.38% reading. He raised his arms in triumph and shouted, "A new record."[65] It was hard to think of a more vivid symbolic repudiation of the crusade christened by Borkenstein and championed by MADD. Conversely, such devices became routine fixtures in Australian drinking establishments, where they were used for their intended purpose, in large part because of the high likelihood that intoxicated drivers would actually be stopped by the police. Breathalyzers also became commonplace in Australian wine country, prompting revelers to wait until they had sobered up before heading to the next vineyard.[66]

There were also interventions that had never been adequately studied. Foremost among these was use of the slogan "Responsible drinking," which the alcohol industry had long championed. A 2009 paper published in the journal *Health, Education & Behavior* found that the term was defined poorly and used imprecisely. The authors concluded that it was as much a "marketing tactic" as a genuine effort to lower the amount of binge drinking, drunk driving, and other problems brought on by excessive alcohol use.[67] Nevertheless, the concept of responsible drinking had gained a legitimacy that went largely unchallenged by most Americans.

Knowing which anti–drunk driving measures should and should not be prioritized was extremely helpful, but such knowledge did not always ensure positive change. The backlash against MADD and other activist groups described above surely sapped enthusiasm and funding for effective interventions. As had always been the case, local officials were often unwilling or unable to help. Robert Borkenstein had long termed the lack of enforcement of DWI laws "shocking," but in jurisdictions that lacked the political will or financial resources, police efforts to identify drivers with BACs of 0.08% and higher through checkpoints, crackdowns, or other means continued to sputter. For example, the number of annual arrests for drunk driving, which had peaked at 2 million in the 1980s, had declined by 30 percent, to 1.4 million, in the early twenty-first century. Similarly, some states balked at the notion of installing ignition interlocks in the cars of recidivist drunk drivers, owing either to cost or to the potential unpopularity of such a move. Enforcement of interlock installation varied in states that allowed them, in part because many judges often believed that this punishment was too harsh, especially for first-time offenders. Finally, saving lives continued to rely on behavioral modification. Intoxicated individuals could continue to get into their cars, decline to use their seat belts, and most distressingly, ask someone else to blow into their ignition interlocks to start their cars.[68]

The backlash also manifested itself by limiting the types of law that were ultimately passed. Looking back on the 1988 surgeon general's workshop, which had advocated a series of interventions for drunk driving control, the results were a mixed bag. While the conference probably did create energy for lowering BACs, help popularize initiatives such as designated drivers and sobriety checkpoints, and focus attention on the problem of teenage drinking and driving, many of the more progressive public health–type measures that were advocated were never adopted. For example, despite an increase in the federal excise tax on beer in 1991 and strong public support for additional tax increases on beer, tax rates at both the federal and state levels remained very low, thus precluding one proven strategy for decreasing heavy alcohol intake and drunk driving.

Most notably, the reflexive association of alcohol, including excessive drinking, with manly feats, sexual conquest, and simply having a good time persisted. In the late 1980s and the 1990s, for example, Anheuser-Busch featured a party dog, Spuds MacKenzie, in its advertisements for Bud Lite beer and introduced the Bud Bowl, an animated football game played by Budweiser beer bottles, during Super Bowl telecasts. Thanks to self-regulation by DISCUS and the beer industry, some of the more outrageous advertisements have disappeared, but the alcohol industry continues to sponsor for college students spring-break sporting and musical events that have been termed a "tsunami of booze."[69] Even as college presidents have expressed legitimate concerns about binge drinking on campus through their Amethyst Initiative, George Hacker, of the Center for Science in the Public Interest, notes that alcohol advertising continues to dominate college stadiums. In 1998, the clothing manufacturer Abercrombie & Fitch even included a list of sweet alcoholic drinks in its "Back to School" catalog, urging students to engage in "some creative drinking this semester."

It is reasonable to conclude that while the alcohol industry was not able to prevent Koop's workshop from happening, the industry's emphasis on responsible drinking and its ability to attract people like Cindi Lamb and Candy Lightner helped it to deflect much of the momentum that came out of the conference. Indeed, when the Institute of Medicine issued its 2003 report, *Reducing Underage Drinking,* many of the recommendations about controlling alcohol availability and marketing were identical to those that Koop had sought to implement fifteen years earlier. This lack of progress is especially disappointing given recent data showing that exposure to alcohol advertisements leads adolescents to drink sooner and more heavily.[70]

Finally, drunk driving control continued to be hindered by a very old problem: experts disagreed as to what the data actually showed. Despite the improvements made with the introduction of the Fatality Analysis Reporting System, traffic safety researchers at the CDC, NHTSA, the Pacific Institute for Research and Evaluation, and elsewhere were always the first to admit how difficult it was to compile definitive statistics. This was true for several reasons.

First, it was rare for a specific intervention aimed against drunk driving to be initiated in a vacuum—that is, without other related programs being introduced as well. To take only one example, if a city initiated a program of roadblocks at the same time the statewide BAC was lowered from 0.10% to 0.08%, and the alcohol-related fatality rate went down, which intervention should be deemed responsible?

Second, the vast majority of epidemiological studies were not prospective randomized controlled trials, which did the best job of eliminating biases when evaluating a given innovation. Rather, this research generally examined events that had already occurred, using sophisticated statistical techniques, such as logistic regression, to try to tease out associations between various interventions and outcomes. Even when such associations were present, it was often impossible to definitively ascertain cause and effect. As the historian of medicine Keith Wailoo has written, "epidemiological 'facts' are notoriously unreliable."[71]

Third, as with William Haddon's original figure of 25,000 annual deaths caused by drunk driving, experts disagreed on the newest figures—and what they meant. In 2009, NHTSA reported that there were still roughly 11,000 annual alcohol-related traffic fatalities involving a driver with a BAC of 0.08% or higher. This number approached a more familiar 15,000 if one also included drivers and pedestrians with any alcohol involvement at all. If one used the 11,000 figure, the percentage of traffic fatalities involving alcohol had declined from roughly 50 percent in 1980 to 32 percent: a 36 percent drop. But other estimates were even higher, citing a more than 50 percent drop.[72] Activist groups used such figures to argue that the initial declines in drunk driving injuries and deaths had leveled off and were still an enormous problem, but critics demurred. These data, they claimed, were unreliable because "alcohol-related" fatalities were just that: related. They did not prove causation.[73]

———

Efforts to control drunk driving between 1990 and 2010 demonstrated the obstacles that face longstanding public health programs that have already achieved significant success. Maintaining focus on a specific problem for a long period of time is an ongoing challenge. When RID and MADD first publicized drunk driving in the early 1980s, most Americans had never conceptualized it as an "issue." But twenty years later, the shock value of images of dead teenagers and smashed cars had begun to wear off. In addition, after years of arguments as to why the liberties of drinking drivers needed to be curtailed, the pendulum was swinging back in the other direction. Finally, the seeming inability of scientists, statisticians, and other leaders in the field to generate definitive data led to an inevitable weariness among the public. Depending on whom one asked, lower BACs either saved lives or just created a hassle for social drinkers, and drunk driving had either come under control or was still an epidemic.

Yet one thing was certain. Stories involving drunk drivers—especially those involving celebrities, fatalities, or both—continued to generate incredibly powerful emotions. Such stories are a fruitful way to revisit the cultural, political, and economic factors that have both propelled and limited the war on drunk driving.

CHAPTER SIX

More (and More) Tragedies

Thousands of terrible stories of alcohol-related fatalities had made the newspapers since the 1980s, but even veteran drunk driving activists were stunned to learn about the mid-afternoon July 26, 2009, crash in which a 36-year-old mother drove her minivan 1.7 miles the wrong way on New York's Taconic Parkway before crashing into an oncoming sport utility vehicle. Diane Schuler killed herself, her 2-year-old-daughter, her three young nieces, and the three occupants of the SUV. Her 5-year-old son survived. Police found a shattered vodka bottle in the rubble. Schuler had a blood alcohol level of 0.19%, more than twice as high as New York's legal limit of 0.08%. She was also high on marijuana at the time of the crash. The Schuler story was particularly gruesome because one of the children in her car had spoken with Schuler's brother (the girl's father) a half hour before the crash and had seemed upset. When Schuler's brother later spoke directly to his sister, she had seemed disoriented. He told her to park and wait for him to come, but she chose to continue driving.[1]

For several weeks, especially in the Hudson Valley, where the accident occurred, the Schuler case pushed concerns about the flagging economy, health care reform, and the war in Afghanistan off people's plates as they tried to make sense of this tragedy. Were the BAC and marijuana readings inaccurate, as Schuler's survivors insisted? Or was Schuler an alcoholic? What did her husband know or not know about his wife's drinking and smoking habits? Did the fact that she drove 1.7 miles into oncoming traffic before crashing mean she was accustomed to driving drunk? And how could anyone—especially someone who was by all accounts an excellent mother and aunt—put children at mortal risk?

Although the New York State legislature would quickly pass a law in response to the Schuler tragedy, making it a felony to drive drunk with a child in one's vehicle,[2] larger lessons from the case were hard to draw. With few satisfying explanations on the issues of Schuler's past substance use and why she did what she did, commentators mostly reacted with bafflement and outrage.

The case also raised a broader issue. What was the significance of such a grisly story in the context of overall drunk driving control? After all, drunk driving in 2010 was nothing like drunk driving in 1950 or, for that matter, 1980. There had been decades of activism, a growing embrace of designated drivers and stiffening of laws, such as automatic license revocation and mandatory minimum sentences, which ensured that justice was much more likely to be served. Efforts to prevent intoxicated people from getting behind the wheel, according to Lawrence P. Lonero, of the American Automobile Association, had been a "spectacular success."[3]

So was the Schuler case simply an aberrancy amid progress? What about other prominent DWI cases—ranging from a celebrity actress with three convictions to a professional football player who killed a man crossing the street to a drunk off-duty police officer who fled after causing a crash? Although these tragic examples are not necessarily representative, they nevertheless show that drunk driving remained a persistent problem in the United States a century after cars had been invented and nearly thirty years after the formation of Mothers Against Drunk Drivers.

More than the words of bereaved parents, solemn pronouncements by legislators, or campaigns for responsible drinking by the beverage industry, the public's reaction to both the Schuler case and these other well-publicized drunk driving stories provides key insights into how American society continues to view a series of intertwining issues: alcoholism, driving, legal restrictions, evidence, activism, risk, blame, and most importantly, the proper balance between safety and liberty. This chapter uses these cases to examine four questions in turn.

- Why has American society continued to tolerate an activity that is morally objectionable and an indisputable public health hazard?
- Is there indeed a right to drink and drive or, to put it another way, to drive in an impaired state?
- How should concerns about drunk driving be balanced with a new series of competing public health issues, some of which are also related to traffic safety?

• How helpful are the concepts of blame and culpability when you are trying to change behaviors and save lives?

Two drunk driving cases, those of the actress Lindsay Lohan and of three drinking buddies in Colorado, address the first question, underscoring some of the reasons that drunk driving, despite negative publicity and stricter laws, continues to be tolerated. Lohan's two drunk driving arrests took place in 2007. In the first episode, on May 26, Lohan's speeding Mercedes-Benz "jumped a sidewalk and got wedged between two trees." Lohan was convicted of DWI, lost her driver's license, and entered a rehabilitation facility. Then, in the early morning hours of July 24, 2007, two weeks after leaving rehab, Lohan drove drunk again. In this case, she was chasing a car driven by the mother of her personal assistant, whom the actress had fired earlier in the day. Police reported that Lohan was unable to walk a straight line, refused a breath test, and had cocaine in her car. They charged her with DWI, driving without a license (hers was still suspended), and drug possession. Eventually, her BAC came back at 0.12%, higher than California's legal limit of 0.08%.[4]

Lohan was hardly the only Hollywood star prone to drink and drive. Others arrested for DWI in recent years have included actors Mel Gibson, Rip Torn, and Tracy Morgan, singer Britney Spears (whose children were in the car), and celebrities Paris Hilton and Nicole Richie. The arrests of these individuals received considerable attention from the media, owing to the offenders' fame. Television and Internet websites readily displayed unflattering mug shots of the celebrities in question, many of whom still looked inebriated. Some commentators hoped to make these stories into cautionary tales. "Make drunk-driving stars do perp walk on red carpet," urged columnist Linda McAvoy of the *Toronto Star*. "Impaired driving should be viewed for what it is: life-endangering behavior, a stupid, needless crime, and a very big deal."[5]

But even McAvoy admitted that such a scenario was unlikely, at least in Hollywood, noting that "shame doesn't play a big part in celebrity-DUI arrests." Indeed, as *USA Today* noted, the cycle of "drugs, clubs, DUIs and rehab" was "glamorous." Just as the public was transfixed with celebrities' marriages and divorces, their crash diets and their parties, it was drawn to their transgressions as well. That is, the "bad habits" of the celebrities—such as infidelity, smoking, partying, drinking, and drunk driving—made them "romantic outlaws" not limited by normal societal rules. As one blogger put it, "They're young, rich, and in Hollywood, what do you expect the stories to be like? Do I condone using drugs and alcohol and driving, no. But I support their right to 'rock n roll' all night and 'party' everyday! Hey I wouldn't want everyone to know what drugs I had in my pocket in my younger years." "Her mug shot is heartbreaking," a worshipful fan remarked about Lohan. "She doesn't deserve to be labeled a criminal because she is obviously ill and needs real help."[6]

Such behavior was not limited to Hollywood. In late 2007, cnn.com reported on a Facebook group, "Thirty Reasons Girls Should Call It a Night," which featured college-aged women getting drunk, vomiting, falling down, and urinating publicly. The group reported having more than 150,000 members. Meanwhile, books with titles such as *Naptime Is the New Happy Hour* and *Daddy Needs a Drink* promoted the virtues of alcohol for parents, as did the blog Drunken Housewife.com. Perhaps the zeitgeist was best conveyed by "Hooray for Beer," a paean to the drink recorded by the Texas punk rock band Bowling for Soup:

> Now everything is hunky dory
> The stars are shining all around me
> There's a happy ending to my story now
> I wanna tell the whole world
> Hooray for Beer!
> I'm really glad you're here
> Let's make this moment last
> You feel so right
> Wanna be with you all night
> Shout it out
> Hooray for Beer![7]

The actions of young Hollywood celebrities (and their college counterparts) had come to represent the exact confluence of alcohol, sex, partying, and fast cars that the Project SMART campaign had warned about in the 1980s. Once again, while ostensibly encouraging responsible drinking and designated drivers, the beverage and hospitality industries tacitly condoned this lifestyle through both their advertisements and their sponsorship of events. For example, Svedka vodka had been planning to sponsor Lohan's twenty-first birthday party at Caesar's Palace in Las Vegas, although the event was canceled after her first DWI. As of 2010, three sports stadiums bore the names of local beer manufacturers: Coors Field (Denver), Busch Stadium (St. Louis), and Miller Park (Milwaukee). At National Football League games, beer advertisements appeared throughout stadiums and vendors sold 24-ounce cups. At Giants Stadium in New Jersey's

Meadowlands, drunken men congregated at Gate D (nicknamed "Gate Drunk") at halftime and urged women passersby to display their breasts.[8] That many of these fans drove home intoxicated was a given: Giants Stadium, like the Capitol Center, which had hosted the 1983 Stevie Wonder concert, was not well serviced by public transportation. Finally, beginning in 2004, distilleries began to sponsor National Association of Stock Car Racing (NASCAR) driving teams, which resulted in the placement of alcohol industry logos on cars that were traveling extremely fast (and not very responsibly). Budweiser and Miller were the official beers of the Daytona and Indianapolis Speedways, respectively. What had emerged was what historian John C. Burnham termed the "vice-industrial complex," in which vices "had become in and of themselves major shapers of American society, culture and history."[9] Drunk driving was not actually encouraged, but it was subtly countenanced, especially for the young adults most prone to the act.

Related to the notion of drunk driving as somehow acceptable was its ongoing reputation as normal behavior—something that everyone did at one point or another. As the columnist Ann Coulter wrote, "Boatloads of people have driven home from a party after having one too many beers at some point in their lives."[10] To the degree that this was true, it was difficult to condemn drunk driving outright.

The lure of driving drunk—and getting away with it—remained most pronounced for men in their late teens and twenties. As William Haddon, Pat Moynihan, and others had noted as early as the 1960s, getting drunk and getting in the car and speeding served as a measure of one's masculinity, one's willingness to take risks, and one's interest in flouting the law. In addition to its connection to dangerous behaviors, wrote communications expert Lance A. Strate in the book *Men, Masculinity and the Media*, beer drinking also challenged inebriated young drivers to take "immediate and decisive action" and demonstrate "fine control" despite their impaired state.

Lyrics from the song *D.U.I.* by the California punk rock band Offspring conveyed this idea. Despite the fact that "the cops they took my license away" and efforts by his friends to call him a cab, the song's protagonist gets into his car, takes a shot, and turns the key. "I drink and drive, feel so alive," he sings. Even though he admits he "can't drive a straight line," he thinks he drives "all right" and even tries to set a speed record for drunk driving. And, to underscore how what he knows he is doing is wrong, the singer adds "Designate someone other than me."[11]

Whereas most speeding drunk drivers still were men, women occasionally participated in such rituals as well. In the early morning of January 18, 2008, three friends from Lafayette, Colorado, Michael Martin Flaherty, 21, Lucas Raymond Snyder, 21, and Amber Dawn Kowalski, 23, all of whom had been drinking beer at a bar, got into a Subaru Impreza WRX with either Snyder or Kowalski behind the wheel. The car reached almost 110 miles per hour before it crashed into a light pole in nearby Louisville, Colorado, splitting in half and immediately killing all three of them. Three children and one unborn child (being carried by Snyder's girlfriend) were among the survivors.

Flaherty loved fast cars, his family said, and decorated his room with photographs of NASCAR drivers. Along with his father, David, and his sister, Lorie, he spent many days and nights at local racetracks. Kowalski's ex-boyfriend, Wes Abila, said that both he and Kowalski liked to race cars, but he had warned her not to drive recklessly. "That car was her baby," Kowalski's friend, Meliny Archuleta, said about the Subaru involved in the crash.[12]

While surely a horrible tragedy worthy of media coverage, the Louisville crash generated particular attention because of a comment made to a reporter by Lorie Flaherty. "The thing that really makes me feel much better about this is they died doing what they loved to do—they were drinking, they were going fast and they were together," she said. "It gives me comfort, it does, to know those three things."[13] *Entertainment Tonight*, among other media outlets, picked up on these remarks and broadcast them across the country. The resultant maelstrom led to provocative discussions, particularly on the Internet, about drinking too much and driving too fast.

A good example was the website of the *Boulder* (CO) *Daily Camera*.[14] Predictably, writers castigated Lorie Flaherty's acceptance of a seemingly preventable catastrophe. "I have never written in about an article/story before but I was so sickened by Lori [*sic*] Flaherty's comments," one correspondent wrote. "How can she think that's OK?" Another author rejected Flaherty's romanticizing the pursuit of speed and booze: "No, I won't respect people who endanger their own lives, other's lives, and who take life so cheaply as to do something this insane and leave kids behind." Finally, responding to a comment about "3 beautiful lives taken too soon," another writer retorted that the lives had not been taken at all. Rather, "they took their own lives by drinking, driving and speeding."

More interesting than these replies, however, were those that either validated what Lorie Flaherty had said or what the three friends had done. Providing any type of justification for such a jarring mistake, while surely done to ease the pain of the survivors, nevertheless demonstrated a willingness to tolerate drunk driving even though it had just taken three young lives. Some characterized what had happened in fatalistic terms. "People die in all sorts of ways," wrote one person. Then, invoking the exact language that anti–drunk driving activists had so long opposed, this author added, "Life is an accident waiting to happen." Some writers invoked religion to make the same point. "God takes us all at different times," one wrote, while another added "God must need them more than we do down here."

Other posters suggested that what the three friends had done was not so out of the ordinary. "We as human beings are not [in]fallible," one wrote. "We are not perfect nor are our choices." Another writer asked readers, "Do any of you remember how you were when you were in your 20's? You cannot sit here and say that you were perfect, that you have never ever had a drink and driven." Perhaps the most perceptive remarks came from someone who connected alcohol abuse to "young people who don't have a sense of purpose or meaning in their lives." Even having children, the writer added, "carries no responsibility whatso-ever." The crash was "symptomatic of a society that views things as drinking heavily and driving fast as acceptable behavior."

This sense of drunk driving as an antidote to unfulfilled lives was conveyed in a *New York Times* article published on September 2, 2006. Entitled "Youthful Binge Drinking Fueled by Boredom of the Open West," reporter Timothy Egan described the heavy drinking that characterized life in rural areas of "frontier" states like Wyoming, Montana, North Dakota, and South Dakota. Not all these drinkers drove, but many did. "Had a kid, drunk, flipped his car going 80 miles an hour, and that killed him," recalled Wyoming sheriff Scott Steward.[15]

Boredom promoted binge drinking, Egan wrote, but drinking and drunk driving were also part of the culture. Drinking was a "rite of passage" for children well under the official drinking age and a way for young men "to prove themselves in the West." Montana had only recently passed an open container law prohibiting unsealed alcohol products in a moving vehicle—and there had been stiff opposition. Wyoming, Egan reported, still allowed open containers as long as the driver was not holding them. According to Rosie Buzzas, a Montana state legislator and alcohol counselor, her typical constituent's attitude was "I work hard and I'll be damned if I'm not going to have a beer or two on the way home." Not surprisingly, Montana was the "worst state for drunken driving" in 2009. Perhaps a documentary on drunk driving, *Drinking and Driving: The Toll, the Tears,* summarized this mindset best: "Driving is freedom. Freedom is a good time. A good time is drinking. That seems to be the cycle of growing up in America."[16]

Wisconsin was another state that critics believed had "a mindset that accepts, even celebrates, getting drunk." As of 2008, it had issued roughly 5,000 liquor licenses, more per capita than any other state. Milwaukee, in particular, was linked with the rise of the beer industry in America, once housing the Miller, Pabst, and Schlitz breweries. Accompanying the heavy drinking in taverns across the state were lenient laws for those on their way home from such establishments. Not until a fifth DWI was someone charged with a felony. Wisconsin was also one of twelve states that prohibited sobriety checkpoints. Most remarkably, in an era concerned about underage drinking, restaurants and bars could legally serve alcohol to teenagers accompanied by parents who gave their consent.[17]

There also continued to be considerable tolerance for drunk driving when there were fatalities. On the morning of March 14, 2009, a car being driven by Cleveland Browns wide receiver Donte Stallworth, who had been drinking at a bar in Miami Beach's fabled Fontainebleau Hotel, struck and killed a pedestrian, Mario Reyes. Reyes, a construction worker, had been crossing the street when he was hit by Stallworth, whose BAC eventually tested at 0.126%, well over Florida's 0.08% limit. Police estimated that Stallworth had been driving at 50 miles per hour in a 40-mph zone.

Stallworth pled guilty to DUI manslaughter and received only a 30-day jail sentence, along with 2 years of house arrest, 8 years of probation, 1,000 hours of community service, and a suspension of his driver's license for at least 5 years and as much as his whole life. Stallworth also reached a "confidential financial settlement" with the Reyes family. To be sure, he had no previous criminal record and had willingly accepted responsibility for what he had done. But being given a month in jail (of which he ultimately only served 24 days) looked a lot like the typical slap on the wrist that RID and MADD had inveighed against for so long.[18]

Some critics believed that the lenient sentence occurred because Stallworth was a celebrity. "Justice wasn't served," said one retired Cleveland police officer. "The well-connected and the money were served. I'm so tired of seeing celebrities beat the law." But things were more complicated. As fate would have it, another National Football League wide receiver, Plaxico Burress, of the New York Giants, was also in the news, having carried a loaded gun to a New York City nightclub and accidentally shot himself in the leg. Burress, who had injured only himself, got two years in prison, even though he had not killed or injured anyone else. It seemed that it was more the nature of the crime—drunk driving—as opposed to who Stallworth was that had once again led to leniency. Moreover, as Bill Lubinger and Gabriel Baird wrote in the Cleveland *Plain Dealer*, plea-bargains after drunk driving crashes were still commonplace in Florida, Ohio, and elsewhere. There was also the issue of Reyes's own partial culpability, as he had apparently been jaywalking at the time of the crash.[19]

There was surprise and disappointment at the judge's decision, even from long-suffering Browns' fans, who desperately wanted the receiver in the lineup. "Stallworth killed a man because Stallworth was drunk as a skunk," one wrote. "Stallworth should rot in jail for 10 years rather than get a get out of jail free card." Another wrote, "I am sick and tired of people making excuses for anyone who gets behind the wheel after even having one drink. I don't do it. Never have. Never will."

But as with the Colorado case, a surprising number of commentators saw things very differently, resurrecting the sort of fatalistic language that drunk driving critics as far back as William Haddon had tried to expunge. That is, Stallworth's conscious act of choosing to get into his car and drive in an intoxicated state was explained away by the old "there but for the grace of God go I" defense.[20] "Look, I bet many of the posters in this forum have driven with a 0.12 BAC before," wrote one correspondent on the *Plain Dealer* website. "It could have happened to anybody." Another poster agreed: "If ANY of you have ever driven after 2 beers or a few drinks, or you rode with someone else who did, you [are] no better than Stallworth or anyone else, you're just luckier." The word *accident* was frequently invoked. "He partied and got busted by a freak accident" one poster wrote. "Accidents happen," another opined. "Nobody can be sure that it was because of drunk driving." Another stated that "both of them were in the wrong place at the wrong time."

Finally, as another poster noted, the legal system continued to thwart efforts to prosecute drunk driving, helping to explain the judge's decision. "I don't know why everyone is stunned at the sentence," he wrote. "Under the causation laws in the great state of Florida, Stallworth's attorneys would have created enough reasonable doubt about the case, and Donte would have walked on DUI manslaughter charges." Indeed, that Reyes may have been jaywalking created the exact sort of legal loophole that Lawrence Taylor and other DWI specialists urged fellow defense lawyers to exploit.

Another case from later in 2009 revealed a different way for a drunk driver to try to avoid severe punishment. In the early morning of September 27, 2009,

Vionique Valnord, a 32-year-old aspiring missionary, was hailing a cab in Brooklyn. Suddenly, a Jeep Cherokee driven by New York City police officer Andrew Kelly struck her, hitting her so hard that her body flew into a traffic light. The three passengers in the car, including fellow officer Michael Downs, fled the scene. Kelly stayed behind, chewing gum and drinking water given to him by another police officer, but refused a BAC test. He later left the crash scene, claiming that a responding officer had given him permission.

It was not until seven hours after the crash that Kelly's BAC was drawn at a hospital. According to the *Daily News*, Kelly had been uncooperative, stating that doctors would have to "tie [him] down" in order to obtain his blood. When the test came back, Kelly's BAC was 0.0%, entirely negative. The news stunned all of New York, especially Valnord's grieving mother Philoisa, who called Kelly and Downs "cowards" who had left her dying daughter as if she were "garbage."[21] A headline in the *Daily News* asked: "No Booze = No Convictions?"

Local prosecutors remained confident, claiming that Kelly had admitted drinking six to eight beers before driving and that he "reeked of alcohol" and was "slurring his speech."[22] There was also said to be a video of him drinking at a local bar that night. Nevertheless, the negative result, quite plausible if obtained more than seven hours after someone's last drink, meant that a conviction was much less certain. Kelly's prosecution, a local lawyer remarked, would now come down to the word of one officer against another. Ultimately, Kelly pled guilty to vehicular manslaughter, but faced a sentence of only 90 days in jail. "90 DAYS!!!!!!" wrote one angry citizen. "Are you kidding me?!!! For drunk driving, killing a young woman and covering it up! AND HE'S A POLICE OFFICER WHOSE JOB IT IS TO UPHOLD THE LAW!! What a travesty of justice!"[23]

It can be argued that because the accused drunk driver in this instance was a police officer, it made a cover-up more likely and thus was not a representative case. But it was only a variation on a theme. According to traffic safety expert James Fell, it has become commonplace—as high as 80 percent in some areas—for ordinary citizens to decline BAC testing, especially if their level is apt to be very high. Even though refusal of testing is admissible in court and can be considered as evidence of guilt, such a strategy may lead to milder punishments. More broadly, both the Stallworth and Kelly cases were examples of clever strategies that increased the likelihood that drunk drivers would either go free or receive relatively minor punishments. That intoxicated drivers also used smartphone apps to identify and avoid sobriety checkpoints underscored how drunk driving was still a game of cat and mouse.[24]

In sum, drunk driving, which all but the most provocative philosophers would characterize as a morally objectionable public health hazard, persists in the United States because it is convenient in a country without adequate public transportation, is a rite of passage, a macho activity, and an inextricable element of partying and good times—a connection persistently emphasized by the alcohol industry. And it still, at times, engenders considerable sympathy in the courtroom, even when deaths result, leading to relatively lenient punishments.

But what about the second question this chapter raises? Is it as acceptable as before for social drinkers to get behind the wheel? What, if anything, has changed about the right to drink and drive, assuming one does not break the law?

Here things are not so different. Responsible drinking, the notion long championed by the beverage industry, has not only become the mantra for drinking itself but has also provided an acceptable guidepost for drinkers who engage in potentially risky activities, such as driving. The furor that erupted after the 1970 Licensed Beverage Industries "Know your limits" advertisements is now hard to find. Part of the explanation for this change is the success of alcohol industry lobbying groups—most notably the Century Council and DISCUS—in making the notion of moderation a mainstream idea. These groups have attained increased credibility by partnering with MADD to advocate for a 0.08% BAC, administrative license revocation, and other anti–drunk driving measures. According to its website, the Century Council fights drunk driving by promoting "responsible decision making regarding beverage alcohol." In 2008, the US Department of Agriculture included DISCUS's "Educational Tool Kit on Beverage Alcohol Consumption," information that enabled health professionals to allow their patients to drink alcohol responsibly, as part of its Dietary Guidelines for Americans.[25] Alcohol was liquid bread once again.

What this sanctioning of responsible drinking means, however, is that the alcohol industry has helped to push more aggressive strategies for limiting impaired driving off the table. Perhaps the best example of industry's power is the almost complete absence of efforts to lower the BAC in the United States to 0.05%, the level at which informed observers know increased risk of crashes begins. Studies since the 1930s have regularly shown that this level impairs driving skills for most people; research updating Robert Borkenstein's Grand Rapids study now estimates that drivers with BACs between 0.05% and 0.08% have a four to ten times higher risk of crash. In addition, as of 2009, most industrialized nations have lowered their legal BACs to 0.05% or less, leaving the United States, once again, as extremely tolerant. These other countries include Norway,

Russia, and Sweden at 0.02% and Australia, Denmark, Finland, France, Germany, Israel, Italy, and Spain at 0.05%. Top researchers, such as James Fell and Robert Voas, of the Pacific Institute for Research and Evaluation, believe that international data clearly show additional reductions of crashes, injuries, and fatalities in countries that have moved to 0.05%. The deterrent effect, they believe, is both specific and general. Some of the prevented deaths result from discouraging those arrested for mildly impaired driving from doing it again, while others result from alerting the public to the more restrictive limits and keeping drunk driving offenses in the news.[26]

Some of this inertia may result from obfuscation. It is common, for example, for critics of drunk driving laws to make the utterly misleading claim that one or two drinks with dinner is enough alcohol to put most drivers into the illegal BAC range.[27] This is simply not true. Getting to 0.05% generally entails two to three drinks on an empty stomach and getting to 0.08% requires even more alcohol. But even activists who know that there is almost always genuine impairment between 0.05% and 0.08% have largely dropped the issue, believing that they have no chance of competing against Washington lobbying groups determined to protect alcohol sales. The political clout of beverage and hospitality industry representatives, like those who took on C. Everett Koop and those who marched over to Capitol Hill after Cindi Lamb's 1991 speech, is simply too strong. MADD, for example, supports legislation that would establish a legal BAC of 0.05% per se for adult drivers previously convicted of DWI—but not for all drivers.[28] And even this idea is not high on its legislative wish list. Thus, in contrast to what happens in many other countries, impaired driving remains a right in the United States. As long as a driver keeps below 0.08%, downing two or three drinks and then hopping in a car—almost certainly buzzed—is still acceptable, as long as he or she is not apprehended or is able to perform roadside sobriety tests adequately.

The notion of responsible drinking is problematic for another reason: it characterizes drinking before driving as either moderate or heavy, implying that a clear distinction exists between the two states. In this sense, responsible drinking has become the social drinking of the early twenty-first century. Mirroring Max Hayman's arguments from the 1960s, such terminology has the potential to minimize very real problems related to alcohol use. Even those persons genuinely planning to limit their intake might not do so because small amounts of alcohol potentially impair not only one's driving but one's judgment as well. As Robert Williams, who killed seven pedestrians at a bus stop in August 1984, later reflected: "When you start drinking, you're not driving. You don't think about driving under the influence of alcohol, because you're not going anywhere at that particular time. Once the alcohol has started setting in, starts working on you, then you lose a sense of thinking."[29]

As anti–drunk driving activists continue to struggle with lax enforcement and the continued acceptance of social drinking and driving, a third potential challenge has emerged: other driving-related activities that cause distractions. This is not an entirely new issue. For example, both before and during the MADD era, car crashes were at times caused by entirely sober drivers who had apparently fallen asleep at the wheel. In August 1946, for example, former First Lady Eleanor Roosevelt may have dozed off while driving on New York's Saw Mill River Parkway before crossing the dividing line and hitting an oncoming car. Fortunately, no one was killed. But a February 13, 1997, article in the *New England Journal of Medicine* announced a new hazard: the cell phone. According to researchers from the University of Toronto, drivers using their portable phones increased their risk of crashing fourfold. Surprisingly, use of hands-free devices, which potentially reduce the distraction, did not lower this risk.[30]

Ten years later, a grisly crash made the issue of cell phone use while driving much more immediate. On the night of June 28, 2007, in Canandaigua, New York, a sport utility vehicle carrying five high school cheerleaders from nearby Fairport, New York, swerved into an oncoming tractor-trailer and burst into flames, killing all five girls. It was later revealed that the cell phone of the driver, 17-year-old Bailey Goodman, had been in use. Shortly before the crash, Goodman had spoken to a friend traveling in an accompanying vehicle. Then, two minutes before the crash, a text was sent from Goodman's phone to a male friend. Moments before the crash, a reply was texted back to Goodman's phone.

In retrospect, several factors may have contributed to the crash: Goodman was speeding, was traveling on a winding two-lane highway, and was driving illegally. Her junior driver's license made it illegal for her to be driving unsupervised at 10 p.m. and to have that many passengers. But the evidence of texting on Goodman's phone just prior to the crash—even if not done by Goodman herself—strongly suggested that it had caused her to lose attention and cross into traffic. The police reported no evidence that drugs or alcohol had been involved.[31]

The crash led to a surge of national interest in the related subjects of cell phone use and texting, in particular, while driving. "Texting While Driving Becoming Death Sentence" read a headline in the *Temple* (University) *News*.

"Driving and Text Messaging: A Deadly Combination?" asked National Public Radio, while ABC News reported that "Texting May Have Played Part in Fatal Teen Car Crash." One group of individuals that did not appear especially interested, however, were anti–drunk driving activists. For example, as of October 2009, the only mention of cell phones on the MADD website was in a list of myths, one of which was that "cell phone use behind the wheel and speeding cause more damage than drunk driving." The website went on to argue that the risk caused by drunk drivers far exceeded that caused by those talking or texting on cell phones.[32]

The relative silence of groups like MADD and RID on cell phone use while driving is surely understandable. After all, depending on one's criteria, there are still between 13,000 and 17,000 deaths attributed to drunk driving each year. Furthermore, it has been estimated that more than 90 million automobile trips still occur annually with a driver at a BAC of 0.08% or greater. True, the drunk driving activists are also fighting teenage drinking, but adopting a new cause, and one that has nothing at all to do with alcohol, has been too much of a stretch. If one believes Hilgartner and Bosk's model of competition among activist movements, cell phone misuse runs the risk of shifting the public's focus away from drunk driving.

But such a narrow focus potentially ignores the important fact that drunk driving, cell phone calls, and texting raise similar concerns. Indeed, the 1997 *New England Journal of Medicine* article made a point of emphasizing that the increased risk caused by drivers on cell phones was roughly equivalent to that of drivers with BACs of 0.08%. Readers commenting on the coverage of the 2007 upstate New York car crash made this connection as well. "Hopefully this will be hyped up big time so as to curb people while talking on their phones and text messaging," one wrote on the ABC News website. "They're just as bad as drunk drivers and should be treated as such." A poster on the *USA Today* website agreed, declaring that "the ban of cell phones while driving should be in the same category as drunken driving." For good measure, the writer added, "The dead could care less about the way they die." Another commentator on the same website wrote, correctly, that "studies have shown that using a cellphone while driving is almost like DUI, unfortunately even hands free is pretty close too." His solution: "a complete ban and significant fines like $2000."[33]

Coverage of tragedies such as the death of Goodman and her friends has led to the growing use of a new term: *distracted driving*. Cell phones were only one of the many possible distractions in the Goodman crash. "The issue here," wrote a poster on the ABC News website, "is that she was speeding, texting, and distracted with other kids in the car, ALL of which have been proven to increase the chances of teens dying in fatal crashes." That is, these indiscretions were all of a piece. "The point is any distraction raises the risk of a crash," read another post from the same site. "Each risk needs to be identified and minimized to avoid future loss." Another writer put it succinctly: "When u drive, u lose rights to be doing other things, plain and simple."

Of course, one does not tend to think of drunk driving as distracted driving. Drunk driving brings to mind impairment, giddiness, and bravado. But whatever labels one uses, all these circumstances make drivers distracted—and less able to carry out the primary task of driving. In September 2009, US Secretary of Transportation Ray LaHood convened three hundred experts in Washington for a conference on distracted driving. The meeting focused mostly on the hot-button issues of cell phone use and texting, although there was also discussion of the dangers posed by other emerging in-vehicle wireless technologies, termed *telematics*, such as adaptive cruise control and Internet access.

Data presented at the conference estimated that between one in four and one in ten drivers use their cell phones at any point in time, representing close to one million people. Also discussed was a study by the Virginia Tech Transportation Institute that found truckers to be 23 times likelier to crash when sending text messages.[34]

Among those speaking at the conference was Chuck Hurley, executive director of MADD. Hurley's attendance signaled two things. First, the wall—real or perceived—between activists fighting drunk driving and those concerned with distracted driving might be crumbling. This alliance raised the possibility that all issues associated with car crashes—not only intoxication and distraction but also drug use, fatigue, speeding, aggressive driving, and seat belt and air bag use—might productively be unified under the dual rubrics of "traffic safety" and "harm reduction." The idea would be to promote the concept that drivers should regularly avail themselves of all available strategies to make their trips safer and avoid behaviors that potentially caused harm. Promotion of traffic safety reached back to William Haddon and was now being championed by groups such as the National Highway Traffic Safety Administration, the Centers for Disease Control and Prevention, the American Automobile Association, the Insurance Institute for Highway Safety, and even the UN General Assembly.[35] Harm reduction had become a unifying principle for public health movements in the United States and elsewhere. But neither phrase has grabbed the public's attention.

Second, the insights gained during decades of anti–drunk driving efforts might be brought to bear on these newer concerns. Indeed, at the conference, Hurley emphatically stated that responsible drinking publicity campaigns had not had much effect on drunk driving rates. Stricter laws, he believed, were the way to go—whether for drunk or distracted drivers. "Asking risk takers to limit their own risk is a proven failure," Hurley added. "That's why good laws, well enforced, is [*sic*] the way to go."[36] Indeed, there was already legislation moving through Congress using the old trick that had produced stricter drunk driving laws across the country: withholding federal highway funding from states that did not ban texting and e-mailing while driving.

Historical lessons were also apparent as the public attempted to process tragedies such as the one that killed Bailey Goodman and her friends. As in the early years of RID and MADD, there was tremendous anger, mostly directed at the parents of the girls, who had apparently condoned the risky outing with an inexperienced, not fully licensed driver. The real culprits "are the brain dead parents that let a kid drive their SUV while having a phone in the vehicle," one man wrote. "These parents should be charged and held in custody while awaiting trial." Another writer cited the "laziness and stupidity" of the parents, as well as the girls' disregard for the law and safety. "How can anyone possibly say that it is not this girl's fault when if she had simply followed the restrictions of her license five people would still be alive?"[37]

Such characterizations framed what had happened in black-and-white terms: the girls and their families were the guilty parties, having acted in ways that were utterly thoughtless and dangerous. The fact that, in this case, only the girls themselves had died probably tempered the accusations of blame and culpability. Fortunately, the driver of the tractor-trailer had experienced only minor injuries, and the drivers of nearby cars had escaped unharmed. One perceptive writer to the *USA Today* website nevertheless identified the man who collided with the girls as himself a victim, possibly playing back the crash over and over in his head, wondering if he could have done more to avoid the oncoming SUV.

These stark characterizations—innocence versus blame, victims versus criminals—are the subject of the fourth question this chapter raises. As we have seen, such characterizations are seemingly mandatory for the early years of a new activist campaign. Just as the image of the morally bankrupt killer drunk had mobilized drunk driving control efforts in the early 1980s, so, too, might "killer texters" in the 2010s. Yet there is already evidence that this type of language is unacceptable to Americans, even those who view what is happening with cell phones in moving automobiles as a grievous problem. Many of those commenting on the Canandaigua crash, like those who had written about the Colorado drag-racing tragedy, were full of forgiveness. "Don't judge," one wrote on the ABC website. "Just pray to God and thank him that it wasn't your child." "No one is perfect," wrote another. "We all do stuff we shouldn't so no one should be pointing fingers."[38]

There was also a lot of use of the word *accident* to describe what had occurred. "In my opinion, it is no one's fault—it was an ACCIDENT—a terrible, horrific accident," one woman wrote. Another writer agreed: "It was an accident [that] could have happened to anybody, day or night, 17 or 37, doesn't matter, it happened." Another said that "this could have just been a freak accident."[39] Such language would surely have made William Haddon apoplectic. After all, it was he and others alarmed at drunk driving rates who pointed out that characterizing car crashes as "God's will" serves to eliminate any exploration of the human agency and corporate greed that actually promote such events and lead to so many injuries and deaths.

But if, after decades of warnings, people still prefer to refer to car crashes as accidents, that says something: the concept of blame can go only so far to help mobilize a movement. MADD recognized this fact when it quietly changed its name from *Mothers Against Drunk Drivers* to *Mothers Against Drunk Driving*. Haddon himself acknowledged it when, coming from the world of drunk driving, he nevertheless began to promote concepts like traffic safety and "packaging of people" in the early 1960s. So, too, did scholars like Laurence Ross, when he put forth the seemingly heretical idea of making cars and the roads safe enough to allow intoxicated people to drive. "Why don't you take some pity on Drunk Drivers?" a correspondent once asked Doris Aiken. "I just wanted to let you know that I feel sorry for them." And, as far as alcoholism goes, blaming is also tricky: scientific research has increasingly shown it to be a disease, one with a significant genetic component.[40]

Perhaps the most symbolic repudiation of blame came in June 2002, when Cindi Lamb, by then a college health sciences instructor, decided to revisit and write about the 1979 crash that had paralyzed her daughter Laura. Laura Lamb had died in 1986, at the age of 6, from a series of brain seizures. She had beaten the odds by living so long with such a severe spinal cord injury, and she spent much of her life in intensive care units battling broken bones, infections, and collapsed lungs. But Laura had also attended school in Maryland, where her classmates and teachers loved her courage and sense of humor.

Still very much bearing the pain of her daughter's short life and death, Cindi Lamb tracked down Russell Newcomer Jr., the habitual drunk driver who had caused the crash and eventually served five years in prison. Lamb later wrote about their meeting, which took place at a Denny's in Frederick, Maryland. Newcomer reported that he had been sober for nine years and had a good job: weatherizing homes for people needing special services. Throughout the encounter, Lamb verbally assaulted Newcomer, screaming at him for having continued to drive despite five DWIs and giving him excruciating details about Laura's medical ailments. "Why did you do this do my daughter?" Lamb yelled. "Why? I just want to know why?" At that point, she started crying.[41]

But once Newcomer began telling Lamb about his own life, she softened. "At first I drank because I wanted to, because it was fun," he told her. "Then I drank because I had to, because I became addicted. Then I drank to forget about what I did to your daughter, to you."

Newcomer talked about the crash. "I think about it every day and every night," he said. "I feel bad always. And you don't know how many times I wished and prayed that it had happened to me instead of your little girl. I wished I could bring her back." Then Newcomer apologized. "I am so sorry for what I did," he said. "I wish it never happened. I am so sorry."

What he did next caught Lamb off guard. "I know this is crazy to ask, but do you think you could forgive me?" Lamb thought about it and said no. Forgiving Newcomer, she thought, would have been spitting in Laura's face.

Soon thereafter, Newcomer, Lamb, and Lamb's husband, Ray, who had accompanied her, got up to leave. On the way out, a woman who had been eavesdropping lashed out at Newcomer. "They never should have let you out of prison," she barked. "You should have rotted and died there."

A few months later, in November 2002, Newcomer and Cindi Lamb were back in the same Denny's. Lamb had undergone a religious conversion and was planning to be baptized. This time, Lamb told Newcomer that she forgave him. "We have something in common," she told him. "Pain. We both have had immense pain in our lives. I think it's time we dumped it. I'm dumping my pain right here, right now, at the counter of Denny's in Frederick. And I want you to do the same."[42]

Lamb felt as passionately as ever that drunk driving was terribly wrong. But she also realized that the lives of those who drove drunk were complicated. This was clearly the case with Diane Schuler, who had been responsible for the deadly crash on the Taconic Parkway in 2009. If she was indeed a secret alcoholic, did that make her more or less blameworthy? Did a cultural mandate that she be a "perfect mother" somehow exonerate her?[43] When the goal is eradicating a public health problem, blame and revenge are only part of the answer.

So, too, is trying to get people to change their behavior, as MADD's Chuck Hurley suggested at the distracted driving conference. Of course, as of the twenty-first century, many Americans act very differently when it comes to drinking and driving, either designating a driver at a three-martini lunch or skipping the martinis altogether. Indeed, some commentators would likely challenge Hurley's statement that the propaganda produced by groups such as MADD have only had a minimal effect, arguing instead that it was a combination of deterrence and education that has changed the culture of drinking and driving. But what remains crystal clear is that whether it is a famous athlete or a movie star out celebrating, three friends with a love of fast cars or a suburban housewife with no known history of alcoholism, millions of inebriated people continue to get into cars utterly certain that they—unlike those other unlucky suckers—will make it home without incident. Scientists call this phenomenon *subjective immunity*, in which people underestimate their own risk of crashing. But it is also a sort of game, one that Kelly Burke, an intoxicated Washington television reporter, lost on July 1, 1984, when he hit an oncoming car in Darnestown, Maryland, killing a transportation worker named Dennis Lee Crouch. In a documentary he was required to make as part of his sentence, Burke aptly called drunk driving "American roulette." Many people play it, he wrote. "It's where they assume just because they made it home many times before, they'll make it home every time."[44]

Burke's documentary, with its powerful personal confession, is quite moving, but it is also a reminder that plenty of people who know better still drive drunk. When the major problem of drunk driving was first "outed" in the Reagan-era 1980s, the best way to draw attention to it was to represent it as a morality play with stories of innocent victims and recidivist culprits. There were a lot of both, and it made sense to pass laws that would maximize the possibility of deterrence. What was harder to do is what came next: study drunk driving and all the proposed preventive and other interventions to see what does and does not work. This is what researchers like Laurence Ross have tried to do.

Their results are often less than satisfying. Many people drink and drive safely. Harsher punishments have not deterred. Focusing on individual responsibility ignores the role played by corporate America and other complicated social and economic factors. What these findings mean is that there are major limits to a law-and-order approach to social problems, something that researchers studying the concurrent moralistic movements of the 1980s are concluding as well. For example, the main impacts of the war on drugs, *New York Times* columnist Nicholas D. Kristof recently wrote, were higher rates of imprisonment, empowerment of criminals abroad, and inadequate allocations for effective drug treatment programs. Fetal alcohol syndrome created a "moral panic," exaggerating the severity of the problem of women drinking alcohol during pregnancy. And the increased prosecution of domestic violence cases, according to Jonathan Simon, has subverted some of the original feminist goals of empowering women victims.[45] Beyond the limitations of a legalistic approach, efforts to control drunk driving were further hampered by never having been fully embraced by the public health community, even though certain strategies, such as roadblocks, had a public health flavor.

The alternative public health model for drunk driving control has the potential advantage of causing less irritation among libertarians than the traditional legal prohibitions. But the proposed interventions—improving public transportation, lowering alcohol availability through taxation, and opposing alcohol-industry sponsorship of events—often seem not to be directly related to drunk driving and still anger those favoring a free-market approach. Caught between a legalistic and a public health approach, anti–drunk driving efforts have stagnated.

Faced with this reality, public health officials, activists, and legislators now increasingly look toward technological solutions to prevent drunk driving. It is no surprise that in 2010, the major initiative favored by most anti–drunk driving activists has been greater use of ignition interlocks, making them mandatory for anyone convicted, even once, of DWI. As of 2009, twelve states had passed such a law, and there were 180,000 interlocks in use nationwide. Moreover, roughly three-quarters of the public supports the use of mandated interlock devices for convicted drunk drivers.

Others in the field look forward to more sophisticated alcohol detection devices, such as infrared absorption spectroscopy, not yet widely available, which prevents a car from starting when a driver places his or her hands on the steering wheel and alcohol is detected in the person's tissues. A great appeal of this particular strategy is that it is entirely passive and not reliant on any specific behaviors by the driver.[46] Strikingly, according to a recent Insurance Institute for Highway Safety survey, two-thirds of Americans favor routine installation of alcohol detection devices in all cars.[47] Another technology currently in use is a bracelet that samples a person's sweat to detect alcohol and sets off an alarm if there is a positive result. A judge mandated that Lindsay Lohan wear such a device.

Activists promoting new technologies have no illusions about them being a "fix" for the drunk driving problem. For example, intoxicated people getting into their cars remain free to ask others to blow into the interlock device or, theoretically, to place their hands on the wheel. In addition, it remains unclear, at least for poor and working-class offenders, who would pay for interlocks and the monthly lease fee, even if the sentencing judge mandates them. And there remains the virulent libertarian objection to any universal requirement for such devices, which is regarded as punishing the many to benefit the few, even though the benefit in question is preventing people from being killed in the prime of life. Remarkably, in 1974, Congress reversed an earlier decision to mandate the manufacturing of cars with seat belt interlocks that would have prevented cars from starting unless front-seat passengers had fastened their lap belts. The *Wall Street Journal* termed these life-saving devices "a gratuitous insult and annoyance," while one opponent from Connecticut said he represented "a growing army of citizens . . . fed up with bureaucratic, ill-advised, and personally restrictive regulations out of the Washington complex."[48]

As of 2011, you would be hard pressed to find any Americans—including teenagers—who have not continually heard anti–drunk driving pronouncements. Legislators have passed many new laws to combat impaired driving, but the laws have been weakly enforced. Strategies that work in other countries either have not been tried or do not work in the United States. Born out of fury, the campaign against drunk driving has become, more than anything, pragmatic. It is, as the expression goes, a problem to be managed but not solved. This is not to say that Joseph Gusfield's contention that drunk drivers often receive special moral opprobrium is no longer true. They do. But in a world where drivers are often overly tired, speeding, high on drugs, texting friends, or exhibiting road rage, it is harder to single out drinking and driving as a particularly egregious sin.

Why is this so? In a nutshell, a full-frontal attack on drunk driving is not "American." Experts in the field have expressed this sentiment in various ways. For example, Robert Borkenstein frequently cited the legal scholar Roscoe Pound, who wrote in 1913 that "legal precepts which failed of enforcement did so because they failed to accurately express and formulate experience of life."

"Like other irresponsible, antisocial behaviors," law professor James B. Jacobs stated in his 1989 book, "excessive drinking and driving is shaped by cultural and social attitudes and values." Or, as the American Automobile Association's Lawrence Lonero wrote in 2007, "law expresses society's values and expectations."[49] Indeed, decades before RID and MADD, early activists had anticipated the difficulties of controlling the problem in a country so wedded to the protection of individual rights, even if the proposed inconveniences would save thousands and thousands of lives. As one North Dakotan wrote to Doris Aiken: "Don't you go & have a few drinks & smile once in a while & have fun with people[?] *I do & I always will & always have.* I'm only human & so are thousands of other people. This is the U.S. & not Russia but at this rate we are going to be just like it in a couple of years. It don't hurt anybody to drink 6–8 beers & drive sensible."[50]

This historical ambivalence about achieving better control of drunk driving—both before and after MADD—raises the interesting possibility that we have reached the limit of what can be achieved in the United States.[51] That is, without new laws designed at substantially limiting alcohol sales or large-scale infusions of funding to apprehend and prosecute more drunk drivers, the annual rate of alcohol-related fatalities may remain around the 15,000 plateau, which some have called an "irreducible minimum." It might even be said that, having permanently reduced alcohol-related fatalities by 30 to 40 percent in a country with such a fierce spirit of individualism, the problem of drunk driving has been "fixed."

It would be a shame, however, to leave the story here. As traffic safety expert Dinesh Mohan has written, "Road traffic injuries are the only public health problem for which society and decision-makers still accept death and disability among young people on a large scale." In looking for additional strategies, it is useful to return to the history of antismoking efforts. As late as the 1980s, the assumption was that America could not do without cigarettes. The twentieth century in the United States, historian Allan M. Brandt has convincingly argued, was the "Cigarette Century," one in which as much as 40 percent of the population found compelling the notion of inhaling a noxious, and ultimately dangerous, combination of tobacco and chemicals into its lungs. Advertisements, often featuring movie stars and athletes, portrayed cigarettes in a similar manner to alcohol: connected to status, fame, sex, and parties—in other words, essential to the good life. When early data emerged after World War II suggesting that cigarettes caused lung cancer and other grave diseases, the tobacco companies dug in their heels, obfuscating and lying about what they knew to be true. To them, the product was so essential to American culture and the economy that it needed to be promoted at any cost.

But this was not to be. First, a series of lawsuits, which revealed the industry's perfidy, did enormous damage to the cigarette companies' reputations. Second, public health researchers latched on to the concept of "side smoke," which referred to the damage done by cigarette smoking to nearby nonsmokers. Even though some critics questioned the actual harm caused by such exposure, the data were compelling enough to win widespread acceptance among the American public. Smoking, once a sign of urbanity and trendiness, became thoroughly stigmatized. Cities banned smoking in restaurants and bars, even in states like Virginia and North Carolina, the heart of tobacco country. The same went for other work establishments. Initially, smokers were forced outside of buildings, even in the bitter cold. Subsequently, certain localities even banned outdoor smoking. It was no exaggeration to suggest that smokers had become pariahs.[52]

It might be argued that the same process has occurred with drunk drivers since 1980. But the ongoing litany of crashes and deaths, such as those discussed in this chapter, show that the comparison is only partially true. And, whether or not one believes that drunk driving—as opposed to other forms of impaired driving—has received more than its share of attention, these tragedies should continue to discourage complacency. We need only look to other countries, such as Norway, Sweden, and Australia, to see that other models are possible. In these places, there are cultural norms that characterize drunk driving as inherently wrong and view personal sacrifices—not driving if drinking and not drinking if driving—as necessary and appropriate. One study carried out in Norway found a BAC of 0.5% or greater in only 3 out of 1,000 randomly tested nighttime drivers.[53] Surely it is hard to argue that someone who smokes, especially away from other people, deserves more scorn than someone who drives drunk.

Jay A. Winsten, the head of the Harvard Alcohol Project, which had great success in the 1980s in getting television shows to publicize the concept of designated driving, likes to contrast what occurs in Scandinavia with what happens in the United States. Hosts at Swedish parties, he reports, routinely ask arriving guests who the designated driver will be, and they offer this person nonalcoholic beverages. A Swedish celebrity told Winsten that "to be arrested and convicted for drunk driving is a social and personal catastrophe."[54] The International Abstaining Motorists Association carries on the work of the old Union of Temperance Drivers. Meanwhile, in 1997, Sweden's Parliament passed an act known as Vision Zero, which established a long-term goal of zero fatalities and zero

Among the barriers to greater use of designated drivers is the perception that they cannot enjoy themselves at parties. www.CartoonStock.com

injuries on the road. Just as the public has the moral duty not to drive drunk, Swedish highway agencies are ethically obligated to implement the best, scientifically proven approaches both to ensure highway safety and to anticipate driver errors.[55]

So even if harsh laws and punishments have not discouraged drunk driving in Scandinavia, moral opprobrium has—and maybe that sort of moralism is not such a bad thing. What the new breed of anti–drunk driving activists first charged in the early 1980s is still true. Innocent Americans die every day at the hands of drunk drivers, and this is unacceptable—even in a country that cherishes liberty and individualism.

Perhaps Wisconsin's Ralph Hudson best expressed the general frustration at having a decades-old public health problem that cannot be adequately controlled. "Personally, I am tired of public wringing of hands over the problem while we allow alcohol impairment we say we deplore," he wrote in advocating a 0.05% BAC. "Society badly needs to make a public statement of a meaningful restriction on alcohol usage prior to driving." Hudson noted that unlimited time, personnel, and funds are available to try to save a child who has fallen into a well. "How about thousands of young lives—snuffed out by alcohol-impaired drivers—sacrificed to our gods of cash, convenience and conviviality?"[56]

When Willard Y. Howell, of the National Highway Traffic Safety Administration, spoke at the 1971 Conference on Public Information Programs on Alcohol and Traffic Safety at the University of Michigan, he told an anecdote from a trip he had recently made to an unspecified Eastern Europe country. During his visit, he inquired of his hosts about people who drank too much vodka and then got in their cars.

"Is not permitted," he was told.

Howell demurred, saying it was not permitted in the United States either, but it happened anyway.

"Oh, you don't understand," was the reply. "Here it is not permitted."[57]

One can only wonder, in a Communist country during the cold war, how the government prevented drunk driving. Howell correctly mused that such a model would probably not work in the democratic United States. But one can be pretty certain that many fewer people—fathers, mothers, sisters, brothers, sons, and daughters—in that country were dying unnecessarily as a result of drinking and driving.

Afterword

This book began by my urging readers to raise their blood alcohol levels to the point at which it would be illegal to drive and then imagine themselves doing so—even though most would be somewhere between "buzzed" and drunk. I then reminded them that as recently as forty years ago, it was possible to drink nearly twice as much as I suggested and still drive legally.

Then I explored the myriad historical reasons for these phenomena. They include Americans' love of drinking, their love of driving, the country's lack of adequate public transportation, and the enduring backlash against the Prohibition experiment of the 1920s. Meanwhile, industry, interested in selling alcohol and cars, has publicly oppposed drunk driving, but never in a manner that would seriously threaten the sales of its products. Finally, a strong American streak of individualism and libertarianism has hampered more aggressive attempts to curb drinking and driving.

The question ultimately raised in this book is: "Is this so bad?" At first glance, one may be tempted to answer no. After all, anti–drunk driving activists have had their day in the sun, leading to many legislative victories, such as lowering the acceptable blood alcohol content from 0.15% to 0.08% and raising the legal drinking age to 21. Almost everyone has heard the phrase "Friends don't let friends drive drunk," and many of them take it seriously. In an era of cell phones and hand-held computers, there are many other causes of distracted driving that compete for our attention. Scholars have also carefully shown how public health issues, such as drunk driving, can be oversimplified and misconstrued. Finally, in the wake of the passage of Barack Obama's health care legislation, charges of a "nanny state," in which the government too aggressively monitors health-related behaviors, have achieved new gusto.

At the end of the day, however, the history of drunk driving control suggests that the answer to the question should be yes. One can make a cogent argument that people who eat fatty foods, smoke, or drink constitute a public health problem because society eventually pays their medical bills. But such individuals only *indirectly* threaten the health of their fellow Americans by raising health care costs. People who choose to drive in an impaired state, whether buzzed or drunk, *directly* threaten others every single time they get behind the wheel. There is a reason that modern public health efforts began with the quarantining of people with contagious infectious diseases. Healthy people, Americans agreed, had the right to be protected from potentially harmful—and deadly—threats.

The efforts of RID, MADD, SADD, NTHSA, the NIAAA, the Insurance Institute for Highway Safety, and their thousands of volunteers and employees notwithstanding, the history of drunk driving control has thrown this idea on its head. Bullied by industry and certain members of the public, legislators and law enforcement officers have frequently paid as much attention to the rights of those who choose to drink and drive as to those who might be victimized by such behavior. As a result, prosecutions based on BACs and other laws have always given significant credence to a number of plausible but ultimately questionable counterarguments: heavy drinkers hold their liquor especially well, even when behind the wheel; people caught driving drunk generally have made a one-time mistake; Breathalyzers regularly generate inaccurate readings; and arresting officers often give misleading testimony. And, ever since the disease of alcoholism became popular in the 1940s, judges, juries, and the general public have at times characterized the perpetrators of drunk driving offenses themselves as victims. With all due respect to the difficulties that such individuals experience before and after making a catastrophic mistake, this notion is utterly absurd. "HISTORY will look aghast at our alcohol/driving record," said Ralph Hudson, the Wisconsin surgeon who became sensitized to the issue of drunk driving when the earnest and polite teenaged son of his nurse was needlessly killed. "This national embarrassment and disgrace has not been just the accumulation of death and injury," he wrote, "but, rather, the strange acceptance of death and injury as the way of life."[1]

As more and more potential distractions for drivers emerge, we should be less—not more—tolerant of a mindset that excuses such behaviors because "everybody does them." The United States may never be like countries in which a communitarian ethic leads to cultural condemnation of activities that put one's fellow citizens at risk. But emulating what these other societies do best is still a worthy goal.

Notes

INTRODUCTION: What's the Harm?

1. Philip B. Linker, "Drinking and Driving Can Mix," *New York Times*, June 3, 1984, LI22.

2. The modern definition of moderate drinking is one drink a day for women and two drinks a day for men. See www.cdc.gov/alcohol/faqs.htm#moderateDrinking.

3. Linker, "Drinking and Driving," LI22.

4. Peter F. Cohalan and Jenifer E. Johnson, "Readers Reply to 'Drinking and Driving Can Mix,'" *New York Times*, June 17, 1984, LI18.

5. There are many excellent books on drunk driving, including Joseph R. Gusfield, *The Culture of Public Problems: Drinking-Driving and the Symbolic Order* (Chicago: University of Chicago Press, 1981); H. Laurence Ross, *Deterring the Drinking Driver: Legal Policy and Social Control* (Lexington, MA: Lexington Books, 1984); Michael D. Laurence, John R. Snortum, and Franklin E. Zimring, eds., *Social Control of the Drinking Driver* (Chicago: University of Chicago Press, 1988); James B. Jacobs, *Drunk Driving: An American Dilemma* (Chicago: University of Chicago Press, 1989); Gerald D. Robin, *Waging the Battle against Drunk Driving: Issues, Countermeasures, and Effectiveness* (New York: Praeger, 1991); H. Laurence Ross, *Confronting Drunk Driving: Social Policy for Saving Lives* (New Haven: Yale University Press, 1992). See also chapter 10 of Leonard Evans, *Traffic Safety* (Bloomfield Hills, MI: Science Serving Society, 2004), accessed January 5, 2009, www.scienceservingsociety.com/ts/text/ch10.htm.

6. The term *freedom machine* comes from Lawrence P. Lonero, "Finding the Next Cultural Safety Paradigm for Road Safety," AAA Foundation for Traffic Safety, 2007, accessed March 9, 2010, www.aaafoundation.org/pdf/lonero.pdf.

7. Books on the history of alcohol and alcoholism include Dan E. Beauchamp, *Beyond Alcoholism: Alcohol and Public Health Policy* (Philadelphia: Temple University Press, 1980); Carolyn L. Wiener, *The Politics of Alcoholism: Building an Arena around a Social Problem* (New Brunswick, NJ: Transaction Books, 1981); Mark E. Lender and James K. Martin, *Drinking in America: A History* (New York: Free Press, 1987); Herbert Fingarette, *Heavy Drinking: The Myth of Alcoholism as a Disease* (Berkeley: University of California Press, 1988); Ron Roizen, "The American Discovery of Alcoholism, 1933–1939" (PhD diss., University of California, Berkeley, 1991); Susanna Barrows and Robin Room, eds., *Drinking: Behavior and Belief in Modern History* (Berkeley: University of California Press, 1991); Andrew Barr, *Drink: A Social History of America* (New York: Carroll & Graf, 1999); Griffith Edwards, *Alcohol: The World's Favorite Drug* (New York: Thomas Dunne Books, 2000); Sarah W. Tracy, *Alcoholism in America: From Reconstruction to Prohibition* (Baltimore: Johns Hopkins University Press, 2005).

8. Jonathan Yardley, "Drunk Driving: Why We Won't Admit the Cause of the Crime," *Washington Post*, October 19, 1981, D1, D8.

9. Ralph P. Hudson to John A. Volpe, April 23, 1984, box 4, folder: Dr. Ralph Hudson, William N. Plymat Papers, State Historical Society of Iowa, Des Moines. Most drunk driving offenses in the United States are characterized as either Driving While Intoxicated (DWI) or Driving Under the Influence (DUI). For the sake of convenience, this book will use DWI throughout, unless DUI is specified.

10. Robert V. Seliger and Lloyd M. Shupe, *Alcohol at the Wheel: A Brief Discussion of Drinking and Driving* (Columbus, OH: School and College Service, 1953).

11. Quoted in Joseph D. Whitaker, "'A National Outrage': Drunken Drivers Kill 26,000 Each Year," *Washington Post*, March 22, 1981, A1, A6.

12. See www.youtube.com/watch?v=n8L-ZZSc8JU&feature=related, accessed March 10, 2010. See also Patricia F. Waller, "Challenges in Motor Vehicle Safety," *Annual Reviews in Public Health* 23 (2002): 93–113.

13. Paul F. Gavaghan, "Remedial Approaches to Drunk Driving," a paper presented to the Transportation Research Board, Colorado Springs, Colorado, July 29–30, 1985, box 113.2, folder: DISCUS, Robert F. Borkenstein Papers, Herman B. Wells Library, Indiana University.

14. Scharline Smith to RID, n.d., RID Papers, Schenectady, NY. Courtesy of Doris Aiken.

15. Transcript of *Good Morning America*, May 3, 2000.

16. Yardley, "Drunk Driving," D8.

17. Bonnie Steinbock, "Drunk Driving," *Philosophy and Public Affairs* 14 (Summer 1985): 278–95, quote on 290.

CHAPTER 1: The Discovery of Drunk Driving

1. "The Conductor Was Drunk," *New York Times*, January 10, 1887, 5; "Sixteen People Killed," *Washington Post*, June 5, 1887, 1.

2. "Howard's Letter: Some Morals about Drink and Drunkards," *Boston Globe*, January 16, 1887, 5.

3. Quoted in J. Marse Grant, *Whiskey at the Wheel: The Scandal of Driving and Drinking* (Nashville, TN: Broadman Press, 1970), 12.

4. "Tried in Vain to Warn Her," *Los Angeles Times*, July 13, 1905, I12.

5. "Auto's History Grows Longer," *Los Angeles Times*, December 30, 1907, I16.

6. "The Coroner's Verdict," *Los Angeles Times*, March 31, 1905, II4.

7. "Revised Auto Rules," *Boston Globe*, May 21, 1909, 11.

8. "Plan to Amend Callan Auto Law," *New York Times*, December 28, 1912, 12. The cartoon is contained in box: Personal Papers, 1956–74, folder: GM visit, 1956, William Haddon Papers, Bethesda, MD. Courtesy of Gene Haddon.

9. John C. Burnham, "New Perspectives on the Prohibition 'Experiment' of the 1920s," *Journal of Social History* 2 (1968): 51–68.

10. The most recent history of Prohibition is Daniel Okrent, *Last Call: The Rise and Fall of Prohibition* (New York: Scribner, 2010). All of the books on alcoholism cited in chapter 1 contain substantial discussions of Prohibition. See also Raymond B. Fosdick and Albert L. Scott, *Toward Liquor Control* (New York: Harper & Bros., 1933); Fletcher

Dobyns, *The Amazing Story of Repeal* (Chicago: Willett, Clark & Co., 1940); Paul Aaron and David Musto, "Temperance and Prohibition in America: Historical Overview," in Mark H. Moore and Dean R. Gerstein, eds., *Alcohol and Public Policy: Beyond the Shadow of Prohibition* (Washington, DC: National Academy Press, 1981), 127–81; Richard F. Hamm, *Shaping the Eighteenth Amendment* (Chapel Hill, NC: University of North Carolina Press, 2008).

11. Thorne Smith, *Topper: A Ribald Adventure* (New York: Grosset & Dunlap, 1926), 15. See also Christine Sismondo, *Mondo Cocktail: A Shaken and Stirred History* (Toronto: McArthur & Co., 2005), 209–10.

12. Marty Mann, "Alcoholism: America's Greatest Unsolved Public Health Problem," unpublished manuscript, n.d., Public and Private Non-Profit Organizations, box 24, Rutgers Center for Alcohol Studies Archives.

13. See chapter 3 of Ron Roizen's dissertation, "The American Discovery of Alcoholism, 1933–1939," accessed March 10, 2010, www.roizen.com/ron/dissch3.htm.

14. Patricia A. Morgan, "Power, Politics, and Public Health: The Political Power of the Alcoholic Beverage Industry," *Journal of Public Health Policy* 9 (Summer 1988): 177–97. See also Roizen, "American Discovery," chaps. 1 and 8; Jonathan Zimmerman, "'One's Total World View Comes into Play': America's Culture War Over Alcohol Education, 1945–1964," *History of Education Quarterly* 42 (Winter 2002): 471–92; Sarah W. Tracy, *Alcoholism in America: From Reconstruction to Prohibition* (Baltimore: Johns Hopkins University Press, 2005), 280.

15. "Distiller Warns Wets," *New York Times*, October 16, 1934, 27.

16. Stuart Elliott, "From a Leader in Moderation Messages, an Aggressive New Campaign Against Drunk Driving," *New York Times*, December 21, 1994, D20. See also Michael R. Marrus, *Mr. Sam: The Life and Times of Samuel Bronfman* (Toronto: Penguin Books, 1992).

17. "Hard Liquor Advertising," *Los Angeles Times*, November 6, 1934, A4. See also "More Drunk Drivers," *Los Angeles Times*, March 15, 1934, A4.

18. "Drunk Driving," *Los Angeles Times*, January 3, 1932, A4; "More Drunk Drivers," A4.

19. "To Fight Tipsy Driving," *New York Times*, May 27, 1939; Robert Alden, "Advertising: Seagram's Drive Is Disarming," *New York Times*, June 12, 1960, 188.

20. See http://lachlan.bluehaze.com.au/books/nsc_safety_facts_1941/index.html, accessed March 12, 2010; Boris Penrose, "Occupational Lead Poisoning in Battery Workers: The Failure to Apply the Precautionary Principle," *Labour History* 84 (May 2003), accessed January 2, 2009, www.historycooperative.org/journals/lab/84/penrose.html.

21. Rune B. Andreasson and A. Wayne Jones, "The Life and Work of Erik M. P. Widmark," *American Journal of Forensic Medicine and Pathology* 17 (September 1996): 177–90.

22. Bert Pierce, "'Drunkometer' Used to Tell Whether and How Much a Driver Is Intoxicated," *New York Times*, April 25, 1948, X21. See also Stephanie Pain, "Catch 'Em on the Rye," *New Scientist* 183 (July 10–16, 2004): 46.

23. Herman M. Gunn, "When Is a Man Intoxicated and Who Is Competent to Testify as to His Condition?" *Fraternal Order of Police Journal*, October 1938.

24. Herman A. Heise to Robert F. Borkenstein, August 29, 1975, box 113.2, folder: Herman Heise, Robert F. Borkenstein Papers, Herman B. Wells Library, Indiana University.

25. Herman A. Heise, "Alcohol and Automobile Accidents," *JAMA* 103 (1934): 739–41.

26. "Alcohol and Safe Driving," *JAMA* 110 (1938): 1617; "Tests for Alcoholic Intoxication," *JAMA* 142 (1950): 523; Robert F. Borkenstein to Samuel T. Green, April 4, 1981, box 113.2, folder: G, Borkenstein Papers.

27. "One Little Nip," *Los Angeles Times*, May 14, 1935, A4.

28. Richard L. Holcomb, "Alcohol in Relation to Traffic Accidents," *JAMA* 111 (1938): 1076–85.

29. Ira H. Cisin, "Social Psychological Factors in Drinking-Driving," in Bernard H. Fox and James H. Fox, eds., *Alcohol and Traffic Safety* (Washington, DC: GPO, 1963), 1–25; Rune B. Andreasson, "Swedish Legislation on Alcohol and Road Traffic and Its Effects," in J. D. J. Havard, *Alcohol and Road Traffic* (London: British Medical Association, 1963), 74–78; Johannes Andenaes, "The General Preventive Effects of Punishment," *University of Pennsylvania Law Review* 114 (1966): 949–83; Johannes Andenaes, "The Scandinavian Experience," in Michael D. Laurence, John R. Snortum, and Franklin E. Zimring, eds., *Social Control of the Drinking Driver* (Chicago: University of Chicago Press, 1988), 43–63; Garrett Peck, *The Prohibition Hangover: Alcohol in America from Demon Rum to Cult Cabernet* (New Brunswick, NJ: Rutgers University Press, 2009), 200.

30. Hans Klette, "Swedish Experiences in Relation to Drunk Driving," unpublished manuscript, n.d., box 113.3, folder: Hans Klette, Borkenstein Papers. See also Werner Wiskari, "Liquor Laws Stiff in Sweden," *New York Times*, April 5, 1959, 46.

31. Quoted in *Proceedings of the First International Conference on Alcohol and Traffic* (Stockholm: Kugelbergs Boktryckeri, 1951), 320.

32. Herman A. Heise, Burt R. Shurly, and Thomas A. McGoldrick, "Report of the Committee to Study Problems of Motor Vehicle Accidents," 1939 and 1942. Courtesy of the American Medical Association Archives, Chicago, IL.

33. David Hackett Fischer, *Paul Revere's Ride* (New York: Oxford University Press, 1994), xv.

34. Heise, Shurly, and McGoldrick, "Report of the Committee," 1942, 4.

35. Ralph F. Turner, Herman A. Heise, and Clarence W. Muehlberger, "Interpretation of Tests for Intoxication," unpublished manuscript, 1957 [?], box 113.2, folder: Herman Heise, Borkenstein Papers.

36. Ibid. It is worth noting that AMA/NSC committee members, at different times, referred to their lenient categories as both liberal and conservative. This might be taken as suggestive evidence that at that particular historical moment, there were no alternatives available to them.

37. Heise, Shurly, and McGoldrick, "Report of the Committee," 1942, 4.

38. Quoted in Richard A. Myren, ed., *Symposium on Alcohol and Road Traffic* (Bloomington, IN: Trustees of Indiana University, 1959), 220. See also an editorial that Heise ghost-wrote for *JAMA*: "Chemical Tests for Intoxication," *JAMA* 166 (1958): 1484.

39. Quoted in Myren, *Symposium*, 192.

40. *Proceedings of the First International Conference*, 176. See also Henry W. Newman, *Acute Alcohol Intoxication: A Critical Review* (Palo Alto, CA: Stanford University Press, 1941).

41. *Proceedings of the First International Conference*, 176.

42. Myren, *Symposium*, 39.

43. "The Public Asks 'Why?'" *Atlanta Constitution*, August 13, 1949, box 137; "Names of Judges in Gravitt Case Cited," *Atlanta Journal*, August 23, 1949, box 116; and "Margaret Mitchell's Death Shows Farcical Nature of Driving Laws," *Abilene Morning Reporter News*, August 21, 1949, box 142, Margaret Mitchell Papers, Hargrett Rare Book and Manuscript Library, University of Georgia.

44. F. A. Merrill, "Atlanta Should Take Preventive Measures," *Atlanta Journal*, August 18, 1949, box 137, and "Dave Boone Says," *New York Sun*, August 18, 1949, box 150, Mitchell Papers.

45. Thomas M. Stubbs to Stephens Mitchell, August 17, 1949, box 151, Mitchell Papers; Barbara Ampolsey and George Groynom, "Letters," *Life*, September 19, 1949, 18.

46. "Let's Be Sensible about Drunk Driving," *Atlanta Journal*, August 18, 1949, and Pierce Harris, "It's Not Hard to Prove That People Are Stupid," *Atlanta Journal*, August 16, 1949, box 137; and "Editorial Was Good, but Not Liquor Ads," *Atlanta Journal*, August 21, 1949, box 116, Mitchell Papers.

47. "Miss Mitchell Death Laid to Public Apathy," *Atlanta Journal*, August 20, 1949, box 116, Mitchell Papers. The clippings can be found in box 138.

48. John R. Marsh to Charles Aycock, July 26, 1950, and John R. Marsh, handwritten notes, April 12, 1951, box 152, Mitchell Papers.

49. "Drunk Driving Toll Highest in History," *Los Angeles Times*, December 5, 1949, 1, 2.

50. Ibid., 2; "The Drunk Driver Problem," *Los Angeles Times*, December 11, 1949, B4.

51. "Drunk Driver-Killer Still Runs at Large," *Los Angeles Times*, December 6, 1949, A1, A7.

52. Clarence H. Lee and G. C. Paine, "Comments on the Drunk Driving Series," *Los Angeles Times*, December 8, 1949, A4; Nathan Newby, "Public Enemy," *Los Angeles Times*, December 20, 1949, A4.

53. Robert V. Seliger and Lloyd M. Shupe, *Alcohol at the Wheel: A Brief Discussion of Drinking and Driving* (Columbus, OH: School and College Service, 1953), 6, 10, 11.

CHAPTER 2: Science and Government Enter the Fray

1. Mickey Mantle with Herb Gluck, *The Mick: An American Hero* (New York: Doubleday, 1985), 219.

2. "Hugh Gravitt Hurt Driving Car in Crash with Truck," *Atlanta Constitution*, November 18, 1949, box 137, Margaret Mitchell Papers, Hargrett Rare Book and Manuscript Library, University of Georgia.

3. "Why Wasn't Gravitt's License Revoked?" *Atlanta Journal*, November 19, 1949, 2.

4. Paul Thompson, "Gravitt Says Beer Didn't Affect Driving," *Atlanta Constitution*, August 21, 1949, box 116, Mitchell Papers.

5. The calling card is preserved in box 137, Mitchell Papers. See also Bem Price, "Atlanta Author Still Near Death," *Savannah* (Georgia) *News*, August 13, 1949, also in box 137.

6. Margaret B. Powers to John R. Marsh, August 17, 1949, box 150, and Rosa Bell Williams to John R. Marsh, August 16, 1949, box 151, Mitchell Papers.

7. Edna Cain Daniel, "It Was an Accident That Did Not Have to Happen—But It Did Happen," *Atlanta Journal*, August 22, 1949, box 116, Mitchell Papers.

8. "Kid-Glove Handling of Reckless Drivers," *Atlanta Journal*, August 16, 1949, and "A Proper Memorial—and a Lesson," *Atlanta Constitution*, August 18, 1949, box 137, Mitchell Papers.

9. Celestine Sibley, "Questions Are Still in the 'Wind,'" *Atlanta Journal and Constitution*, July 5, 1989, C1; Gary Pomerantz, "An Old Cabbie's Anguish," *Atlanta Journal and Constitution*, August 11, 1991, A1; and Sara H. Armstrong, "Peace for Man Whose Car Hit Margaret Mitchell," *Atlanta Journal and Constitution*, August 25, 1991, B6.

10. In this manner, those harmed by drunk drivers became examples of victims who paradoxically get blamed. Others in this category have included rape and domestic abuse victims.

11. "Drunk Driver Avoids Long Jail Terms," *Los Angeles Times*, December 7, 1949, A1, A2.

12. Thomas Nuzum, "Drunk Driver Defenses Also Pretty Shaky," *Chicago Daily Tribune*, May 13, 1957, A6. See also Eugene Meyer, "How to Get Alcohol Off the Highways," *Family Circle*, July 1, 1981, 65, 108, 110, 116; Doris Aiken to the author, August 10, 2008.

13. "Too Much Sympathy for Drunk Drivers," *Chicago Daily Tribune*, April 24, 1957, 18; Robert McKinley, "Comment from the Floor," in Richard A. Myren, ed., *Symposium on Alcohol and Road Traffic* (Bloomington: Trustees of Indiana University, 1959), 40–41; Robert F. Borkenstein, H. J. Trubitt, and R. J. Lease, "Problems of Enforcement and Prosecution," in Bernard H. Fox and James H. Fox, *Alcohol and Traffic Safety* (Washington, DC: GPO, 1963), 137–88, esp. 147, 153.

14. McKinley in Myren, *Symposium*, 41; Borkenstein et al., "Problems of Enforcement and Prosecution," 152; Stephanie Pain, "Catch 'Em on the Rye," *New Scientist* 183 (July 10–16, 2004): 46, accessed March 13, 2010, www.sandiegodrunkdrivingattorney .net/2010/01/birth-of-breathalyzer-discovery-of.html.

15. Daniel P. Moynihan to William Haddon Jr., March 7, 1961, box: Moynihan, folder: Moynihan, 1961, William Haddon Papers, Bethesda, MD. Courtesy of Gene Haddon.

16. Barron H. Lerner, *Contagion and Confinement: Controlling Tuberculosis along the Skid Road* (Baltimore: Johns Hopkins University Press, 1998).

17. Mark S. Foster, *A Nation on Wheels: The Automobile Culture in America since 1945* (Belmont, CA: Wadsworth, 2003), 67, 68.

18. Ibid., 68; "Statement of Daniel Patrick Moynihan before the Committee on Interstate and Foreign Commerce of the House of Representatives," May 4, 1966, box: Moynihan, folder: Moynihan, 1966, Haddon Papers; Horace Porter, "Open Letter to Governor Merriam," *Los Angeles Times*, June 13, 1934, A4.

19. Foster, *A Nation on Wheels*, 72; Ford is quoted in Lawrence P. Lonero, "Finding the Next Cultural Safety Paradigm for Road Safety," AAA Foundation for Traffic Safety, 2007, accessed March 9, 2010, www.aaafoundation.org/pdf/lonero.pdf; Moynihan, "Statement of Daniel Patrick Moynihan." For more on the postwar cult of the automobile, see David L. Lewis and Laurence Goldstein, eds., *The Automobile and American Culture* (Ann Arbor: University of Michigan Press, 1980); James J. Flink, *The Automobile Age*

(Cambridge, MA: MIT Press, 1990); Michael L. Berger, *The Automobile in American History and Culture* (Westport, CT: Greenwood Press, 2001).

20. Jonathan Zimmerman, "'One's Total World View Comes into Play': America's Culture War over Alcohol Education, 1945–1964," *History of Education Quarterly* 42 (Winter 2002): 471–92, quote on 488; Patricia A. Morgan, "Power, Politics, and Public Health: The Political Power of the Alcoholic Beverage Industry," *Journal of Public Health Policy* 9 (Summer 1988): 177–97; Carl Spielvogel, "Advertising: Post Joins Liquor Media List," *New York Times*, August 31, 1958, F6.

21. Fletcher Dobyns, *The Amazing Story of Repeal* (Chicago: Willett, Clark & Co., 1940), 420.

22. John Crosby, "The Actors Sure Do Enjoy Those Quantities of Beer," *Washington Post*, October 5, 1953, 23.

23. Robert V. Seliger and Lloyd M. Shupe, *Alcohol at the Wheel: A Brief Discussion of Drinking and Driving* (Columbus, OH: School and College Service, 1953), 22.

24. Quoted in Richard A. Myren, ed., *Symposium on Alcohol and Road Traffic* (Bloomington: Trustees of Indiana University, 1959), 16.

25. See http://supreme.justia.com/us/352/432/case.html, accessed March 17, 2010.

26. See http://supreme.justia.com/us/384/757/case.html, accessed March 17, 2010.

27. Thomas J. Donovan, "Review of Selected Public Information Campaigns on Alcohol and Highway Safety," in James W. Swinehart and Ann C. Grimm, eds., *Public Information Programs on Alcohol and Highway Safety* (Ann Arbor, MI: Highway Safety Research Institute, 1972), 32–39, quote on 34.

28. Ibid., 34. For another example of industry funding of academia, in this case support of the Rutgers Center of Alcohol Studies by the United States Brewers Association, see Horace E. Campbell, "Studies of Driving and Drinking," *Quarterly Journal of Studies on Alcohol* 30 (1969): 457–58.

29. On Borkenstein's and Indiana University's role in the history of alcohol testing, see D. M. Lucas, "Professor Robert F. Borkenstein—An Appreciation of his Life and Work, 2000," accessed March 17, 2010, www.borkensteincourse.org/borkenstein_appreciation .pdf. See also Kurt M. Dubowski, "A Brief History," 2008, accessed March 17, 2010, www .borkensteincourse.org/faculty%20documents/Dubowski_History.pdf.

30. James Karns, quoted in Myren, *Symposium*, 36–37; "55 Traffic Aides View Liquor Tests," *New York Times*, June 5, 1959, 25.

31. Myren, *Symposium*, 43. See also William N. Plymat, "For Members of the National Commission on Drunk Driving," unpublished manuscript, September 6, 1982, box 1, folder: Presidential Commission, William N. Plymat Papers, State Historical Society of Iowa, Des Moines.

32. Howard Whitman, "Plain Facts on Drunk Driving," *Los Angeles Times*, December 10, 1958, 6. See also "Half Drunk Drivers Are Dangerous Too!" unpublished document, 1977, box 7, folder: RID, Plymat Papers.

33. Myren, *Symposium*, 274–77; "Strict Test Urged for Drunkenness," *New York Times*, November 30, 1960, 76; Kurt M. Dubowski to the author, April 14, 2010.

34. Constance A. Nathanson, "The Contingent Power of Experts: Public Health Policy in the United States, Britain, and France," *Journal of Policy History* 19 (2007): 71–94.

35. William Haddon Jr. and V. A. Bradess, "Alcohol in the Single-Vehicle Fatal Accident: Experience of Westchester County, New York," *JAMA* 169 (1959): 1587–93.

36. J. R. McCarroll and William Haddon Jr., "A Controlled Study of Fatal Automobile Accidents in New York City," *Journal of Chronic Diseases* 15 (1962): 811–26. See also "Alcohol and Highway Deaths," *Maine AAA News Report*, April 1965.

37. Quoted in "Drunk Drivers and Highway Safety," a pamphlet by Allstate Insurance Company, January 1969. See also William Haddon Jr., P. Valien, J. R. McCarroll, and C. J. Umberger, "A Controlled Investigation of the Characteristics of Adult Pedestrians Fatally Injured by Motor Vehicles in Manhattan," *Journal of Chronic Diseases* 14 (1961): 655–78; William Haddon Jr. to Daniel P. Moynihan, April 15, 1958, box: Moynihan, folder: Moynihan, 1958, Haddon Papers; William N. Plymat, "A Second Look at Alcohol and Traffic," unpublished speech, 1957, box 5, folder: Miscellaneous Speeches, Plymat Papers.

38. Haddon's personality was well captured in three eulogies from his funeral by Joan Claybrook, Donald Schaffer, and Brian O' Neill. See also Leon S. Robertson, "Groundless Attack on an Uncommon Man," *Injury Prevention* 7 (2001): 260–62, a defense of Haddon written after the publication of a critical and controversial article by Malcolm Gladwell, "Wrong Turn: How the Fight to Make America's Highways Safer Went Off Course," in the June 11, 2001 issue of the *New Yorker* magazine. On Moynihan, see Douglas Schoen, *Pat: A Biography of Daniel Patrick Moynihan* (New York: Harper & Row, 1979).

39. William Haddon Jr. to Daniel P. Moynihan, November 23, 1964, box: Moynihan, folder: Moynihan, 1964–65, Haddon Papers.

40. David Hemenway, "The Public Health Approach to Motor Vehicles, Tobacco, and Alcohol, with Applications to Firearms Policy," *Journal of Public Health Policy* 22 (2001): 381–402.

41. For a discussion of how Haddon incorporated De Haven's work, see William Haddon Jr., Edward A. Suchman, and David Klein, *Accident Research: Methods and Approaches* (New York: Harper & Row, 1964).

42. William Haddon Jr. to Daniel P. Moynihan, October 20, 1961, box: Moynihan, folder: Moynihan, 1961, Haddon Papers; Moynihan, "Statement of Daniel Patrick Moynihan."

43. Ford is quoted in Lonero, "Finding the Next Cultural Safety Paradigm"; William Haddon Jr. to Ross A. McFarland, May 17, 1966, box: Personal Papers, 1956–74, folder: GM Visit, 1956, Haddon Papers.

44. Haddon to Moynihan, October 20, 1961.

45. William Haddon to Daniel P. Moynihan, September 14, 1960, box: Moynihan, folder: Moynihan, 1960, Haddon Papers.

46. William Haddon to Daniel P. Moynihan, May 8, 1963, box: Moynihan, folder: Moynihan, 1962–63, Haddon Papers; Bernard Stengren, "New Laws Attack Drunken Driving," *New York Times*, August 3, 1959, 18; Charles McCarry, *Citizen Nader* (New York: Signet, 1972), 69.

47. Daniel P. Moynihan, "Epidemic on the Highways," *Reporter*, April 30, 1959. See also Moynihan, "Statement of Daniel Patrick Moynihan."

48. Daniel P. Moynihan to William Haddon Jr., December 23, 1959, box: Moynihan, folder: Moynihan, 1959, Haddon Papers.

49. Quoted in Steven Waldman, "Governing under the Influence," *Washington Monthly*,

January 1988, accessed July 25, 2008, http://findarticles.com/p/articles/mi_m1316/is_n12_v19/ai_6306545/pg_8/.

50. Douglas Dales, "Auto Law Signed to Curb Drinking," *New York Times*, March 16, 1960, 39; Don Ross, "The Traffic Accident Epidemic: Harvard Probes Hidden Causes," *New York Herald Tribune*, March 13, 1961, 1; Department of Transportation, *1968 Alcohol and Highway Safety Report* (Washington, DC: GPO, 1968), 109–14.

51. Robert F. Borkenstein, F. R. Crowther, R. P. Shumate, W. B. Ziel, and Richard Zylman, *The Role of the Drinking Driver in Traffic Accidents* (Bloomington: Department of Police Administration, Indiana University, 1964).

52. McCarry, *Citizen Nader*, 80–96; James C. Fell and Robert B. Voas, "Mothers Against Drunk Driving (MADD): The First 25 Years," *Traffic Injury Prevention* 7 (2006): 195–212, esp. 195–96; Jerry L. Mashaw and David L. Harfst, *The Struggle for Auto Safety* (Cambridge, MA: Harvard University Press, 1990).

53. Michael D. Laurence, "The Legal Context in the United States," in Michael D. Laurence, John R. Snortum, and Franklin E. Zimring, eds., *Social Control of the Drinking Driver* (Chicago: University of Chicago Press, 1988), 136–66.

54. Department of Transportation, *1968 Alcohol and Highway Safety Report*.

55. Joseph R. Gusfield, "The Control of Drinking-Driving in the United States," in Laurence, Snortum, and Zimring, *Social Control of the Drinking Driver*, 109–35.

56. Department of Transportation, *1968 Alcohol and Highway Safety Report*, 86. This language paraphrased Hugh DeHaven.

57. Quotations are from ibid., 1, 86, 87.

58. J. Marse Grant, *Whiskey at the Wheel: The Scandal of Driving and Drinking* (Nashville, TN: Broadman Press, 1970), 7, 16, 69.

59. Ibid., 26, 68, 81.

60. Ibid., 23.

CHAPTER 3: The MADD Mothers Take Charge

1. Mark Starr, William J. Cook, Marsha Zabarsky, Joe Contreras, and Donna Foote, "The War Against Drunk Drivers," *Newsweek*, September 13, 1982, 34–39.

2. Frank Jacobs, *Sing Along with MAD* (New York: Signet, 1970).

3. R. Johnson to Doris Aiken, 1982 [?], RID Papers, Schnectady, NY. Courtesy of Doris Aiken.

4. The ad appeared between pages 32 and 33 in the July 27, 1970, issue of *Time*.

5. William N. Plymat to the Federal Trade Commission, October 12, 1970, box 1, folder: Bill Sr., 1970–71, William N. Plymat Papers, State Historical Society of Iowa, Des Moines.

6. William N. Plymat to John A. Volpe, November 4, 1970, Plymat Papers.

7. Julian A. Waller to Federal Trade Commission, November 30, 1970, Plymat Papers.

8. Guy Halverson, "Liquor Industry Plays Dr. Jekyll and Mr. Hyde," *Christian Science Monitor*, August 20, 1970, 11.

9. Robert B. Voas to Thomas J. Donovan, November 16, 1970 and "DOT News," box 2, folder: DOT, Plymat Papers.

10. Max Hayman, "The Myth of Social Drinking," *American Journal of Psychiatry* 124 (1967): 585–94.

11. James E. Wilson to William N. Plymat, December 30, 1970, box 1, folder: Bill Sr., 1970–71, Plymat Papers.

12. Morris E. Chafetz, *Liquor: The Servant of Man* (Boston: Little, Brown, 1965).

13. William N. Plymat to Clark Mollenhoff, May 25, 1971, box 1, folder: Bill Sr., 1970–71, Plymat Papers. See also William Montague, "Health-Foundation Chief Linked to Alcoholic Beverage Industry," *Chronicle of Philanthropy*, July 25, 1989, 14; Jack Anderson, "Liquor Adviser Criticized Over Ties to Industry," *Washington Post*, April 14, 1984, F21. On the public health model of alcohol control, see Dan E. Beauchamp, *Beyond Alcoholism: Alcohol and Public Health Policy* (Philadelphia: Temple University Press, 1980).

14. Paul J. C. Friedlander and Morris E. Chafetz, in James W. Swinehart and Ann C. Grimm, eds., *Public Information Programs on Alcohol and Highway Safety* (Ann Arbor, MI: Highway Safety Research Institute, 1972), 142–45, 179–81; Robert F. Borkenstein to Mark Keller, September 10, 1973, box 113.3, folder: Mark Keller, Robert F. Borkenstein Papers, Herman B. Wells Library, Indiana University. Paul Friedlander's three articles appear in the December 19, 1971, December 26, 1971, and February 27, 1972, issues of the *Times*.

15. William N. Plymat to Gerald Klerman, May 11, 1978, box 2, folder: Ernest P. Noble, Plymat Papers.

16. Carolyn L. Wiener, *The Politics of Alcoholism: Building an Arena Around a Social Problem* (New Brunswick, NJ: Transaction Books, 1981), 233, 239.

17. H. Laurence Ross, " Deterrence-Based Policies in Britain, Canada, and Australia," in Michael D. Laurence, John R. Snortum, and Franklin E. Zimring, eds., *Social Control of the Drinking Driver* (Chicago: University of Chicago Press, 1988), 64–78.

18. Ralph K. Jones and Kent B. Joscelyn, *Alcohol and Highway Safety 1978: A Review of the State of Knowledge* (Ann Arbor, MI: Highway Safety Research Institute, 1978), 72.

19. These public service announcements are discussed in James W. Swinehart and Ann C. Grimm, eds., *Public Information Programs on Alcohol and Highway Safety* (Ann Arbor, MI: Highway Safety Research Institute, 1972); see esp. 70, 88, 103, 114, 119. See also www.youtube.com/watch?v=MsSIpDK16c4, accessed March 23, 2010.

20. Jones and Joscelyn, *Alcohol and Highway Safety*, 75; James C. Fell and Robert B. Voas, "Mothers Against Drunk Driving (MADD): The First 25 Years," *Traffic Injury Prevention* 7 (2006): 195–212.

21. Jones and Joscelyn, *Alcohol and Highway Safety*, 1, 44, 53, 89, 90; H. Laurence Ross, "Reflections on Doing Policy-Relevant Sociology: How to Cope with MADD Mothers," *American Sociologist* 18 (Summer 1987): 173–78. A more recent estimate is one arrest per 772 episodes of driving two hours after drinking. See Paul Zador, Sheila Krawchuk, and Brent Moore, *Drinking and Driving Trips, Stops by the Police, and Arrests* (Washington, DC: Department of Transportation, 2000).

22. Jones and Joscelyn, *Alcohol and Highway Safety*, 41, 78.

23. Ibid., 78.

24. Connie, "A Mother's Fight against the System," n.d., RID Papers. On the crafting of stories, see Barron H. Lerner, *When Illness Goes Public: Celebrity Patients and How We Look at Medicine* (Baltimore: Johns Hopkins University Press, 2006), 12, 13.

25. Janet S. Besse to RID-USA, 1979, RID Papers.

26. Richard J. Warren, "Little Hue and Cry," *Los Angeles Times*, September 23, 1973, F2.

27. William S., "Ann Landers: A Drunk Driver's Victim," *Washington Post*, September 25, 1973, B4.

28. Bob Rohr to the author, December 31, 2008, and January 2, 2009.

29. Katherine DuTreil to the author, January 6, 2009.

30. Ralph P. Hudson to the author, December 15, 2008, and July 22, 2009.

31. Robert M. Carney to the author, December 15, 2008.

32. Barry Siegel, "Drunk Drivers and the Courtroom Sieve," *Los Angeles Times*, November 16, 1977, A1, A8, A9.

33. Susan Goodemote to Doris Aiken, August 15, 1980, RID Papers.

34. Stewart Rosenkrantz to RID, 1982, RID Papers.

35. Mr. and Mrs. Herbert Rouse to Doris Aiken (three letters), n.d., RID Papers.

36. Carlton Turner to Martin Anderson, December 29, 1981, Presidential Commission on Drunk Driving Papers, Ronald Reagan Presidential Library, Simi Valley, CA. Obtained through Freedom of Information Act request # 2008-090/1.

37. Doris Aiken, *My Life as a Pit Bull* (San Jose, CA: Writers Club Press, 2002), 1.

38. Ibid., 2.

39. Ibid., 4.

40. Ibid., 5, 245; Doris Aiken to DMV Commissioner Melton, 1980, RID Papers; "Law: They're MADD as Hell," *Time*, August 3, 1981, accessed July 28, 2009, www.time.com/time/magazine/article/0,9171,949291,00.html.

41. Doris Aiken to the author, July 20, 2009. See also Peggy Mann, *Arrive Alive* (New York: Woodmere Press, 1983), 65–66.

42. Aiken, *My Life*, 8–10; Mann, *Arrive Alive*, 122; Doris Aiken to Charles Wilcox, August 21, 1980, RID Papers.

43. Doris Aiken to James Brown, April 5, 1982, RID Papers.

44. Aiken, *My Life*, 5; Linda A. Campion, RID DWI-Victims Assistance Project, January 1992, RID Papers.

45. Monica Shairer, "Swerving Car Shatters Couple's Idyllic Life," *Damascus* (Maryland) *Weekly Courier*, May 7, 1980, A1, A11.

46. Interview with Cindi Lamb, February 24, 2009.

47. Eugene L. Meyer, "Victims Testify on Drunk Driving," *Washington Post*, September 23, 1980, C1; "Why Laura Lamb Can't Move," *Washington Post*, September 25, 1980, A18.

48. Mann, *Arrive Alive*, 56; Eugene Meyer, "How to Get Alcohol Off the Highways," *Family Circle*, July 1, 1981, 65, 108, 110, 116. See also an excellent four-part retrospective on Cindi and Laura Lamb published in the *Frederick* (MD) *News Post* on November 8, 2009.

49. Candy Lightner and Nancy Hathaway, *Giving Sorrow Words* (New York: Warner Books, 1990), 1–16.

50. Ibid., 9.

51. Cindi Lamb, "The Visitor," was published in the *Dundalk* (MD) *Eagle* between September 26, 2002, and February 26, 2003. Copy courtesy of Cindi Lamb.

52. Lightner and Hathaway, *Giving Sorrow Words*, 11.

53. Joseph D. Whitaker, "'A National Outrage': Drunken Drivers Kill 26,000 Each Year," *Washington Post*, March 22, 1981, A1, A6; Mac Marshall and Alice Oleson, "MADDer than Hell," *Qualitative Health Research* 6 (February 1996): 6–22.

54. Lightner and Hathaway, *Giving Sorrow Words*, 11; Lamb interview, February 24, 2009.

55. Frank Weed, "The MADD Queen: Charisma and the Founder of Mothers Against Drunk Driving," *Leadership Quarterly* 4 (1993): 329–45; Otto Friedrich et al., "Man of the Year," *Time*, January 7, 1985, accessed March 24, 2010, www.time.com/time/magazine/article/0,9171,956231,00.html; Fell and Voas, "Mothers Against Drunk Driving," 197–98.

56. Mann, *Arrive Alive*, 124; Gaylord Shaw, "Crackdown Urged on Drunk Drivers," *Los Angeles Times*, October 2, 1980, B4.

57. Fell and Voas, "Mothers Against Drunk Driving," 197; Whitaker, "A National Outrage"; Starr et al., "War against Drunk Drivers."

58. Holly Everett, *Roadside Crosses in Contemporary Memorial Culture* (Denton, TX: University of North Texas Press, 2002).

59. Mann, *Arrive Alive*, 61; "Law: They're MADD as Hell"; "Maryland Plans All-Out Effort Against Intoxicated Drivers," *Washington Post*, May 1, 1981, A42. The man who killed Tommy Sexton only served a year of probation and paid a $200 fine.

60. Interview with James C. Fell and Robert B. Voas, November 24, 2009; Candy Lightner to Robert F. Borkenstein, January 7, 1985, and Robert F. Borkenstein to Candy Lightner, January 19, 1984, box 113.4, folder: MADD, Borkenstein Papers.

61. Candy Lightner to Robert F. Borkenstein, February 7, 1985, and Robert F. Borkenstein to Candy Lightner, February 15, 1985, Borkenstein Papers.

62. Aiken, *My Life*, 52.

63. Mann, *Arrive Alive*, 127–28; Fell and Voas, "Mothers Against Drunk Driving," 197; Starr et al., "War against Drunk Drivers," 35.

64. Gerald D. Robin, *Waging the Battle against Drunk Driving: Issues, Countermeasures, and Effectiveness* (New York: Praeger, 1991), 12–14.

65. *Cedar Rapids Gazette*, October 12, 1981, 7A; Celeste Dauherty to William N. Plymat, September 2, 1982, box 2, folder: Cedar Rapids Gazette, Plymat Papers.

66. James C. Fell, *An Examination of the Criticisms of the Minimum Legal Drinking Age 21 Laws in the United States from a Traffic-Safety Perspective* (Washington, DC: NHTSA, 2008).

67. The Reagan quote is in Steven R. Weisman, "Reagan Signs Law Linking Federal Aid to Drinking Age," *New York Times*, July 18, 1984, A15. See also Morris E. Chafetz, "The 21-Year-Old Drinking Age," *Huffington Post*, August 18, 2009, accessed March 25, 2010, www.huffingtonpost.com/morris-e-chafetz/the-21-year-old-drinking_b_262264.html; Aiken, *My Life*, 54; Rich Ceppos, "The Rise and Fall of Ralph Nader," *Car and Driver*, September 1982, 64–71; Robert B. Voas and James C. Fell, "Impaired Driving: Opportunities and Problems," *Alcohol Research and Health* (in press).

68. Jonathan Simon, *Governing Through Crime: How the War on Crime Transformed American Democracy and Created a Culture of Fear* (New York: Oxford University Press, 2007); Kevin A. Sabet, "The 'Local' Matters: A Brief History of the Tension Between Federal Drug Laws and State and Local Policy," *Journal of Global Drug Policy and Practice* 1 (2006), accessed February 5, 2010, www.globaldrugpolicy.org/1/4/3.php.

69. Craig Reinarman, "The Social Construction of an Alcohol Problem: The Case of Mothers Against Drunk Drivers and Social Control in the 1980s," *Theory and Society* 17 (January 1988), 91–120. Jim Fell and Bob Voas disagreed with Reinarman. See Fell and Voas, "Mothers Against Drunk Driving," 200.

70. Linda C. Fleet, "What Should Be Done about Drunk Driving?" *Washington Post*, March 30, 1981, A18.

71. John Leo, "One Less for the Road?" *Time*, May 20, 1985, accessed July 1, 2008, www.time.com/time/printout/0,8816,956316,00.html.

72. David F. Musto, "Tower Flap Another Sign Alcohol's on Way Out," *Houston Chronicle*, March 8, 1989, 15A; Desson Howe, "'Arthur': A SADD Sequel," *Washington Post*, July 8, 1988, N30. Reviewers found a 2011 remake of *Arthur* to be similarly "boring and tiresome." See A. O. Scott, "A Lush Life, with Nanny on Board," *New York Times*, April 18, 2011, C10.

73. Dorothy Townsend, "2 Counts of Drunk Driving Charged to Johnny Carson," *Los Angeles Times*, March 3, 1982, A2. Carson pled no contest and was given three years probation and a $603 fine.

CHAPTER 4: The Movement Matures and Splinters

1. Richard Zylman, "A Critical Evaluation of the Literature on 'Alcohol Involvement' in Highway Deaths," *Accident Analysis and Prevention* 6 (1974): 163–204.

2. Ibid., 201.

3. Richard Zylman, "Commentary," in Robin Room and Susan Sheffield, eds., *The Prevention of Alcohol Problems: Report of a Conference* (Berkeley, CA: Social Research Group, 1974), 206–8.

4. Joseph R. Gusfield, *The Culture of Public Problems: Drinking-Driving and the Symbolic Order* (Chicago: University of Chicago Press, 1981), xii.

5. Ibid., 79.

6. Ibid., 63–66.

7. Ibid., 74; Joseph R. Gusfield, "The Control of Drinking-Driving in the United States: A Period in Transition?" in Michael D. Laurence, John R. Snortum, and Lawrence E. Zimring, eds., *Social Control of the Drinking Driver* (Chicago: University of Chicago Press, 1988), 109–35.

8. Gusfield, *Culture of Public Problems*, 82.

9. Ibid., 41, 174; Gusfield, "Control of Drinking-Driving," 120.

10. Joseph R. Gusfield, "Remarks," in Room and Sheffield, *The Prevention of Alcohol Problems*, 116–18.

11. Gusfield, *Culture of Public Problems*, 174; Gusfield, "Control of Drinking-Driving," 120.

12. H. Laurence Ross, *Settled Out of Court: The Social Process of Insurance Claims Adjustment* (Chicago: Aldine Publishing, 1970); H. Laurence Ross, "Reflections on Doing Policy-Relevant Sociology: How to Cope with MADD Mothers," *American Sociologist* 18 (Summer 1987): 173–78.

13. Quoted in "Transport Minister Launches Drink and Drive Publicity Campaign," press release, September 19, 1967, box 113.1, folder: Barbara Castle, Robert F. Borkenstein Papers, Herman B. Wells Library, Indiana University. See also H. Laurence Ross, "Deterrence-Based Policies in Britain, Canada, and Australia," in Laurence, Snortum, and Zimring, *Social Control of the Drinking Driver*, 64–78.

14. Arlen J. Large, "Drunk Driving, Cause of 70 Fatalities a Day, Is Under Rising

Attack," *Wall Street Journal*, April 20, 1982, 1, 18; Robert F. Borkenstein to Henry van Engeln, October 25, 1968, box 113.2, folder: Herman Heise, Borkenstein Papers.

15. H. Laurence Ross, *Deterring the Drinking Driver: Legal Policy and Social Control* (Lexington, MA: Lexington Books, 1984), 22, 68–69; H. Laurence Ross, "The Scandinavian Myth: The Effectiveness of Drinking-and-Driving Legislation in Sweden and Norway," *Journal of Legal Studies* 4 (1975): 285–310; John R. Snortum, "Deterrence of Alcohol-Impaired Driving," in Laurence, Snortum, and Zimring, *Social Control of the Drinking Driver*, 189–226.

16. Ross, *Deterring the Drinking Driver*, 68.

17. Ibid., xxv and back cover. See also Ross, "Reflections," 176.

18. H. Laurence Ross and Graham Hughes, "Drunk Driving: What Not to Do," *Nation*, December 13, 1986, 663–64. See also Allan F. Williams, "Reflections on the Highway Safety Field," *Injury Prevention* 10 (2004): 330–33.

19. Thomas M. Stout, "Cheers, Not Sneers," and Graham Hughes, "Hughes Replies," *Nation*, February 14, 1987, 166.

20. Ross, "Reflections"; H. Laurence Ross, "The American War on Drunk Driving: A Constructionist Critique," *Contemporary Drug Problems* 18 (Spring 1991): 1–8. Ross mistakenly called Laura Lamb "Cindi Lamb" in the latter piece. Cindi Lamb insists her daughter was properly belted.

21. Ross, "Reflections," 177. See also Ross and Hughes, "Drunk Driving," 664.

22. Gusfield recounted Edwards's objection in his book. See Gusfield, *Culture of Public Problems*, 186, 187, 189.

23. Doris Aiken, *My Life as a Pit Bull* (San Jose, CA: Writers Club Press, 2002), 53.

24. Interview with Cindi Lamb, February 24, 2009; Willard Gaylin, "Who Killed Libby Zion?" *Nation*, October 9, 1995, 394–97; Margaret Rankin, "Diary of a MADD Housewife," *Washington Times*, October 10, 1990, E1.

25. This last recollection came from Ralph P. Hudson to the author, July 27, 2009. See also Rankin, "Diary"; "Fired MADD Leaders Forming New Group," *San Francisco Chronicle*, December 21, 1988, A13; James Harper, "MADD's Direction Causes Dispute," *St. Petersburg Times*, October 8, 1990, 12; Frank Weed, "The MADD Queen: Charisma and the Founder of Mothers Against Drunk Driving," *Leadership Quarterly* 4 (1993): 329–45; interview with Candace Lightner, October 28, 2010.

26. Pamela E. Pennock, *Advertising Sin and Sickness: The Politics of Alcohol and Tobacco Marketing, 1950–1990* (DeKalb: Northern Illinois University Press, 2007), 153, 173; Allan M. Brandt, *The Cigarette Century: The Rise, Fall, and Deadly Persistence of the Product That Defined America* (New York: Basic Books, 2007), 241–77; Leonard Evans, *Traffic Safety* (Bloomfield Hills, MI: Science Serving Society, 2004), accessed January 5, 2009, www.scienceservingsociety.com/ts/text/ch10.htm; Philip J. Cook, "The Effect of Liquor Taxes on Drinking, Cirrhosis, and Auto Accidents," in Mark H. Moore and Dean R. Gerstein, eds., *Alcohol and Public Policy: Beyond the Shadow of Prohibition* (Washington, DC: National Academy Press, 1981), 255–85.

27. See www.cspinet.org, accessed March 30, 2010. See also Pennock, *Advertising*, 172; Dan E. Beauchamp, *Beyond Alcoholism: Alcohol and Public Health Policy* (Philadelphia: Temple University Press, 1980).

28. Michael Jacobson, Robert Atkins, and George Hacker, *The Booze Merchants: The Inebriating of America* (Washington, DC: CSPI, 1983). See also Pennock, *Advertising*,

66–81, 171; Garrett Peck, *The Prohibition Hangover: Alcohol in America from Demon Rum to Cult Cabernet* (New Brunswick, NJ: Rutgers University Press, 2009), 202; David F. Musto, "New Temperance vs. Neo-Prohibition," *Wall Street Journal*, June 25, 1984, 26.

29. Jacobson, Atkins, and Hacker, *Booze Merchants*, vii.

30. Ibid., 5; Peck, *Prohibition Hangover*, 211; Robert Lewis Thompson, "The Long Shadow of Prohibition," *Washington Post*, December 11, 1983, G1, G4; Jonathan Rowe, "Liquor Foes Unite: Tax Hike, Restrictions Sought," *Christian Science Monitor*, May 6, 1988, accessed August 5, 2009, www.csmonitor.com/1988/0506/adrink2.html.

31. Jacobson, Atkins, and Hacker, *Booze Merchants*, 28, 40; Christopher Conte, "Crusaders against Drunk Driving Split Over Whether to Fight Alcohol Broadly," *Wall Street Journal*, November 6, 1985, 35.

32. Jacobson, Atkins, and Hacker, *Booze Merchants*, 49–51, 57; Colman McCarthy, "Politics and Alcohol Abuse," *Washington Post*, January 1, 1984, G4, and Mark Potts, "Battle Brews over Broadcast Beer, Wine Ads," *Washington Post*, December 9, 1984, F1.

33. Jacobson, Atkins, and Hacker, *Booze Merchants*, 82–99.

34. Ibid., 112.

35. Ibid., 139–43.

36. Ibid., 156; Pennock, *Advertising*, 206–8; "Opposition to Alcohol Ad Reforms Continues," *Project SMART Newsletter*, May 1985, courtesy of George Hacker. Not surprisingly, perhaps, the NAB had done a lackluster job of monitoring the content of cigarette advertisements in the 1960s, hoping to ensure that the tobacco companies continued to advertise on television. See Brandt, *Cigarette Century*, 259–60.

37. The warning labels legislation resulted from a rare collaboration between conservative Senator Strom Thurmond and liberal Representative John Conyers. Most commentators believe it did little to control alcohol abuse and drunk driving. See Pennock, *Advertising*, 197, 220.

38. McCarthy, "Politics," G4.

39. Aiken, *My Life*, 71–75.

40. Rowe, "Liquor Foes"; John Gannon, "RID vs. MADD: The Battle Over Booze Ads on TV, Radio," *Sacramento Bee*, June 17, 1987; Aiken, *My Life*, 71; Bard Lindeman to Doris Aiken, May 31, 1988, RID Papers, Schenectady, NY. Courtesy of Doris Aiken.

41. William DeJong and Anne Russell, "MADD's Position on Alcohol Advertising: A Response to Marshall and Oleson," *Journal of Public Health Policy* 16 (1995): 231–38; Barron H. Lerner, *The Breast Cancer Wars: Hope, Fear, and the Pursuit of a Cure in Twentieth-Century America* (New York: Oxford University Press, 2001), 260–62.

42. Quote is from Conte, "Crusaders," 35. See also Aiken, *My Life*, 57; Craig Reinarman, "The Social Construction of an Alcohol Problem: The Case of Mothers Against Drunk Drivers and Social Control in the 1980s," *Theory and Society* 17 (January 1988): 91–120; Lightner interview, October 28, 2010.

43. William Montague, "Drunk-Driving Foes Accept Big Gifts from Alcoholic-Beverage Producers," *Chronicle of Philanthropy*, July 25, 1989, 1, 12–14; Donald B. Shea, "Saving Lives Is Important Enough to Merit Financial Aid from the Brewing Industry," *Chronicle of Philanthropy*, September 5, 1989, 29.

44. E. Gene Patterson to George Hacker, July 23, 1984, box 2, folder: Center for Science in the Public Interest, William N. Plymat Papers, State Historical Society of Iowa, Des Moines; "MADD as Hell and Not Going to Take It Anymore," *Broadcasting*

Magazine, April 15, 1985; E. R. Shipp, "Alcohol Abuse Is Becoming a Public Policy Issue," *New York Times,* October 1, 1985, A18; Lightner interview, October 28, 2010.

45. Reinarman, "Social Construction," 111. See also Gannon, "RID vs. MADD"; Montague, "Drunk Driving Foes," 13.

46. Reinarman, "Social Construction," 105.

47. James F. Mosher, "Alcohol Policy and the Presidential Commission on Drunk Driving: The Paths Not Taken," *Accident Analysis and Prevention* 17 (1985): 239–50.

48. H. Laurence Ross, "Final Report of the Presidential Commission on Drunk Driving," *Accident Analysis and Prevention* 17 (1985): 199–206; Ross, "Reflections," 174.

49. Aiken, *My Life,* 59.

50. Minutes of the Board of Directors of the National Commission Against Drunk Driving, December 11, 1984, box 6, folder: NCADD, 1984–1985, and Candy Lightner to the NCADD, January 24, 1985, box 6, folder: 1984–1985, Plymat Papers.

51. Aiken, *My Life,* 58. See also Brandt, *Cigarette Century,* 256–58.

52. William N. Plymat to Elizabeth H. Dole, December 4, 1985, box 6, folder: Elizabeth Dole, and Ralph F. Hudson, "A Public Health Concept—BAC 0.05 Illegal Per Se," unpublished manuscript, 1986, box 4, folder: Dr. Ralph Hudson, Plymat Papers. See also Geoffrey Rose, *The Strategy of Preventive Medicine* (New York: Oxford University Press, 1994).

53. Morris E. Chafetz, "How to Deal with Drunk Driving," *Boston Globe,* October 3, 1985, 23; Morris E. Chafetz, "Dangerous, But to Whom?" *Des Moines Register,* January 3, 1985, 8A.

54. F. Scott Deaver and Robert C. Hickle, "Drunken Driving," *Des Moines Register,* January 16, 1985, 9A.

55. Interview with James C. Fell, December 22, 2009; interview with John V. Moulden, March 18, 2010.

56. Stephen Hilgartner and Charles Bosk, "The Rise and Fall of Social Problems: A Public Arenas Model," *American Journal of Sociology* 94 (1988): 53–78.

57. James S. Kunen, *Reckless Disregard: Corporate Greed, Government Indifference, and the Kentucky School Bus Crash* (New York: Simon & Schuster, 1994).

58. Dirk Johnson, "Carrollton Journal: Murder Charges Are Met by Cries of Compassion," *New York Times,* August 8, 1988, A14; Paul Hoverston, "'88 Crash Awoke U.S. to Peril of DWI," *USA Today,* September 1, 1999, 3A.

59. Edward O. Fritts to C. Everett Koop, November 17, 1988, box 149, folder 46, C. Everett Koop Papers, National Library of Medicine, Bethesda, MD.

60. Edward O. Fritts to C. Everett Koop, November 29, 1988, in ibid.

61. Ronald R. Rumbaugh to C. Everett Koop, December 1, 1988, box 149, folder 43, Koop Papers.

62. V. J. Adduci to C. Everett Koop, December 5, 1988, in ibid.

63. John E. Toole to C. Everett Koop, November 28, 1988, in ibid. See also Aiken, *My Life,* 59.

64. C. Everett Koop to V. J. Adduci, December 1, 1988, and C. Everett Koop to Edward O. Fritts, November 22, 1988, box 149, folder 46, Koop Papers; *Proceedings of the Surgeon General's Workshop on Drunk Driving* (Washington, DC: US Department of Health and Human Services, 1989), 96.

65. *Proceedings,* 48, 57, 58, 88.

66. Interview with Robert W. Denniston, January 9, 2009. See also Randall Bloomquist and Kevin McCormack, "A Major Koopla," *Adweek*, December 19, 1988.

67. Alexander C. Wagenaar and Frederick M. Streff, "Public Opinion on Alcohol Policies," *Journal of Public Health Policy* 11 (1990): 189–205.

68. Interview with C. Everett Koop, January 3, 2008.

69. Interview with David A. Sleet, March 19, 2010. See also interview with Amy Barkin, January 4, 2009; Denniston interview, January 9, 2009; Koop interview, January 3, 2008.

70. Koop interview, January 3, 2008.

71. Enoch Gordis to Surgeon General, December 12, 1988, box 149, folder 45, Koop Papers.

72. On the precautionary principle, see Sandra Steingraber, *Living Downstream: A Scientist's Personal Investigation of Cancer and the Environment* (New York: Vintage, 1998). See also Pennock, *Advertising*, 186–87, 220. Pennock uses the term *secular morality* to characterize this mindset.

CHAPTER 5: Lawyers, Libertarians, and the Liquor Lobby Fight Back

1. Micky Sadoff, *Get MADD Again, America!* (Irving, TX: MADD, 1991).

2. Ibid., 2, 97.

3. Ibid., 50, 52, 80.

4. Ibid., 71.

5. Mac Marshall and Alice Oleson, "In the Pink: MADD and Public Health Policy in the 1990s," *Journal of Public Health Policy* 15 (1994): 54–68.

6. William DeJong and Anne Russell, "MADD's Position on Alcohol Advertising: A Response to Marshall and Oleson," *Journal of Public Health Policy* 16 (1995): 231–38.

7. Jill Abramson, "Selling Moderation: Alcohol Industry Is at Forefront of Efforts to Curb Drunkenness," *Wall Street Journal*, May 21, 1991, A1, A14. See also Francine I. Katz to Robert F. Borkenstein, June 25, 1993, box 113.1, folder: A, Robert F. Borkenstein Papers, Herman B. Wells Library, Indiana University.

8. Abramson, "Selling Moderation." For a more nuanced assessment of industry's role, see H. Laurence Ross, "Brewers View Drunk Driving: A Critique," *Accident Analysis and Prevention* 19 (1987): 475–77.

9. Interview with Cindi Lamb, February 24, 2009.

10. Doug Bandow, "Targeting the Most Dangerous Drunk Drivers," *Washington Times*, January 28, 1994, A23; Connie Koenenn, "The Company She Keeps," *Los Angeles Times*, January 26, 1994, 1.

11. Bandow, "Targeting"; "Koenenn, "The Company"; Katherine Griffin, "No Longer MADD," *This World*, August 7, 1994, 6, 7; Michael Fumento, "Catch Drunks, Don't Harass Drivers," 1997, accessed January 7, 2007, www.fumento.com/drunk.html.

12. James D. Stuart, "Deterrence, Desert, and Drunk Driving," *Public Affairs Quarterly* 3 (1989): 105–15.

13. Ibid.; H. Laurence Ross, "Reflections on Doing Policy-Relevant Sociology: How to Cope with MADD Mothers," *American Sociologist* 18 (Summer 1987): 173–78.

14. James B. Jacobs, *Drunk Driving: An American Dilemma* (Chicago: University of Chicago, 1989), 43, 52, 77.

15. Bonnie Steinbock, "Drunk Driving," *Philosophy and Public Affairs* 14 (1985): 278–95.

16. Douglas N. Husak, "Is Drunk Driving a Serious Offense?" *Philosophy and Public Affairs* 23 (1994): 52–73.

17. Ibid., 71–73.

18. Rosemary L. Calhoun to Robert F. Borkenstein, May 18, 1988, box 113.1, folder: Rosemary Calhoun, and Robert F. Borkenstein to Candy Lightner, February 15, 1985, box 113.4, folder: MADD, Borkenstein Papers.

19. Gerri Hirshey, "'Lady D.U.I.' Comes to Her Own Defense," *New York Times*, January 4, 2009, CT1.

20. Lawrence Taylor, *Drunk Driving Defense*, 2nd ed. (Boston: Little, Brown, 1986), 45–49. Taylor's blog is www.duiblog.com.

21. Judge X, *How to Avoid a Drunk Driving Conviction* (Port Townsend, WA: Loompanics Unlimited, 1993), 103, 106. *Beat the Breathalyzer*, by Chris Jamessen, was actually published in 1979.

22. Judge X, *How to Avoid*, 6. See also Taylor, *Drunk Driving Defense*, 7.

23. Roger Lowenstein, "On the Defensive: How a Lawyer Gets Drunken Drivers Off the Hook," *Wall Street Journal*, April 14, 1986, 1, 20. Jere Joiner to the author, March 30, 2010.

24. Eric Peters, "MADD House," *National Review*, September 28, 1998, 36–37; Judy Rakowsky, "MADD Board Resigns, Citing Change in Focus," *Boston Globe*, May 19, 1993, 16, accessed April 9, 2010, www.fundinguniverse.com/company-histories/Mothers-Against-Drunk-Driving-MADD-Company-History.html. See also David J. Hanson, "Mothers Against Drunk Driving: A Crash Course in MADD," accessed April 1, 2010, www.alcoholfacts.org/CarashCourseOnMADD.html.

25. Quoted in Sam Bresnahan, "MADD Struggles to Remain Relevant," *Washington Times*, August 6, 2002, B1. See also Hanson, "Mothers," 12.

26. Robert Davis, "French Struggle: Drinking and Driving," *USA Today*, September 3, 1997, 3A.

27. "Princess Di's Death Should Raise Public Consciousness about Drunken Driving," *Washington Times*, September 8, 1997, A20.

28. Ibid., A20. See also Andrea Stone, "Diana Invoked in Alcohol Bill," *USA Today*, September 4, 1997, 8A; Andrew Barr, *Drink: A Social History of America* (New York: Carroll & Graf, 1999), 281.

29. Barr, *Drink*, 283. See also Rick Berman, "MADD Doesn't Differentiate between Drunks and Social Drinkers," *Washington Times*, September 26, 1997, A18.

30. Berman, "MADD," A18; Garrett Peck, *The Prohibition Hangover: Alcohol in America from Demon Rum to Cult Cabernet* (New Brunswick, NJ: Rutgers University Press, 2009), 205.

31. Ralph Hingson, Timothy Heeren, and Michael Winter, "Lowering State Legal Blood Alcohol Limits to 0.08 Percent," *American Journal of Public Health* 86 (1996): 1297–99; Robert Apsler, A. R. Char, Wayne M. Harding, and Terry M. Klein, *The Effects of 0.08% Laws* (Washington, DC: NHTSA, 1999).

32. Barr, *Drink*, 282–83.

33. "Power MADD," *Washington Times*, March 6, 2000, A16; http://activistcash.com/organization_quotes.cfm/o/17-mothers-against-drunk-driving, accessed April 10, 2010.

34. Alfred Lubrano, "My Job Is to Defend Drinking and Driving," *Philadelphia Inquirer*, November 26, 2000, J1.

35. See www.responsibledrinker.com, accessed April 11, 2010.

36. See www.motorists.org/roadblocks, accessed April 11, 2010; interview with Candace Lightner, October 28, 2010.

37. Pamela E. Pennock, *Advertising Sin and Sickness: The Politics of Alcohol and Tobacco Marketing, 1950–1990* (DeKalb: Northern Illinois University Press, 2007), 171–76; Janet L. Golden, *Message in a Bottle: The Making of Fetal Alcohol Syndrome* (Cambridge, MA: Harvard University Press, 2005). For a critique of these types of initiatives, see Jacob Sullum, *For Your Own Good: The Anti-Smoking Crusade and the Tyranny of Public Health* (New York: Simon & Schuster, 1998).

38. "Power MADD," A16; Chris Overbey, *Drinking and Driving: War in America* (Lulu.com, 2006), 39. It is worth noting that provocative quotes, such as that made by Pena, get picked up and repeated by numerous anti-MADD websites, which may make them appear more influential than they actually are.

39. Ralph P. Hudson to the author, July 27, 2009; John Lee, "The Prohibition Times," n.d., accessed April 11, 2010, http://piratenews.org/theprohibitiontimes.html.

40. Balko is quoted in Peck, *Prohibition Hangover*, 207; Hanson, "Mothers Against Drunk Driving," 2; "MEMO to MADD's New Celebrity Board," September 17, 2003, accessed September 23, 2009, www.consumerfreedom.com/print.cfml?id=2125&page=headline.

41. Eric Zimmermann, "Beer Summit Sparks Fight Between MADD, Restaurant Group," The Hill's Blog Briefing Room, August 3, 2009, accessed October 29, 2009, http://thehill.com/blogs; Doris Aiken, "The Beer Summit Gift from Obama," July 31, 2009, accessed April 11, 2010, http://rid-usa.org/blog.

42. Quoted in Peck, *Prohibition Hangover*, 213. See also Jonathan Freedland, "Second Front: Battle of the Bottle," *Guardian*, May 28, 1996, T2.

43. Peck, *Prohibition Hangover*, 199. See also Lubrano, "My Job," J1.

44. Richard A. Grucza, Karen E. Norberg, and Laura J. Bierut, "Binge Drinking among Youths and Young Adults in the United States, 1979–2006," *Journal of the American Academy of Child and Adolescent Psychiatry* 48 (2009): 692–702; "Quick Stats Binge Drinking," accessed December 2, 2009, www.cdc.gov/alcohol/quickstats/binge_drinking.htm; Robert B. Voas and James C. Fell, "Impaired Driving: Opportunities and Problems," *Alcohol Research and Health* (in press).

45. These lyrics are available at www.lyricsmode.com. For a clever critique of the DDAM mindset, see Kathryn Lindskoog, "They Call Themselves MADD? Well, We Are DAMM Mad!" *Christian Century*, June 2, 1982, 655–56.

46. Hanson, "Mothers Against Drunk Driving," 7; Overbey, *Drinking and Driving*, ii; Llewellyn H. Rockwell Jr., "Legalize Drunk Driving," November 3, 2000, accessed February 7, 2008, http://lewrockwell.printthis.clickability.com. Because motorcyclists are putting themselves—as opposed to others—at risk by not wearing helmets, this issue is somewhat less contentious than strict prohibitions against drunk driving. See www.iihs.org/research/qanda/helmet_use.html and Marion M. Jones and Ronald Bayer, "Paternalism and Its Discontents: Motorcycle Helmet Laws, Libertarian Values, and Public Health," *American Journal of Public Health* 97 (2007): 208–17.

47. See http://drunkard.com/issues/08_02/08_02_fighting_madd.htm, accessed September 23, 2009.

48. Dinitia Smith, "A Serious Business for a Humorous Drunkard," *New York Times*, October 30, 2004, B9. See also www.drunkard.com/md_editors_rant.htm, accessed September 23, 2009.

49. Gerri Hirshey, "Teenagers and Cars: A Deadly Mix," *New York Times*, December 9, 2007, LI1.

50. Barbara Holland, *The Joy of Drinking* (New York: Bloomsbury, 2007), 88, 111, 117. See also Christine Sismondo, *Mondo Cocktail: A Shaken and Stirred History* (Toronto: McArthur & Co., 2005), esp. re: Hemingway.

51. Holland, *Joy*, 127; Brigid Schulte, "Critics say District's DUI Policy Goes Too Far," *Washington Post*, October 13, 2005, B1; Amy Alkon, "You Don't Have to Be Drunk to Be Arrested for Drunk Driving," November 3, 2007, accessed January 21, 2008, www.advicegoddess.com.

52. For additional criticisms of DWI prosecutions, see www.dui.com/dui-library/victims/personal-tragedy#comments, accessed October 4, 2010.

53. Peck, *Prohibition Hangover*, 209; Mark Schone, "Over the Legal Limit," *Boston Globe*, March 19, 2006, C1. On the use of the law as a public health strategy, see Tom Christoffel, "Using Roadblocks to Reduce Drunk Driving: Public Health or Law and Order?" *American Journal of Public Health* 74 (1984): 1028–30; Jonathan P. Shepherd, "Criminal Deterrence as a Public Health Strategy," *Lancet* 358 (2001): 1717–22.

54. Lee Green, "The College Alcohol Study," in: Stephen L. Isaacs and David C. Colby, *To Improve Health and Health Care*, vol. 13 (San Francisco: Jossey-Bass, 2009), 201–26.

55. Sarah Slavin, "The Social World and Political Community of Head-Injured People," in Mary Lou Kendrigan, ed., *Gender Differences: Their Impact on Public Policy* (New York: Greenwood Press, 1991), 189–219; accessed February 15, 2010, www.youtube.com/watch?v=bHpAgVYlBow.

56. Insurance Institute for Highway Safety, "DUI/DWI Laws," January 10, 2010, accessed February 15, 2010, www.iihs.org/laws/dui.aspx.

57. Ruth A. Shults, Randy W. Elser, Davis A. Sleet, et al., "Reviews of Evidence Regarding Interventions to Reduce Alcohol-Impaired Driving," *American Journal of Preventive Medicine* 21 (4S) (2001): 66–88; James C. Fell and Robert B. Voas, "Reducing Illegal Blood Alcohol Limits for Driving: Effects on Traffic Safety," in J. C. Verster, S. R. Pandi-Perumal, J. G. Ramaekers, and J. J. de Gier, eds., *Drugs, Driving and Traffic Safety* (Basel: Birkhauser Verlag, 2009), 415–37; interview with James Fell and Robert Voas, November 24, 2009.

58. Shults, Elser, Sleet, et al., "Reviews of Evidence," 72, 73; NHTSA, *Traffic Safety Facts: Lives Saved in 2008 by Restraint Use and Minimum Drinking Age Laws* (Washington, DC: Department of Transportation, 2009).

59. Shults, Elser, Sleet, et al., "Reviews of Evidence," 75–78. See also the discussion with Radley Balko in Peck, *Prohibition Hangover*, 205–7.

60. Allan F. Williams, "Reflections on the Highway Safety Field," *Injury Prevention* 10 (2004): 330–33; www.ghsa.org/html/stateinfo/laws/checkpoint_laws.html; Fell and Voas interview.

61. Paul L. Zador, Adrian K. Land, Michele Fields, and Karen Weinberg, "Fatal Crash

Involvement and Laws against Alcohol-Impaired Driving," *Journal of Public Health Policy* 10 (1989): 467–85; Ann Dellinger and David A. Sleet, "Preventing Traffic Injuries: Strategies That Work," *American Journal of Lifestyle Medicine* 4 (2010): 82–89; Traci L. Toomey, Darin J. Erickson, Kathleen M. Lenk, Gunna R. Kilian, Cheryl L. Perry, and Alexander C. Wagenaar, "A Randomized Trial to Evaluate a Management Training Program to Prevent Illegal Alcohol Sales," *Addiction* 103 (2008): 405–13; Philip J. Cook and Maeve E. Gearing, "The Breathalyzer Behind the Wheel," *New York Times*, August 31, 2009, A19; Fell and Voas interview.

62. Dellinger and Sleet, "Preventing Traffic Injuries," 84–85.

63. Matthew L. Wald, "Highway Safety Agency Unveils New Campaign against Drunken Driving," *New York Times*, August 17, 2006, A17; Lawrence P. Lonero, "Finding the Next Cultural Safety Paradigm for Road Safety," AAA Foundation for Traffic Safety, 2007, accessed March 9, 2010, www.aaafoundation.org/pdf/lonero.pdf.

64. Paul Vitello, "Alcohol, a Car and a Fatality: Is it Murder?" *New York Times*, October 22, 2006, sec. 4, 1, 4.

65. Virginia Inman, "On This Quarter-Eating Machine, a High Score Could Be Dangerous," *Wall Street Journal*, November 29, 1982, 29.

66. Nancy Lewis, "In Australia, the Wines Have Funny Names—and Go Down Easy," *Washington Post*, October 31, 2004, P1.

67. Adam E. Barry and Patricia Goodson, "Use (and Misuse) of the Responsible Drinking Message in Public Health and Alcohol Advertising: A Review," *Health, Education and Behavior*, published online on August 10, 2009. See http://heb.sagepub.com/cgi/rapidpdf/1090198109342393v1.pdf.

68. "Research Material," n.d., box 113.6, folder: Voas, Borkenstein Papers; Cook and Gearing, "The Breathalyzer," A19; Fell and Voas interview.

69. "Spring Break—Awash in the Alcohol Industry's Tsunami of Booze," www.traumaf .org/featured/03-06-03index.html, accessed December 8, 2010.

70. Peck, *Prohibition Hangover*, 222, 226–29; Vikas Bajaj, "Retailer to Pull Catalog Showing Use of Alcohol," *Dallas Morning News*, July 30, 1998, 27A; Richard J. Bonnie and Mary Ellen O' Connell, eds., *Reducing Underage Drinking: A Collective Responsibility* (Washington, DC: Institute of Medicine, 2003); Peter Anderson, "Is it Time to Ban Alcohol Advertising?" *Clinical Medicine* 9 (2009): 121–24. The alcohol industry has argued that such measures are not necessary given that overall rates of alcohol consumption in the United States have dropped despite marketing efforts. See Pennock, *Advertising*, 195.

71. Keith Wailoo, *How Cancer Crossed the Color Line: The Transformation of Health and Race in a Nation Divided* (New York: Oxford University Press), 2011. See also Robert B. Voas, A. S. Tippetts, and James C. Fell, "The Relationship of Alcohol Safety Laws to Drinking Drivers in Fatal Crashes," *Accident Analysis and Prevention* 32 (2000): 483–92.

72. Dellinger and Sleet, "Preventing Traffic Injuries," 83; Eric Peters, "Drinking and Driving Deaths Plummet," *National Review Online*, December 27, 2002, accessed, www .nationalreview.com/comment/comment-peters122702.asp; Leonard Evans, *Traffic Safety* (Bloomfield Hills, MI: Science Serving Society, 2004), accessed January 5, 2009, www .scienceservingsociety.com/ts/text/ch10.htm.

73. For a representative critique of NHTSA data, see "NHTSA Admits Their Data Is Misinterpreted," accessed February 7, 2008, www.ridl.us/phpBB2/viewtopic.php?t =532.

chapter 6: More (and More) Tragedies

1. Al Baker and Lisa W. Foderaro, "Tests Show Driver Was Drunk in Parkway Crash That Killed 8," *New York Times*, August 5, 2009, A1.

2. Jeremy W. Peters, "New York Is Set for Strict Stand on D.W.I. Cases," *New York Times*, November 18, 2009, A1.

3. Lawrence P. Lonero, "Finding the Next Cultural Safety Paradigm for Road Safety," AAA Foundation for Traffic Safety, 2007, accessed March 9, 2010, www.aaafoundation .org/pdf/lonero.pdf. See also Patricia F. Waller, "Challenges in Motor Vehicle Safety," *Annual Reviews in Public Health* 23 (2002): 93–113.

4. Beverley Lyons and Laura Sutherland, "Lindsay Has Hit a New Lo: Troubled Actress Is Arrested Again," *Daily Record*, July 25, 2007, 15.

5. Linda McAvoy, "Make Drunk-Driving Stars Do Perp Walk on Red Carpet," *Toronto Star*, June 2, 2007, W6.

6. Karen Thomas, "What Has Gotten into Them? Young Celebs' Lives Filled with Drugs, Clubs, DUIs, and Rehab," *USA Today*, June 6, 2007, 1D; John C. Burnham, *Bad Habits: Drinking, Smoking, Taking Drugs, Gambling, Sexual Misbehavior, and Swearing in American History* (New York: New York University Press, 1993), 145; www.celebitchy .com/4008/lindsay_lohan_arrested_for_dui, and www.crushable.com/entertainment/lindsay -lohan-arrested, accessed April 17, 2010.

7. Elizabeth Cohen, "Young Women Drink, Party, Post," CNN.com, December 10, 2007, accessed December 11, 2007, www.cmm.com/2007/HEALTH/12/10/face.book/ index.html; Ada Calhoun, "Moms Who Drink: No Joking after the Schuler Tragedy," Time.com, August 11, 2009, accessed August 19, 2009, www.time.com/time/nation/ article/0,8599,1915467,00.html; http://lyrics.wikia.com/Bowling_For_Soup:Hooray_For _Beer. See also Alessandra Stanley, "Where Alcoholism Drinks in the Laughs," *New York Times*, December 3, 2010, C1, C3.

8. Doug Camilli, "Sobering News for Lohan," *Montreal Gazette*, May 29, 2007, D8; David Picker, "State Senator Appalled by Unruly Fans," *New York Times*, November 21, 2007.

9. Burnham, *Bad Habits*, 292. See also Garrett Peck, *The Prohibition Hangover: Alcohol in America from Demon Rum to Cult Cabernet* (New Brunswick, NJ: Rutgers University Press, 2009), 221.

10. Quoted in "Drink Tank," *Salon*, November 3, 2000, accessed April 18, 2010, www .salon.com/news/politics/feature/2000/11/03/reacts/index.html.

11. See www.metrolyrics.com/dui-lyrics-offspring.html, accessed January 24, 2010; Lance A. Strate, "Beer Commercials: A Manual on Masculinity," in Steve Craig, ed., *Men, Masculinity, and the Media* (Newbury Park, CA: Sage, 1992), 78–92.

12. Heath Urie, "Trio Loved Speedy Cars," *Boulder* (CO) *Daily Camera*, January 20, 2008, accessed June 17, 2009, www.dailycamera.com/news/2008/jan/20/trio-loved-speedy -cars-families-friends-remember.

13. Ibid.

14. See ibid. for the quotations in this and the two subsequent paragraphs.

15. Timothy Egan, "Youthful Binge Drinking Fueled by Boredom of the Open West," *New York Times*, September 2, 2006, A1, A12.

16. Ibid., A12; Samuel Warren, "Worst States for Drunken Driving," February 24, 2009, accessed August 30, 2010, http://autos.aol.com/article/worst-states-for-drunken

-driving; Kelly Burke, *Drinking and Driving: The Toll, the Tears*, WETA/TV, Washington, DC, May 7, 1986, RID Papers, Schenectady, NY. Courtesy of Doris Aiken. As of January 2010, seven states still had no open container laws. See "DUI/DWI Laws," accessed February 15, 2010, www.iihs.org/laws/dui.aspx.

17. Dirk Johnson, "Where the Beer Flows Easy, Calls to Sober Up," *New York Times*, November 16, 2008, A16.

18. Bill Lubinger and Gabriel Baird, "Cleveland Browns Fans Stunned by Donte Stallworth's 30-Day Jail Term for DUI Manslaughter," *Cleveland Plain Dealer*, Tuesday, June 16, 2009, accessed June 17, 2009, www.cleveland.com/browns/index.ssf/2009/06/cleveland_browns_fans_stunned.html.

19. Ibid.

20. The comments about the Stallworth case follow the Lubinger and Baird article and an article by Mary Kay Cabot, "Cleveland Browns Terminate Donte Stallworth's Contact," February 8, 2010, accessed April 20, 2010, www.cleveland.com/browns/index.ssf/2010/02/cleveland_browns_terminate_don/2932/comments.html.

21. Matthew Lysiak and Rich Schapiro, "Mother of Brooklyn Woman Mowed Down by Accused Drunk Cop Rips Officers Involved as 'Cowards,'" *New York Daily News*, September 29, 2009, accessed April 20, 2010, www.nydailynews.com/news/ny_crime/2009/09/30/2009-09-30_grieving_mother_of_brooklyn_woman_rips_cops.html.

22. Matthew Lysiak, Rocco Parascandola, Wil Cruz, and Rich Schapiro, "No Alcohol Found in DWI Charge Cop Andrew Kelly's Blood in Tests That Were Delayed by 7 Hours," *New York Daily News*, September 30, 2009, accessed April 20, 2010, www.nydailynews.com/news/ny_crime/2009/09/29/2009-09-29_no_alcohol_found_in_fatal_dwi_charge_cop_andrew_kelly_in_tests_that_were_delayed.html.

23. The comment was posted by hslew in response to William Sherman and Corky Siemaszko, "Officer Andrew Kelly Pleads Guilty to Killing Vionique Valnord While Driving Drunk," *New York Daily News*, September 8, 2010, accessed September 29, 2010, www.nydailynews.com/ny_local/2010/09/08/2010-09-08_tk.html.

24. Interview with James Fell and Robert Voas, November 24, 2009. Nine states have recently put in policies to thwart BAC avoidance, in which judges are on call to issue search warrants mandating breath or blood testing. See www.msnbc.msn.com/id/21113454o/vp/40838549#40838549. See also Randall Stross, "Helping Drunken Drivers Avoid Tickets but Not Wrecks," *New York Times*, April 17, 2011, BU3.

25. "Distilled Spirits Council Recognized by USDA for Promoting Federal Dietary Guideline on Responsible Alcohol Consumption," *Drug Week*, June 27, 2008. See also www.centurycouncil.org.

26. James C. Fell and Robert B. Voas, "The Effectiveness of Reducing Illegal Blood Alcohol Concentration (BAC) Limits for Driving: Evidence for Lowering the Limit to .05 BAC," *Journal of Safety Research* 37 (2006): 233–43. Great Britain and Canada, like the United States, remain at a 0.08% BAC.

27. Atul Gawande, "One for My Baby, but 0.08 for the Road," *Slate*, February 27, 1998, accessed April 20, 2010, www.slate.com/id/2672; Karolyn V. Nunnallee, "MADD Strives to Keep Drunken Drivers off the Road," *Washington Times*, August 19, 1998, A18; Peck, *Prohibition Hangover*, 205.

28. Laura Dean-Mooney, "Don't Be Mad at MADD," *Washington Times*, May 4, 2009, A20.

29. Quoted in Burke, "Drinking and Driving."

30. "Police Not to File Charges against Mrs. Roosevelt," *Washington Post*, August 16, 1946, 3; Donald A. Redelmeier and Rob J. Tibshirani, "Association between Cellular-Telephone Calls and Motor Vehicle Collisions," *New England Journal of Medicine* 336 (1997): 453–58.

31. "Text Messaging May Be Factor in Fatal Teen Car Crash," *FoxNews.com*, July 15, 2007, accessed October 26, 2009, www.foxnews.com/story/0,2933,289365,00.html.

32. "New Jersey Roadways Scariest Thing This Halloween," MADD New Jersey Press Release, October 31, 2008, accessed October 26, 2009, www.madd.org.

33. These comments and those in the following paragraph can be found at http://abcnews.go.com/GMA/comments?type=story&id=3379012 and www.usatoday.com/news/nation/2007-07-14-ny-crash_N.htm, both accessed October 26, 2009.

34. Ashley Halsey III, "What Does It Take to Get Texting Off Roads? Consequences Are Only Way, Some Say," *Washington Post*, October 5, 2009, B1, B8.

35. The most comprehensive document on traffic safety is *Improving Traffic Safety Culture in the United States: The Journey Forward* (Washington, DC: AAA Foundation for Traffic Safety, 2007), available at www.aaafoundation.org/pdf/safetyculturedocument.pdf. See also "A 10-Year Plan to Reduce Road-Traffic Accidents," *Lancet* 375(2010): 866.

36. Quoted in Halsey, "What Does It Take," B1.

37. See note 32.

38. http://abcnews.go.com/GMA/comments?type=story&id=3379012.

39. All of the quotes are from ibid.

40. Unsigned letter to Doris Aiken, June 21, 1984, RID Papers. For a more skeptical view about the importance of changing language, see Lonero, "Finding the Next Cultural Safety Paradigm."

41. Cindi Lamb, "The Visitor," was published in the *Dundalk* (MD) *Eagle* between September 26, 2002, and February 26, 2003. Copy courtesy of Cindi Lamb. This piece is the source of the conversation between Lamb and Newcomer detailed in the subsequent paragraphs.

42. Of note, Candy Lightner also publicly forgave Clarence Busch. See transcript of *Good Morning America*, May 3, 2000.

43. Susan Dominus, "A 'Perfect Mother,' a Vodka Bottle and 8 Lives Lost," *New York Times*, August 8, 2009, A1.

44. Burke, "Drinking and Driving." The phrase "subjective immunity" comes from Allan F. Williams, "Reflections on the Highway Safety Field," *Injury Prevention* 10 (2004): 330–33.

45. Elizabeth M. Armstrong, *Conceiving Risk, Bearing Responsibility: Fetal Alcohol Syndrome and the Diagnosis of Moral Disorder* (Baltimore: Johns Hopkins University Press, 2003); Janet Golden, *Message in a Bottle: The Making of Fetal Alcohol Syndrome* (Cambridge, MA: Harvard University Press, 2005); Jonathan Simon, *Governing through Crime: How the War on Crime Transformed American Democracy and Created a Culture of Fear* (New York: Oxford University Press, 2007), 180, 181; Nicholas D. Kristof, "Drugs Won the War," *New York Times*, June 13, 2009, WK10.

46. Jeremy W. Peters, "New York Is Set for Strict Stand on D.W.I. Cases," *New York Times*, November 18, 2009, A1; Bertil Hok, Hakan Pettersson, Annika K. Andersson, Sjoerd Haasl, and Per Akerlund, "Breath Analyzer for Alcolocks and Screening Devices," *IEEE*

Sensors Journal, 2010, accessed April 20, 2010, www20.vv.se/fud-resultat/Publikationer_000801_000900/Publikation_000828/IEEE_Sensors_H%C3%B6k_etal.pdf.

47. "New Survey Results: Stop Anyone Impaired by Alcohol from Driving Any Vehicle," Insurance Institute for Highway Safety Press Release, September 17, 2009, accessed April 20, 2010, www.iihs.org/news/rss/pr091709.html.

48. "Regulatory Overkill," *Wall Street Journal*, August 15, 1974, 10; Edwin R. Linz, "Buchwald and Safety Belts," *Washington Post*, April 25, 1974, A19. I thank David Sleet for pointing out this historical episode.

49. Robert F. Borkenstein, "History of Attempts to Deter Driving While Impaired by Alcohol," unpublished manuscript, June 1986, box 113.1, folder: APA Conference, Robert F. Borkenstein Papers, Herman B. Wells Library, Indiana University; James B. Jacobs, *Drunk Driving: An American Dilemma* (Chicago: University of Chicago, 1989), 200; Lonero, "Finding the Next Cultural Safety Paradigm."

50. Unsigned letter, Fargo, North Dakota to Mrs. Aiken or RID, n.d., RID Papers.

51. Jacobs, *Drunk Driving*, 193; Mark E. Lender and James K. Martin, *Drinking in America: A History* (New York: Free Press, 1987), 201–4. For an excellent essay on how to determine the success of advocacy movements, see Steven Epstein, "Measuring Success: Scientific, Institutional, and Cultural Effects of Patient Advocacy" in Beatrix Hoffman, Nancy Tomes, and Mark Schlesinger, eds., *Patients as Policy Actors* (Piscataway, NJ: Rutgers University Press, 2001).

52. Allan M. Brandt, *The Cigarette Century: The Rise, Fall, and Deadly Persistence of the Product That Defined America* (New York: Basic Books, 2007), 440–45.

53. Johannes Andenaes, "The Scandinavian Experience" in Michael D. Laurence, John R. Snortum, and Franklin E. Zimring, eds., *Social Control of the Drinking Driver* (Chicago: University of Chicago Press, 1988), 43–63, esp. 51.

54. Jane E. Brody, "Personal Health," *New York Times*, December 29, 1988, B8; Jay A. Winsten, "The Case for Designated Drivers," unpublished manuscript, January 13, 1992, courtesy of George Hacker.

55. Geni Bahar and Nesta Morris, "Is a Strong Safety Culture Taking Root in Our Highway Agencies?" In *Improving Traffic Safety Culture in the United States*, 367–78.

56. Ralph F. Hudson to John A. Volpe, April 23, 1984, box 4, folder: Dr. Ralph Hudson, William N. Plymat Papers, State Historical Society of Iowa, Des Moines.

57. Willard Y. Howell, "Review of Public Information Efforts by Selected Alcohol Safety Action Programs," in James W. Swinehart and Ann C. Grimm, eds., *Public Information Programs on Alcohol and Highway Safety* (Ann Arbor, MI: Highway Safety Research Institute, 1972), 65–67.

AFTERWORD

1. Ralph F. Hudson, "A Public Health Concept—BAC 0.05 Illegal Per Se," unpublished manuscript, 1986, box 4, folder: Dr. Ralph Hudson, William N. Plymat Papers, State Historical Society of Iowa, Des Moines.

Index